PRAYER
in JUDAISM

PRAYER
in JUDAISM

Continuity and Change

edited by
Gabriel H. Cohn and Harold Fisch

JASON ARONSON INC.
Northvale, New Jersey
London

BM
660
.T4413
1996

This book was set in 10 pt. Times by AeroType, Inc.

Copyright ©1996 Gabriel H. Cohn and Harold Fisch

10 9 8 7 6 5 4 3 2 1

All rights reserved. Printed in the United States of America. No part of this book may be used or reproduced in any manner whatsoever without written permission from Jason Aronson Inc. except in the case of brief quotations in reviews for inclusion in a magazine, newspaper, or broadcast.

Library of Congress Cataloging-in-Publication Data

Tefilah ha-Yehudit. English.
   Prayer in Judaism : continuity and change / edited by Gabriel H.
Cohn, Harold Fisch.
     p. cm.
   Based upon the proceedings of an international conference held in
the summer of 1973.
   Includes index.
   ISBN 1-56821-501-0 (alk. paper)
   1. Prayer—Judaism—Congresses. 2. Judaism—Liturgy—Congresses.
I. Cohn, Gabriel. H. II. Fisch, Harold. III. Title.
BM660.T4413 1996
296.4—dc20   95-51821
                                                                                                                        CIP

Manufactured in the United States of America. Jason Aronson Inc. offers books and cassettes. For information and catalog write to Jason Aronson Inc., 230 Livingston Street, Northvale, New Jersey 07647.

Contents

Introduction — vii

PART I

1. Prayer and Modern Man — 3
   Elie Wiesel

2. Some Thoughts on the Subject of Prayer — 13
   Dov Sadan

3. The *Siddur* — A Closed Book? — 25
   Jakob J. Petuchowski

4. Jewish Prayer in Our Days — 31
   A Discussion with Joseph Heinemann, Harold Fisch, Akiva Ernst Simon, Yehudah Nini, Yehudah Friedlander, Yohanan Silman, Eliezer Berkovits, Rikvah Katz, Yehudah Moriel, Moshe Litov, Gabriel H. Cohn

PART II

5. The Fixed and the Fluid in Jewish Prayer — 45
   Joseph Heinemann

6. Prayer and *Halakhah* — 53
   Joseph Tabory

7	Prayer and Jewish Thought: Approaches and Problems (A Survey) *Shalom Rosenberg*	69
8	Prayer in the Thought of Yehudah Halevi *Eliezer Schweid*	109
9	Prayer in the Thought of Maimonides *Marvin Fox*	119
10	The Meaning of Prayer in the Spanish *Kabbalah* *Ephraim Gottlieb*	143
11	The Idea of Prayer in Franz Rosenzweig's "Star of Redemption" *Moshe Schwartz*	163

PART III

12	Education for Prayer *Adin Steinsaltz*	179
13	Teaching *Siddur* to Enhance Devotion in Prayer *Uriel Simon*	189
14	The *Siddur* and the Contemporary Community *Jules Harlow*	199

PART IV

15	Prayer in Hasidism *Sources Arranged and Edited by Samuel Dresner*	217
16	My New Prayer Book *S. Y. Agnon*	241
Glossary		245
Index		249

Introduction

One who sees the sun rising and does not pronounce the blessing to "Him who creates light," who sees it setting and does not bless "Him who brings on the evening," who eats and drinks and does not say the appropriate blessings, is considered as though not truly alive.[1]

Prayer, according to this *Midrash,* is an expression of man's constant awareness of the Divine.[2] The person who praises the Creator for each and every manifestation is a man of prayer—truly alive—and maintains an ongoing dialogue with the Creator. However, as noted in the pages of this book, classical Judaism has demanded more than a personal faith relationship. While there is a place for individual spontaneous prayer—and this is demonstrated in several of the essays in this book—Jewish prayer in the main has a clear, definite framework and content.

It also penetrates into all areas of life, private as well as public, endowing them with a definite style and character. From birth to death, from the early-morning hours to late at night, and through all the days of the year, the Jew has traditionally engaged in a faith response to every time and situation, arranging his service of devotion accordingly. Prayer comes to envelop all aspects of his communal as well as his personal life experience. This universal and all-pervading character of Jewish prayer accounts for the special interest the subject has had for students of Judaism in every generation.[3]

The central role of prayer in Judaism becomes apparent through a perusal of the contents of the *Siddur*, a work that faithfully reflects the total collective historical experience of the Jewish people. One wonders whether any other liturgical canon has so wide and inclusive a range. Somehow it touches on every single stage in the life of the individual and in the history of the people. From the Creation of the world, the election of Abraham, and the Exodus from Egypt, down to our own times, all major events have found expression in one form or another in the *Siddur*. The Jew relives his history through prayer and doing so forges and strengthens his identity.

The Jewish preoccupation with history, however, is not limited to the past. If anything the prayer book turns more often and more decisively to the future. One prays for the welfare of one's children, for God's continuing favor to the House of Israel, for the rebuilding of the Temple. Redemption and the need for Redemption are the theme much more than the celebration of past achievements and past ways of living. Rarely do we find a description of "days of old," and even the account of the Temple service found in the *Musaf* service for the Day of Atonement is enclosed—in its traditional form—in the formula "We will do, and we will offer up," echoing the Children of Israel's "We will do, and we will obey" (Exodus 24:7) proclamation at Mount Sinai. Prayer—like the Covenant itself—is dynamic, an ongoing drama. Needless to say, all the prayers contained in the "Eighteen Benedictions," of the *Amidah* are phrased in the present and future tense, and one is bidden to join the blessing on historical redemption (*ge'ulah*) to these benedictions (*tefillah*) without any break or pause between them (B. T. *Berakhot*, folio 9b). Here too the dimension of historical purpose and fulfillment appears as an overriding theme of Jewish prayer.

This emphasis on the existential immediacy of the prayer act as a response to the challenges of history now and to come gives point to the question raised by many of the contributors to this volume concerning the failure of the modern Jew (and of the traditional liturgy) to formulate an adequate response to the challenges posed by the Holocaust and the establishment of the State of Israel to the traditional prayer system. A number of directions are attempted, but none of the contributors is prepared to accept the notion that the prayer book has become unchangeable, fossilized, rooted in the past. If we have not yet found a way of responding to the mighty changes of our own time, then that response must still be found and uttered.

Judaism notoriously lacks a formal "creed" or set of dogmas. Even Maimonides' attempt to draw up a systematic statement of belief met with limited acceptance. His thirteen articles of faith are indeed included in many versions of the prayer book (as is the hymn—*Yigdal*—based on these), but these have only a marginal place in the prayer cycle. On the other hand, it may be argued that the basic tenets of Judaism are encoded in the prayer book in the form of *testimony*. Each individual testifies to a communion of shared beliefs. Thus thrice daily, the divine unity is affirmed in the *Shema,* a dramatic cry from the individual to the collectivity of Israel. Thrice daily also, the longed-for redemption of the Jewish people, together with that of all nations of the world, finds expression in the *Alenu* prayer. Israel's chosenness and uniqueness are the theme of the blessing repeated (with variations) twice daily (*haBoher be'ammo Yisrael be'ahava* in the morning and *ohev ammo Yisrael* in the evening). The blessing formula ("blessed art thou, O Lord our God . . ."), as Emmanuel Levinas has argued, basing himself on R. Hayyim of Volozhin's *Nefesh haHayyim* (1824), is the fundamental act of worship. It precedes belief or knowledge; it is the "saying" that precedes the "said." Such primary religious response is at the heart of the prayer book.

The most eloquent testimony is often achieved indirectly—through the positioning of the prayers and through their literary imagery. The *Shema,* for instance, is preceded by a benediction on the creation of light, and a second benediction, as already mentioned, on the election of Israel, specifically, through the giving of the Torah. The third blessing (which follows the *Shema*) concerns the future Redemption. Here we find a clear syntax of Creation, Revelation, Redemption. Creation implies purpose, a purpose that will be achieved by means of the Torah, the fundamental instrument for the Redemption of Israel and the world.

The same triadic pattern, identified by Franz Rosenzweig as the heart of the biblical covenant, may be noted in the central benediction of the Sabbath *Amidah* for the evening, morning, and afternoon prayers. In the first of these, God, having completed the work of six days, is said to sanctify the Sabbath day as "the end of the creation of heaven and earth"; in the morning *Amidah,* the scene of sanctification changes to Mount Sinai, with Moses receiving the two tablets of stone "upon which the observance of the Sabbath was prescribed"; in the third form of the blessing during the afternoon *Amidah,* we look forward to an ultimate Sabbath of rest and holiness, when "Abraham will be glad, Isaac will rejoice and Jacob and his sons will be at ease," when "God will be One and his name will be One." Here the theme of Redemption finds expression, but not in the form of a philosophical statement. Instead, three scenes of a universal drama are enacted. The Sabbath is the sign that links them together. The worshipper in uttering these three forms of the central benediction—evening, morning, and afternoon—becomes a partner in sanctifying the Sabbath. It is a speech-act of a special kind.

Examples such as these demonstrate the literary power of the prayer book. Its authors and compilers had a sure sense of poetic structure and the force of poetic imagery, especially as these were found in the Bible. For the most part, they wisely let the biblical texts speak for themselves. The Psalms figure prominently throughout, supplying the accents of both praise and supplication. And there are substantial extracts from other books of the Bible. Later writings are also represented in frequent chapters of the *Mishnah,* excerpts from the Talmud, selections of *Midrash,* as well as liturgical poetry (*piyyut*) actually composed with an eye to synagogue use. Thus the *Siddur* reflects Jewish literary creativity of all times and places, spanning Jewish experience through the ages from the biblical period to the present day.

In addition to historical time, however, the *Siddur* has reference to another kind of time measurement, namely, that of the cycle of the year. The same event is often symbolic on both levels. Passover, for instance, commemorating the Exodus from Egypt, is not only the festival of human freedom; it also heralds the coming of spring. Sukkot, the festival of booths, commemorates the desert sojourn but also marks the season of ingathering. The seasons reflected in the *Siddur* are those of the Land of Israel. Indeed, the bond between the Jewish people and the Land of Israel as a site of special holiness (expressed also in the requirement that the *Amidah* be recited while the worshipper faces Jerusalem) is among the major motifs of the *Siddur.* Thus the man of prayer creates within himself an awareness of the different dimensions of what may be termed Jewish time and space.

A major concern of the present volume is the relationship between thought and act as exemplified in prayer. While the prayers themselves express a spiritual inwardness, the framework in which they are recited is formal, halakhic, involving definite obligations and clearly defined parameters of time, place, and community. One area in which this dialectic is played out is the relationship between the text and melody of the liturgy. While nearly all the liturgical *texts* have become standardized over the course of history, the *melody* of the prayers has remained an ever-changing, often individual expression. In this way, the liturgy gives priority to the uniformity and eloquence of the classic formulations while allowing freedom to "act out" with both soul and thought.

The Jew stands before God not only as an individual but also as member of a faith community, and this is reflected throughout the *Siddur.* Prayers are formulated in the plural; thus, even as one prays for his own private needs, he prays for the needs of the entire Jewish people, affirming his membership in an entity so much larger than himself. This membership is both horizontal and vertical: horizontal in that the worshipper is a member of the community of all living Jews and vertical in that he is a member of the historical nation of the Covenant, with all its shared memories of the past and aspirations for the future. In prayer, the Jew reaffirms his status as a link in the chain reaching from Abraham via Sinai to the messianic future. The repeated encounter with

Introduction xi

shared memories and beliefs strengthens the worshipper's feeling of attachment and belonging no matter where he finds himself. The individual does not stand before God in awful solitude but rather sees himself as part of a group bound by a common destiny. In times of trouble, when a person seeks relief from his personal distress, prayer gives him an opportunity to feel part of a larger whole—he belongs to his people, and joining with them, he reaches out to the God of his ancestors.

The fact that Jewish prayer is not only a conversation between the individual and God but also a conversation of man with himself and his fellowmen in the presence of God, bringing the whole gamut of Jewish experience to bear on this dialogue, makes prayer, in the words of Elie Wiesel, the secret language of the Jew in all places and at all times. Any Jew familiar with the liturgy can join a traditional prayer service anywhere and feel at home. Thus prayer becomes a mode of speech for signifying the unity of the Jewish people. In short, Jews communicate by means of prayer.

The present volume seeks to cover the main topics and questions related to prayer in Judaism, with special reference to the problems of our time, approaching these from five main directions: the existential encounter, halakhic-historical development, philosophical foundations, educational and social issues, and literary form. All the contributors to this volume, as well as having a "professional" interest in the subject, are also personally committed, each in his own fashion and by way of his group affiliation (authors range from Orthodox to Reform and secular).

Most of the writers have a well-established scholarly interest in one or another aspect of the subject, and the essays that follow record their meeting in an interdisciplinary framework with the objective of clarifying the question of "prayer and modern man," and in particular "prayer and the modern Jew."

The book begins with Elie Wiesel's essay, which gives us something of the existential encounter. This is followed by a discussion of prayer in our time, opened by Professor Dov Sadan, and further developed by Jakob Petuchowski, in which the key issues are raised and brought into focus.

The halakhic-historic section of the book includes two major contributions by Joseph Tabory and the late Joseph Heinemann. Shalom Rosenberg offers an analysis of the main trends in Jewish philosophy and mysticism as they touch on the phenomenon of prayer. His study concentrates mainly on the different philosophical schools and on the special questions that they raise for the present-day student. Four main theories of prayer are then discussed in detail: that of Yehuda Halevi by Eliezer Schweid, that of Maimonides by Marvin Fox, that of the Spanish mystics by the late Ephraim Gottlieb, and that of Franz Rosenzweig by the late Moshe Schwartz.

Rabbi Adin Steinsaltz and Uriel Simon write on education for prayer and its possibilities. Rabbi Jules Harlow discusses various efforts to publish new prayer books and anthologies for contemporary Jews and the influence of these efforts on the praying community.

Hasidism contributed new insights into the phenomenon of prayer, but the main way of teaching taken by the hasidic masters was through stories and sayings (not abstract ideas). The contribution of Rabbi Samuel Dresner is based on hasidic reflections. Agnon's story "My Prayer Book," with which this collection concludes, conveys something of the special place the *Siddur* has in Jewish life.

The volume is based upon the proceedings of an international conference held by the David and Batya Kotlar Institute for Judaism and Contemporary Thought at the Nir Etzion Guest house near Haifa and at Bar-Ilan University. A Hebrew version, entitled *HaTefillah HaYehudit: Hemshekh VeHiddush*, edited by Gabriel H. Cohn, was published by Kedem, Jerusalem, on behalf of the Institute for Judaism and Contemporary Thought in 1978. Its contents are herein presented in a revised and updated form and with additions. A number of the articles originally presented in Hebrew were translated into English by Rabbi Leonard Oschry, whose help we hereby acknowledge.

The chapters that follow emphasize Jewish prayer from biblical times to our own as an extraordinary example of continuity in the face of change.

Notes

1. *Midrash Tanhuma*, "Vezoth Haberacha" 7.
2. Compare on this subject A. J. Heschel, "Al Mahut Hatefillah," *Bitsaron* 2 (1940/1941): 346–352.
3. A detailed bibliography of articles on the subject of prayer may be found in Joseph Tabory, *Reshimat Ma'amarim beInyanei Tefillah uMo'adim, Kiryat Sefer,* suppl. to vol. 64 (Jerusalem: Jewish National and University Library, 1992–1993).

Part I

1
Prayer and Modern Man

Elie Wiesel

Make prayers out of my tales, said Rabbi Nahman of Bratzlav. His followers obeyed and went even further: they made tales out of his prayers. As for his distant disciple, Franz Kafka, he simply stated: to write *is* to pray.

Literature and prayer have much in common. Both take everyday words and give them meaning. Both appeal to what is most personal and most transcendent in man. Both are rooted in the most obscure and mysterious zone of our being. Nourished by anguish and fervor, both negate detachment and imitation—and are negated by them. The writer and the worshipper both draw from one source—the source where sound becomes melody, and melody turns into language which becomes offering. What inspiration is to the writer, *kavvanah* is to the beseecher. Both are as open as an open wound—both live tense and privileged moments. If one may assume that man could not live without literature, one may equally affirm that neither could he survive without prayer.

Except that in our society it is becoming increasingly difficult for modern man to pray: He has conquered space but forgotten his prayer.

This is particularly true of our young people. Remember their outburst of emotion when they reached the Western Wall in 1967? Many did not know what to do, what to say. Remember the Simhat Torah celebration in Moscow? Many students sang and danced since they knew nothing else—and no other way—to affirm their Jewishness. Their religious thirst is greater, and more genuine, than that of their parents. What they yearn for is not knowledge but devotion; they seek fervor more than erudition. More and more youngsters, especially of secular background, want to be taught *how* to pray, in what to believe—and in whom as well.

But if worship suggests humility, a discourse of worship implies the opposite. Therefore, I would rather tell you a story.

It's about a man who stumbles in his prayers. Day after day, every time he is about to say *Ahaba rabba ahabtanu,* "You have loved us very much, O Lord," he must stop. He *must.* Every word turns into an obstacle. He feels a shadow enveloping his gaze and weighing on his breath. He feels pain and the pain makes him sad, profoundly sad, and the sadness overwhelms him with memories and nostalgic images and tunes, bringing back a vanished world, his childhood and the fervently innocent prayers of that childhood. His pain increases and, for a moment, he feels trapped: no matter what he would do, what he would say, it would be a lie, a betrayal. Then. . . .

Here again, let us make a brief pause. And have a look at the hero of this story. Who is he? Obviously—our contemporary. From what preceded we already know that he is religious and observant, that he says his prayers every day—and also that he says them with *kavvanah*—otherwise his problem would not touch us at all. If it does, it is *because* of his desire to pray while at the same time being unable to do so. His dialectical situation is such that none of his options seem right. No one has more reasons than he to bow before God, and no one has more reasons to turn away from him. As an individual, he cannot but praise God's mercy for having survived, but as member of the most cursed generation in history, he cannot but refuse God such praise.

So—we understand his difficulties in uttering *Ahaba rabba ahabtanu.* Each of us may encounter similar inner opposition when saying any prayer. The inhibitions are the same; so are the doubts. Between the words we may try to articulate and their content, there exists a wall or an abyss. Either we lie or the words lie. What we wish to say cannot be said, what we want to offer has been taken away from us. And yet, once upon a time, these very words helped us live through the night and wait and wait for dawn—these very words helped link us to what constitutes man's truth if not his immortality. Have we changed? We alone? Not everything has changed. Only the words remain the same—and this is one of the reasons why we find it so painful to use them: as though they had betrayed us—and themselves.

Once upon a time it was all so simple. To live meant to implore, to survive— to express gratitude. In the midst of torment and tempest, one knew what to say and when and how. There was a prayer for every circumstance; a melody for every prayer. A certain order prevailed inside exile itself. Certain sentences had to be formed at a given hour, neither earlier nor later. Nothing was left to chance. In a world both dismembered and demented, one chose to cling to the *Siddur*—hence to *Seder*. Lost in geography, in space, Jews oriented themselves in time, making it their refuge and haven. And prayer lent time its splendor and its depth.

What was prayer to them, to us? An encounter with God and with oneself. A moment of grace, of abandonment, of affirmation—of recognition. If art is man's way of saying no, prayer is his way of saying yes. Yes to the universe and its creator, yes to life and its meaning, yes to faith, to hope, to joy. A beacon to the lost wanderer, Jacob's ladder to the dreamer in search of dreams, a window to the soul: prayer is what is most indispensable in man's passage on earth. Consolation or compensation to some, sublimation to others, prayer also means power and adventure. The famous outcry: "Don't rely on miracles, say Psalms," expresses more than a desperate people's sense of humor; it also communicates its lasting faith in the power of prayer. If the study of Torah has kept *us* alive, then prayer has kept our *hope* alive. Prayer was the shortest way to reach out for answers to misfortune. It was enough to pray—to pray well—for man to reconcile himself with destiny and to achieve some happiness, some peace either as gift or as reward. God may have created man so as to make him sing—and sing Himself. God loves not only to receive prayers but also to recite them, according to the Talmud. What are God's prayers? *She-ekbosh ka'asi vaarahem 'al banai.* . . . "May I contain my anger and have pity on my children."

Thus the history of prayer is as old as the history of man. Remember the Talmud? Adam was the first liturgical author: it was he who composed *Mizmor shir leyom ha-Shabbat*, "A Psalm, a Song, for the Sabbath day." Abraham, Isaac, and Jacob are said to have divided among themselves the three daily services: *Shaharit, Minha, and Maariv*. And so as not to offend the women, one *Tikkun* was granted to Rachel and another to Leah. Kings and prophets, philosophers and kabbalists have all sought to be identified, if not remembered, by a prayer. The *'Aggada* is a song, the *Kabbalah*, a song of that song. What is Hasidism if not one endless prayer offered sometimes in a whisper and sometimes in a shout? Rabbi Nahman believes that every tree and every leaf and every blade of grass say their own prayers to God. Only the dead don't pray.

Israel's entire destiny was contained in its prayer: pleas for help and pleas for food, thanks for blessings received and shared. Gravity and joy, whispers and lamentations, jubilant outcries and melancholy litanies: all the longings, all the metamorphoses of Jewish existence are reflected in Jewish prayer.

Israel's very concept of Israel is in its prayer. Whereas Torah came from above, given by God, *tefillah* was composed by man. In matters of Torah everything has already been said by Moses or to Moses; but not *tefillah*. As he repeats a certain prayer, man identifies with its author and recreates it over and over—and every man can and must give birth to his own prayer.

Naturally, like everything else in our tradition, prayer exists and vibrates on more than one level. All of Jewish humanism can be illustrated by the talmudic saying that silence in prayer has been instituted so as not to embarrass sinners. Jewish philosophy stresses certain conclusions from prayer, namely, that God is not indifferent to what happens to His creation. Jewish literature would be much poorer without the innumerable *piyyutim*—and so would Jewish history: certain *piyyutim* tell more about the Crusades than all the historians' accounts and contain more artistic poetry than many poetic works. Jewish poetry suffuses prayer and is suffused by it: true prayers are inevitably beautiful. And ethical prayers offered on behalf of one's fellowman are granted first. Those uttered against man are rejected—and perhaps that is the reason why *Ve-la'malshinim* (the prayer against slanderers) was added much later to the *Shemoneh-'Esreh,* and why *we-hafer azatam we-kalkel mahshavtam* "cancel their thoughts and thwart their counsels" is said at the end. Prayer must involve man. Because Moshe prayed at the Red Sea crossing, God admonished him: "My creatures are drowning and you indulge in prayer?" "A prayer that is not on behalf of one's community is worthless," said Rabbi Pinhas of Koretz. A prayer from which man's fate is absent—his anguish ignored—is not called prayer.

Yes, it was all so simple and gratifying. Prayer was meant to engage man and God in eternal dialogue. Thanks to prayer, we know that God is present, better still: that God is presence. Hence, that everything is possible and meaningful. Thanks to prayer God descends from heaven and dwells among His creatures; thanks to prayer man's soul leaves *its* dwelling and ascends into heaven. The substance of language and the language of silence—that is prayer. It brings together more than reason and reasoning; it both causes and shapes events. By explaining existence, it gives rhythm and density. Take away prayer from our people and you will have silenced its soul.

As in other traditions, prayer responds to a need—to man's need to understand and be understood, to speak and be heard, to sing, to believe, to remember, to share, to dream, and to worship. Prayer stems from the need to go under in order to emerge again, more serene than before—atoned and purified. Man wants to justify good and evil in the present; he needs to glorify his ordeal and then weep over it. Man cannot hold back too long, at one point he must let go—and he does so in prayer, which then becomes a mode of liberation.

It is possible to live without hope and perhaps without truth—but not without prayer, which is a quest for both. Prayer then means impulse, movement—inward and outward. Movement toward God, movement toward His creatures—

become one with Him, one with them. Prayer means being alive—moving toward life.

For prayer is basically, and in the fullest sense, an act of faith. Faith in God and in history—in God as source of history and therefore just and not only almighty and compassionate; faith in words, faith in faith. Without faith, prayer approaches parody. To pray means to be able to measure what one has and what one lacks, what one is and what one wishes to be; to accept what one is given and give it back. Without this ability, man is deprived of an essential dimension. To be closed to prayer is more punishment than sin, for prayer may contain its own reward. To pray is to break through solitude, through fear of solitude. Prayer is a remedy for solitude even more than for sadness and torture. Had Elisha ben Abuyah *entered* the *Bet-Midrash,* had he chosen Jewish prayers even while rejecting Jewish philosophy, his fate would have been less tragic. In another century, and on another level, it was prayer that saved Franz Rosenzweig and moved him to return to his people. Raba's attitude was not accepted in our tradition: prayer is not *Hayye-shaa,* a fleeting moment, though Torah leads to *Hayye-olam,* eternity. Both are needed for the Jew to fulfill his condition. Without either, he would be unbalanced. Raba was wrong in opposing the two. Prayer and study are both given to man to lift himself to higher spheres; they are not mutually exclusive. Indeed, they complement one another. What Torah does for the mind, prayer does for the soul. But while man may study and still feel lonely, the same is not true of the man who prays.

A Jew who prays, ties himself to the collective body of Israel. That is why *tefillah-bezibbur,* collective worship, is stressed in Judaism. The loneliest Jew ceases to be lonely the moment he joins a *minyan.* The fact that he is saying words that other Jews, elsewhere, are reciting to commemorate the same occasion, is a source of strength. He is no longer alone, his voice is not lost in emptiness. The fact that, for centuries and centuries, millions and millions of Jews of all ages and conditions have repeated the same words to express the same anguish and the same gratitude, cannot but make him realize that he belongs to an immense community where he can find not only forerunners but allies as well. In repeating what Rabbi 'Akiba and Rabbi Shimon said when they faced adversity, when they discovered awe in learning and joy in *Shabbat,* the Jew knows that he is no longer a stranger in God's creation.

Now—you will agree that this need to pray, to communicate, still exists in contemporary man—and even more than before. It exists not only among Jews but among Gentiles as well. The Russians' adoration of Stalin had a religious quality—and even a mystical one. Read or reread the silly and pompous Odes to the ruler of the Kremlin; they are not unlike litanies. Read the confessions of his famous victims; they even use religious vocabulary. The Communist regime may have abolished religion but not prayer.

Outside Russia, we have witnessed recently an awakening of religiosity. Scientists make no secret of their desire to rediscover things spiritual. At a famous NASA base, scores of physicists study the Talmud. They are best suited to realize that technology has solved the wrong problems. Man walks on the moon but no one cares to look. We have conquered space but not the heart. The distance separating one work from another is greater than the one separating us from Mars. Man has never fled so fast from so many places; he has never been so alienated, so traumatized. Since a certain event one generation ago we know that our civilization is bankrupt: it lost its fervor, its sense of adoration, its ability to worship.

Yet the need is there, though it is no longer simple to fill it. The Talmudic saying *Mi-she-nihrab bet-hamikdash nin'alu sha'arei tefillah,* "since the destruction of the Temple, the gates of prayer have been shut," applies more to the present than to the distant past. We have known the taste both of ashes and of wine—and both experiences lie beyond words: no lament would be somber enough, no praise exulting enough. We have seen what no one before was privileged to see: the Temple in flames and the survivors undertaking to rebuild it. In the face of so many tears, so much courage and determination, one feels impotent and humble, too humble to judge or even to react. Like Beckett's heroes, man cannot but utter primitive, disjointed sounds.

What is true in literature is true in liturgy as well. In literature the failure seems total. Among the hundreds of volumes devoted to the two themes that curse and bless our generation, none does them justice, which is only natural. The two events, by their sheer magnitude, transcend imagination and defy perception. No artistic endeavor could even begin to reflect the despair accumulated in the ghettoes and the pride and glory that ensued. No poet, unless he is mad, could even begin to reveal what lies at the core of his madness. Auschwitz and Jerusalem: two mysteries hinting at the same truth—but man is too weak to comprehend such truth. Once upon a time, artistic imagination preceded reality; now it follows it at a great distance, as though ashamed, defeated.

In liturgy, too, one is overcome by helplessness. The existing prayers sound inadequate, or to use a modern cliché, irrelevant. How is one to proclaim and extol divine justice, divine mercy in the century of Majdanek and Treblinka? How well we understand the hero of my tale who stumbles while reciting *Ahaba rabba ahabtanu. Ahaba rabba* "a great love" and Auschwitz? *Hemla gedola viyetera* "great and exceeding mercy" and Belsen? How can one say these words without turning them into lies, into blasphemy? It must be either-or. Either we assume that prayer, though timeless, is relevant to every man and his needs, or we see in it an abstraction of the mind, a luxury of the spirit. We Jews naturally believe the former to be true. How, then, can we pronounce words that have been denied before our own eyes? A thousand communities uprooted and *'Amka ahabta?* One million Jewish children massacred, some of them thrown into the flames alive—and *Ata behartanu mikol ha-'amim?* "Thou hast chosen us from all peoples."

In other words: how is one to pray after what happened? How is one to address God when His ways seem more obscure than ever, His mercy more hidden than ever?

Don't tell us that God had nothing to do with these events. That is a view which runs counter to whatever Judaism stands for. God is involved in man's destiny—good or bad. To thank Him for Jerusalem and not question Him for Treblinka is hypocrisy. God is at the beginning as well as at the outcome of all our endeavors. He is the question and He is the answer. Hence the treacherous trap confronting man: just as one cannot conceive of Auschwitz with God, one cannot comprehend it without God. Thus—how is one to worship Him; how is one not to worship Him? Is one to pray to Him as before—as though nothing ever happened? Would that not be cowardice—does He want our cowardice?

Here we are again at the very heart of the problem which seems to disturb you this year.

For the nonbeliever, the whole question seems . . . academic. That is why the drama of the believer seems more terrifying, his torment more human. Faced with the immense scandal that is the Holocaust, what should be—what could be—his position? What can he say?

His options are limited. He could rebel. And stop practicing—stop worshipping. And no one would have the right to reprimand him. The Jewish tradition, alone among all others, allows man to protest against heaven. From Abraham to Moses, from Jeremiah to Levi Yizhak of Berditchev, there were many who questioned God and His peculiar presence in history. Wasn't it a disciple of Rabbi Ishmael who exclaimed: *Mi kamoka ba'elim ha-shem*—no: *Mi kamoka ba-ilmim ha-shem she-roe be-'elbon banaw we-shotek* "Who is like You among the gods oh Lord!" No: rather, "Who is like You among the dumb, oh Lord, who sees the outrage done to His children and is silent!"? For contemporary man to shout with anger is not compatible with our tradition. Remember the *Anshe keneset ha-gedolah* the men of the Great Synagogue who refused to say *Ha-el ha-gadol ha-gibbor we-ha-nora,* that God is great and mighty and awesome? Today, too, one can choose rebellion and remain within Judaism. But one's rebellion must be constant; meaning: it must be renewed, reexamined, reaffirmed day after day, night after night. One must live one's rebellion and not let it slide into indifference. One must say again and again: *Ribbono shel 'olam,* Master of the Universe, I know and you know that it's time to pray . . . but I will not; do you hear me? I will not! Whoever opts for such an attitude and does so with sincerity, well, his no becomes a yes, and his refusal of prayer becomes . . . prayer.

One might also continue to pray—as before—forcing God to resemble his attributes. As the Kotzker rebbe said: One implores God our father, one implores Him until He becomes our father. One calls Him *rahum we-hanun,* "merciful and gracious"—until He becomes *rahum we-hanun.* This attitude implies—paradoxically—the notion that He is not. Prayer then becomes a form of protest. And defiance. One calls Him loving—because He is something else. Because He permitted bloodshed, one extols His justice. In other words: prayer becomes a means of sanctifying His name *in spite* of the mass graves. And of proclaiming His glory *in spite* of the flames that consumed the night. *Mi-ma-ma'akim karrtika,* "From the depths I have cried unto Thee, oh Lord," would then mean: in spite of the *mi-ma-ma'akim,* in spite of the depth, *karatika,* I am calling for you. In spite of what has been done to Your people, we believe in You, we praise You. *Ekh nashir et shir ha-shem 'al admat neka,* "How shall we sing the Lord's song in a strange land?" would read: *we'od eik nashir*—and how we shall sing! The more numerous the trials, the harsher the ordeal, the more powerful the song and the greater the fervor.

The problem appears even more disturbing when we discover how it was handled by Jews *during* the catastrophe, inside the ghettoes, within the fiery walls.

One of the most poignant mysteries of that period is contained in the religious response of religious Jews who risked their lives continuing to observe as many commandments of the Torah as possible. Some fasted on Yom Kippur and refused to eat bread on Pesah. Some managed never to eat *Tref.* I remember, I will always remember, the gray dawns *over there* when hundreds of Jews would line up, behind the barracks, to lay *tefillin.* I remember, I will always remember, the outdoor Rosh Hashanah services, the *Kol Nidre,* the *Neilah.* I remember, I will always remember, the ancient words, now distorted if not demented, praising God for His goodness, for His compassion, for His love of Israel—His chosen people.

How could they, how could we say these things *over there?* I don't know how. Perhaps it was our way of indicting the Judge—so to speak! Our way of protesting against the inhumanity, the helplessness of the human condition. For that may be the depth and the secret of Jewish faith: to turn every gesture into a challenge, every prayer into an appeal. To rebel in spite of one's belief, to believe in spite of one's rebellion.

Never before did God and man confront one another as they did *over there.* Never before was either tested with such force. Never before has the outcome been as obscure. The great theological protest was enacted there but it contained no words of heresy. On the contrary, the words were those of acceptance and praise. In reciting the *Kaddish, Yitgadal we-yitkadash sheme rabba,* "May his great name be exalted and sanctified" there, at the edge of the ditches and the altars, those Jews succeeded in indicting Him more powerfully than ever before.

Is this the solution? No—it cannot be. No one would dare—today—repeat those words and those deeds: no one has the right or the strength to do so. We can only try to be worthy of what they tried to teach us, perhaps, to our shame, unsuccessfully.

Is that the answer? That is the question. Is belief an art or a necessity? An expression of weakness or of strength? I proclaim—*be-emuna shelemah* "with a perfect faith" that the pious Jew over there was stronger than his predecessors anywhere, stronger than the forces that crushed him, stronger than the forces that tested him. There, he made the impossible possible.

One last example: the Gaon of Vilna said that *we-samahta be-hageka* is the most difficult commandment in the Torah. I could never understand this puzzling remark. Only during the war did I understand. Those Jews who, in the course of their journey to the end of hope, managed to dance on Simhat Torah, those Jews who studied Talmud by heart while carrying stones on their back, those Jews who went on whispering *Zemirot shel Shabbat,* (the Sabbath table-hymns) while performing hard labor—they taught us how Jews should behave in the face of adversity. For my contemporaries, one generation ago, *we-samahta be-hageka* "and thou shalt rejoice in thy festival" was one commandment that was impossible to observe—yet they observed it.

Permit me, in conclusion, to return to the poor hero of my sad tale. We left him at the moment when, sad and crushed, he felt unable to say *Ahaba rabba ahabtanu.* Yet, in the end, he will say it. He will clench his teeth but he will say it. Because other Jews, *over there,* said it before him. No matter what, he feels he should not be the last in the chain: the adventure that Judaism is should not stop with him.

Now—without his hesitation, his prayer would be an act of complacency. With it, his prayer becomes an act of remembrance. And a story as well. For, ultimately, we all share Rabbi Nahman's aspirations. Except that in my case I would like to make tales out of my tales, and prayers out of my prayers, with no one knowing the difference, not even myself—least of all, myself.

This English version of Elie Wiesel's (Hebrew) presentation first appeared in *Rabbi Joseph H. Lookstein Memorial Volume,* edited by Leo Landman (New York: Ktav Publishing House Inc., 1980). It is reprinted by kind permission of the author.

2
Some Thoughts on the Subject of Prayer

Dov Sadan

1

I must admit that I have no idea why I have been given the honor of opening this discussion of prayer and related areas. Let me simply say that since I have been called on, I will write that which "God puts in my mouth" and hope that my readers will be charitable.

But even as I invoke the attribute of mercy, I cannot pretend that I am completely ignorant of the great subject on which we are embarked. Prayer sustained me in my childhood, when the lamp of pure, innocent faith shone over my head but I moved away from it in my youth and early manhood, and the saying, "If you forsake her for one day, she will forsake you for two," was fulfilled in me. Now that I have returned to her in my latter years, at a time of confusion for our generation, I may say that I approach the subject with no little difficulty. I am aware of the struggle which prayer imposes—the struggle between the forms of tradition and the wish for novelty; and I would deceive myself and others if I said that all hesitations are now done with and the account between the prayer tradition and myself is settled.

2

This may lay me open to critics on both sides who have a more clearcut position, but the truth has to be acknowledged—and also the interests of critical candor. I simply find it hard to reflect on prayer in the abstract, or in a general way, as a literary phenomenon or as a means of approaching the Creator. I cannot think of it as gesture without form. For me, whenever prayer comes to mind it is with the definite article attached, I see it in its fixed form, I hear each prayer with its specific melody. Of course, I know the ancient regulation against fixed prayer, in the same way as I know the later legend about the man who did not know the order of prayer but whose halting, inarticulate stammerings found favor with God. I know the attraction of these models. Yet this does not change my deep feeling, acquired in the course of my upbringing, which was commonplace enough, and the tradition I absorbed with it. I will mention a few examples from my own life, which may have a wider bearing on our subject.

As I search my memory for my first experiences of prayer, there comes to mind the image of five small orphans, myself among them, whose mothers had died in childbirth the very night when each was born, evidently of an infection carried by the midwife. The city, which saw in this fivefold bereavement a punishment for the sins of its heretics, made the *Yahrzeit* observed by these five infants into an event, and the *gabbai* (layleader) of each of the synagogues in town attempted to persuade our teacher to bring us to their house of prayer. Once, he acceded to the request of the *gabbai* of a certain *Bet-Midrash* (house of study), that of the great author of the work, *Mate Efraim*. On the way to the synagogue, he instructed us that, while reciting the *Kaddish,* we were to cry out at the top of our lungs, "*Va-yatsmah purkenay ve-karev Meshihay*" ("May His salvation spring forth and His Messiah come quickly"))the words added to the *Kaddish* in the *hasidic* community—and so we did. The worshippers grumbled aloud when they heard us, but we did not know why they were grumbling. At the end of the service, the *gabbai,* a handsome, strapping young man, came over to us, patted us on the cheek, and said, "*Kinderlakh, a shad eyere heldzelakh. Andere hobn shoyen hekhr geshrign, und der rekhta iz nisht gekummen, un ver iz yo gekummen iz gven a ligner.*" That is, "Children, it's a pity for your throats! Others have yelled louder than you, and the one they wanted didn't come (i.e., the Messiah), and the one who came was an impostor." The significance of those words was only understood by me years later, yet, whenever I remember that incident, what impresses me more than the recollection of the five little orphans standing on the steps of the Ark, opened in deference to the multiple orphanhood, was the tension between the teacher and the worshippers—which I came to understand in the course of time, as standing at the heart of the dispute of the last generation and the reason for their differing traditions. One should know that my home city, which was renowned for its scholarship and enlightenment, had eighty-two different synagogues, the majority of which were *Nosah Sefarad* (or adopted by the *hasidim*) and the minority *Nosah Ashkenaz* as followed by the *mitnagdim*. It is against this background that one may understand the double strategy or, if one wishes, the double diplomacy of our teacher, the representative of the stubborn, victorious majority, and the *gabbai*, the representative of the defensiveness of the defeated minority, for both of whom these five little orphans served as forces in their long, drawn out war. For the point was that the words we shouted were part of the Sefaradi or hasidic rite but were omitted in the Ashkenazi prayer book of the *mitnagdim*.[1]

I would not go on at such length about my childhood experiences were it not that there is a sequel attached to it. It is also a case of a majority and a minority—here too the majority being the older stream and the minority being the later stream. In the non-Jewish high school where I studied in our city, the Jewish students were required to attend classes on Saturdays as well, but were excused from the first two hours of classes in order to attend services held in the Jewish primary school and, later on, in the old synagogue (though it was in fact called the "New Synagogue"). These were conducted by our instructor in religion, a rabbi with a doctorate belonging to the new "enlightened" school, who had completed his studies at the rabbinical seminary in Berlin—that of Maybaum. On the face of it, it was a perfectly acceptable, *kosher* service, except that, due to the short time period allotted, the Torah reading was abbreviated, and the pronunciation used was that of the Reform temples (which made us call it the "Bow-wow accent" because it reminded us I am afraid of the barking of dogs.) Students such as myself, who had been raised in pious, traditional homes, rose at dawn and recited the entire service in our rooms, down to the last detail—all due to doubt as to whether we would fulfil our obligations in participating in the students' service. This went so far that when I chanced to go to Lewow-Lemberg and my curiosity brought me to the so-called "enlightened" synagogue, I first went and *davened* with the early *minyan* in the traditional synagogue on the outskirts of town. Further, since it was taken for granted in my family that I would myself become an "enlightened" rabbi, I expected to continue the same strategy, willy-nilly. Before I would go to "Tempel" to minister and to conduct services, I would recite the entire service in my home in the *nosah* and melody to which I was accustomed from the little synagogue in our town and, later, from the *Bet-Midrash* in the village nearby.

3

I must make a confession. Even during those many years of apostasy when I was far from observing the commandments, the taste of prayer was alive in me, with all its richness of tradition and form, and I could apply to myself the well-known folk witticism, containing more truth than a dozen arguments against heresy. It is related of an old *apikoris* (heretic) that he used to say to himself, *Amol oz ikh fargess mikh, oz es iz nisht kayn Borey-Olam, tu ikh mikh a tsudavnen.* The approximate sense is, "Sometimes, forgetting the fact that there is no God, I catch myself praying." It goes without saying that this "deviation" comes to him in the traditional *nosah,* with all of its details and its familiar melody. And in confidence I may reveal that I have found myself "deviating" in this fashion even without the forgetting part. You pray, and you even pray with enthusiasm, even if that Rock toward which you turn no longer exists for you, for it is enough that it existed for you yesterday, so long as it is exactly the same Rock upon which you and those around you depended in your earliest childhood. And last of all: even after my conversion to religion I didn't feel any real difference in this respect. (You will excuse me for using the alien expression, "conversion," even though that is not my usual style. What happened to me and to others like me is not adequately expressed by the term *teshuvah,* or "repentance," for I do not negate that long period during which I was not religious as if it had not been, nor do I regret it or feel embarrassed by it.) But in order not to stray too far away from our subject, I will briefly say that, even though my return is not like the simple retying of a thread which has been cut off (on the contrary, one's view of the world when one "returns" is not the same, and cannot be the same, and perhaps ought not to be the same, as before the point of departure), nevertheless, the feeling of prayer, as it was in my early years, *is* the same. I could easily delude myself that this is that *vertebra* which the rabbis termed "luz," which cannot be fractured either by the flint of denial or the diamond of renewed faith—as if to witness the falseness of all transformation. Yet saying something like that is really a form of self-flattery. The more I apply my critical faculties to this subject, the clearer it becomes that we are dealing here, not with the power of a faith constructed of paradoxes, but with the weakness of simple nostalgia, which means: subjection to an upbringing which has become simply a form of escape, and the further removed one is whether in place or time, the greater its hold over us.

In the light of this analysis, I am aware how much nostalgia is involved in all this—a nostalgia encouraged by habit and routine. That being so, the first step toward freeing myself must be to look at a wider and more inclusive range of prayers—although it is possible that the end result of this bid for freedom may be a renewed, further enthrallment to origins, so let me add to my own examples a pair of examples from people greater than myself.

4

My first example is Shlomo Bickel's book, *Yidn Davenen* ("Jews Praying"). This is an enjoyable pictorial tour of the ways of prayer in sixteen synagogues in New York City made, for the most part, at the height of the Second World War, It includes groups of *hasidim* of the various major and minor dynasties: Lubavitch and Boyan, Kupishnits and Lashkovitz; the varieties of German Jewry, from Frankfort Orthodoxy to the congregants of Temple Emanuel; and the various Sephardic communities—the descendants of the Portuguese exiles and the Jews of Syria. He even finds his way to a *minyan* of black Jews. But the reader who envies the author this opportunity to breathe in so many varied worlds of prayer, which would add up to knowledge and awareness of the totality and diversity of Jewry, will find that he has nothing to envy. The author reveals, in the introduction to the book, what his intention was and to what extent it was fulfilled, and the answer is both positive and negative. He sought, as he says in his third person narrative, "the tones and gestures of the old Jewish world of his boyhood," and he continues, now in the first person, "I wandered through the synagogues of New York, I sought the faces and melodies of *Kolomiah*. I sought—and was consoled; I sought but was not satisfied with the encounter. I was consoled because I was able to recite and to pray in a group and to feel that good taste which my grandfather used to call 'the taste of *Tehillim* (Psalms).' But I was not satisfied, because the symbolic forms, with all their holiness and history, all too frequently retained too weak a measure of genuine celebration. More than once, they evinced too great a measure of the weekday and the commercial."

The criticism, as criticism of what happens when prayer becomes stereotyped, is a subject in itself. But what I found particularly interesting in that multifaceted tour and its impressions was not what Bickel found, but what he sought—namely, the restoration of his childhood, of the atmosphere of the community in which he grew up, which at that very moment was being erased from the face of the earth. That same nostalgia, which caused him to broaden his search, caused me to narrow mine. In my travels in both Americas, I could only truly pray in those places which were closest to me—in the Galician synagogue of Buenos Aires, and in New York in the synagogue named after my birthplace, Brod, where the last of the rabbis of Brod still served.

5

My second example will be S. Y. Agnon's story, "That We Not Stumble" (*Shelo Nikashel*), in which he tells the tale of his life wanderings – from his birthplace, Buczacz, in which he spent his childhood and youth, to Jaffa, the gateway to Zion, where he lived for a while in his youth; and then to Germany, both its cities and villages on the right and left banks of the Elbe, where he passed his early manhood; finally returning to the city of Jerusalem, where he became permanently resident in his middle and later years. All this took him among many different styles of prayer, until he became familiar with them all, and at home in all of the *nushaot*, until all that was left of the basic *nosah* of his early childhood was a pair of words in the Grace after Meals. These two words served, in the unfolding of the story, not for his own salvation as a member of the group obligated to preserve its own tradition, but for that of another person, one not sharing that tradition. I interpreted this story to mean that the different forms of prayer, each with its own *nosah* and melody and components, are hints or symbols of the various incarnations of Judaism. The great author is confessing to us how he learned to live the totality of Judaism through attention to its particular strands, great and small.

But if we are being precise, we must ask: Did he truly learn to live the totality, and if he did, has he also taught it to us? And the answer cannot be an unqualified "yes," because of one glaring omission.

6

I refer to the fact that, despite Agnon's travels through prayer houses over the length and breadth of Ashkenazi Jewry to acquire, via the medium of prayer, a knowledge of the fullness of Jewish experience, in practice he acquired the old ways and ignored the new ones. That is, he remained ignorant of the forms which had sprung up in the various kinds of Reform synagogues (including also the "Counter-Reform"). I have tried to demonstrate elsewhere that this omission, here, is similar to that in, *Hakhnasat Kalah,* set at the height of the stormy struggles of the Enlightenment when many bastions of the faith had already fallen. There, except for a faint echo, itself almost submerged, there is no trace of these great events. The reason for this omission is a romantic desire for harmony which, in the final analysis, amounts to romantic distortion or falsification. Our narrator certainly knew well enough the true state of things at the time, the reality compassed by his great epic but also by this, his short story, "'*Ad Henah,*" where one can see the extent of his involvement in what happened within German Jewry, its internal crises, and then further reverberations outside. So that we are entitled to assume that the above-mentioned omission was designed to save the romantic illusion of a harmony, both in place and in time—a harmony that never really existed. For such is romanticism. It cannot tolerate the present, and in the urgency of its escape, it reaches out not only to yesterday, but to the day before yesterday. It seizes upon the old grandfather who is the image of wholeness and who, because of this wholeness, real or imagined, is an image which needs neither addition nor dimunution.

7

To return to our two examples, Bickel's *Yidn Davenen* and Agnon's "*She-lo Nikashel.*" We have seen from the former book how the image of his grandfather is a constant presence just as it was in fact for Agnon also. Certainly, there is a great difference between the essayist and the storyteller, for the former did not live the life of observance, and thus, the prayer he writes of is that of someone else, a fleeting reminder of the past, while the latter lived an intensely traditional life and prayer formed an integral part of it. Yet this means that while, for Shlomo Bickel, prayer was a temporary fancy, a flight from reality, for S. Y. Agnon it was firm and permanent, a way in fact of holding on to reality. Thus, if the former was somehow entitled to the romantic illusion of his old grandfather, the latter was not.

Allow me to quote a reliable witness who, because he stands above both of them and indeed above all the other writers of his generation, may determine the issue between them. I refer to Hayim Nahman Bialik, who also evoked the image of the old grandfather in passages of his poetry, yet who also knew how to criticize him. A sharp and witty expression of this is to be found in a fragment of his unpublished writings, in which he describes the grandfather figure as follows:

> He sits and serves God. . . . He serves Him and serves Him like a faithful workman, by the sweat of his brow and the toil of his hands, with a true and faithful service. . . . And how short the day is, and how great the task. And how strict and exacting the master is! Midnight Prayers, Psalms, and how many petitions long and short.; three full-length prayers every day with their introductions and codas, with their *kavvanot,* including those of Isaac Luria as recorded in Azulai's *Avodat Ha-Kodesh; Hok-Le-Yisrael,* a chapter of *Mishnah,* lessons in Talmud and *Zohar* and ethical works; one hundred blessings every day and heaps of *mizvot* and minutiae of *mizvot* and details of the details. . . . A Jew is required to carry all this heavy baggage of service, he may not slacken or run away from it for even one hour. . . . However, God is also a God of kindness, merciful and gracious and full of righteousness, and out of His great

kindness and love He gives a man strength to carry all his burden on his bent back unaided. . . . To complete the daily quota of work to its full, to return and repeat it again the next day, and the next, and the day after that as well – and so on forever, day after day, without hesitation, without any change or alteration or innovation in the work. To begin every morning from the beginning, exactly like yesterday and the day before, as if he had never done it all before! So had our fathers and grandfathers performed their tasks of devotion for thousands of years . . . without ever losing heart. The spirit did not break and the soul did not grow impatient. Yes, how great are Your mercies, Master of the World!

These subtle, but transparently ironic remarks of the grandson further strengthen the image of the heavy, blinkered naivety of the grandfather:

For thus must it be – a servitude complete and abject. His actions for the sake of heaven are the product of a simple, clear recognition of what he owes, almost by natural necessity, a matter of habit and education passed on by inheritance, required almost from birth, and not the product of the mind, of free choice or of will. For had a slave the right to examine, to choose and to will? He never had an hour in which he could examine and choose; before his soul was yet awakened and before he knew himself, he was already launched on the same path in which he is now set, the path which had been paved since eternity by his fathers and forebears. He himself does not remember when this life of his began. His entire future life, his customs and deeds and actions, all of his thoughts until his dying day, all his mental perturbations as well as his feelings and desires – everything was laid out for him in precise detail, by letter and number, from earliest childhood by his parents and teachers, his studies and his books. Thus and thus shall you think, thus and thus shall you desire, thus and thus shall you do and say . . . and without adding to or subtracting from what is set down.[2]

8

I have quoted the greater part of this passage, which is practically unmatched for the combination of wonder and critical disapproval which marks the attitude of a grandson belonging to the dynamic world of the new, to the grandfather who belongs to the static world of the old. For our purposes it would have been enough to quote those phrases only which discuss the prayers of the old man who, in keeping with his habit and education, can neither enquire nor criticize, while the grandson, led by his intelligence, his will and desire, is bound to criticize and to choose for himself. Through inquiry he comes to know what it means to choose—and how others before have chosen.

For our present purpose, let it be said that unlike the grandfather, for whom the entire order of the prayer service, to the last detail, had been fixed from time immemorial, the grandson knows that such is not the case. Research by scholars has demonstrated that the history of the basic elements of the prayer book is not the same as that of the additions and amplifications. Here we find earlier and later elements; items have been added and removed according to the exigencies of each period. For the community the urgent need is to express faith—the urgent need of the poet is to answer this demand with his poem. Such is the history of the thousands of prayers and *piyyutim*, scattered through the generations, some of which found their way into the *Siddur* or *Mahzor* and thus survived, and some of which did not merit inclusion and were forgotten. Even an examination of the text of the prayers themselves cannot reveal why some merited inclusion and others did not. So that we cannot escape the conclusion that for the most part it was a matter of chance. But the old grandfather found himself confronted by a canon, closed before the struggles and confusions of the last several hundred years or so, and since these cannot reach him, he is as it were deaf to them. And as he utters nothing of his own he is mute also. One who would apologize by saying that the words of the earlier generations in any event include what the later generations would have liked to say is engaging in false comfort, for the earlier generations were not impressed by that argument but rather left their own imprint on the prayer book. Thus, those grandsons who long for their grandfathers' mode of worship, in all its purity, long for a closed canon which, because it lacks the voices of the last generations, also so to speak freezes the voices of earlier generations. It is like a river which, when it no longer receives a fresh flow of water, turns yesterday's flow stagnant. Moreover, recent generations have been generations of great turmoil bringing stirring discoveries in the natural world and in the field of psychology; they have also been generations which have achieved great verbal expressiveness—witness the birth and growth of its poetry. Yet all this went its way, but did not penetrate the heart of prayer toward which it yearned.

In saying this, we refer not only to the last generation, in which our language achieved poetry of supreme quality, but also to that which preceded it. Even if we limit ourselves to the two great movements of the early modern period—Hasidism and *Haskalah,* we find that Hasidism created nothing except for the *tehinot* (special supplications) of a few individuals which, as is the case with *tehinot,* and in particular those written for women, were consigned to an out-of-the-way corner of the prayer book. Then the main impact of Hasidism in the liturgical area was melodies without words. As for the *Haskalah,* which was rich in odes and invocations, only very few ever got to be mumbled hastily in the synagogue, and these withered away as they sprang up, so that the fruit of the Enlightenment was many words but few melodies. Thus each movement in its own way was condemned to a kind of silence.

9

If we now return to our two chief sources, the author of *Yidn Davenen* and the author of *She-lo Nikashel;* even though they saw personal models in their respective grandfathers, they did so in an ambivalent manner. This I know from personal discussion with each of them and my criticism of them is also a type of self-criticism, for I too have a double focus—romantic approval on the one hand and critical distance on the other. When I pointed out to the first writer that he, in effect, sanctifies the canon, he did not deny it and even cited the critic Baruch Rivkin who considered our literature, even if limited to that in the Yiddish language, as a substitute for faith, religion, and territory. But he added that Jacob Glatstein, who is thought of as the greatest Yiddish writer of the age, aspires above all things to gaining admission into the *Siddur* for even two lines of his verse—this surely testifies to the yearning of poetry to break into the canon. This shows the right sense of proportion. And when I criticized the author of *She-lo Nikashel* for sanctifying the canon, he did not deny it either. Instead, he proceeded to paint a verbal picture of the conquest of the *Siddur*— whether total or partial—by Rabbi Isaac Luria (the *Ari*) and his disciples, as if to say, "We would look fine wouldn't we, without the *Lekhah Dodi?*" He then continued to think out loud as to who had been the last poet introduced into the *Siddur,* and he remembered a *piyyut* of Rabbi Aryeh Modina and of his younger contemporary, Rabbi Yisrael Najara and then, with an elegant leap into the more recent past, remembered Naphtali Hertz Imber, whose poem, "Hatikvah" which later became Israel's national anthem, wriggled its way into the semiofficial prayers of some communities in Italy and then of our own country. His face then became serious in his ironic way, and he said, *"Nu Nu!* A fine trio. Card players and drunkards, drunkards and card players!" But what was not said in this ironic discussion was that even for Agnon himself his deepest wish was somehow to get into the *Siddur;* moreover, this had been realized, for many are the synhgogues in which his prayer for those killed in *Erets-Yisrael* is recited. Yet an analysis of his language there is sufficient to convince us that, more than one finds there the uniqueness of that author, one finds the standard forms of language—the same fixed forms which are to be found in several other prayers instituted by rabbis of our generation and written as if against their will.

And how great their reluctance was we can see from the case of the *Hallel* for Yom Ha'atzmaut (Day of Independence) and the sterile argument, as to whether it should be preceded by the full blessing containing God's name or not. It is sterile because the argument is between those whose ears are opened to hear the commandment issued out of the storm of these terrible and wonderful days, and those whose ears are stopped up so that they have not heard it.

10

I return, in conclusion, to the matter of the closed canon. While clinging to it, we cannot silence the vital element of criticism in regard to it. I will illustrate the necessity for this by means of three short sketches, to the truth of which I can personally testify.

First, an incident on Yom Kippur, during that very period when the news came to us of the destruction of the last of our brothers in the slaughterhouse of Europe. Musing bitterly about a piece of religious bombast which I had heard and read during the Days of Penitence including exaggerated words of confidence from some salesman of faith, I passed by a *shtiebel* (prayer-house) of *Hasidim,* who were lifting up voices of anguish and pain and protest into the empty night. Suddenly, they all took off their prayer shawls: "We cannot *daven,*" and they disappeared, their faces filled with anguish. True, two hours later they came back, put on their *tallesim,* and resumed their prayers. Yet who can measure what happened during those two hours? The revolt of the souls of those believers and the agitation shaking them to their very foundations. With no words to express such a situation, it died in the silence, lost both to their generation and to those following.

Second, an incident in the home of the rabbi of Buenos Aires on *Shabbat Nahamu* (the Sabbath following the ninth of Ab), in which those present engaged in a heated discussion as to whether it is possible, without insincerity, to recite on the Fast of the ninth of Ab the prayer dealing with the degradation of the people Israel and the city of Jerusalem, in light of the rebirth of the people in its Land and its holy city. Arguments were presented on both sides, and one was reminded of the mixture of weeping and joyful shouts in the days of Ezra and Nehemiah. One of the discussants stood up, full of anger, and said, "Kill me if you like, but my whole being rebels against this falsehood." Again I ask: Who can measure the rebellion in the soul of the people at such moments—the rebellion and conflict in the soul of the believer? And what has been lost to our generation and to those who succeed as through the unfeeling silence of the dumb.

Finally, in a visit to a class of schoolchildren in Toronto, in a supposedly religious school, I listened to a discussion between the pupils and their rabbi. The essence of their objection was that they were required to pray mechanically in the words of others, ancient and far away from this world. Neither I nor the rabbi could find an answer for them, or to the question implied in it: "Is everything for yesterday, and for today—nothing?" As I learned in that *shtiebel* that "from the old I gain understanding" (Psalm 119:100), so in that class I learned that "from the mouths of babes and sucklings you have founded strength?" (Psalm 8:3).

Notes

1. Hence the immediate resentment of the worshippers who objected to these unaccustomed words.

2. H. N. Bialik, *Literary Remains* (in Hebrew), ed. Moshe Ungerfeld (Tel Aviv: 1971), pp. 225–227.

3
The *Siddur*—A Closed Book?

Jakob J. Petuchowski

Professor Sadan has explored for us the problem of the "closed prayer book" both in depth and in breadth; and he has authenticated his remarks by a number of intriguing reminiscences. No doubt, every one of us can add to this body of evidence—both from his reading and from his personal experience.

I am reminded of a story related by Agnon in his contribution to the *Siegfried Moses Festschrift*. It is about Samuel Holdheim, the ex-*yeshivah bocher* who became the most radical Reform rabbi of the nineteenth century. Holdheim's congregation, the Berlin *Reformgemeinde,* did not have all-day services on Yom Kippur. They only had a morning service and a *Ne'ilah* service. In the long wait between these two services, so Agnon relates, Holdheim could be seen in a nearby café. Not, Heaven forbid, eating his lunch, but reading all the *piyyutim* which had been cut out from his congregation's prayer book.

Nearer home, I, a professor at the Hebrew Union College, find myself quite frequently attending Shabbath morning services in a little German Orthodox synagogue (*Frankfort*-style)—because I like the *nosah* there, and because I like the "*yekke*" way in which the Torah is read there. And I believe I am in good company. It was only after I had begun attending services in that little synagogue that I was told on reliable authority that the late Ismar Elbogen, who, among other things, taught Jewish Liturgy at the *Hochschule für die Wissenschaft des Judentums,* and who was one of the three editors of the *Einheitsgebetbuch,* the standard Liberal prayer book of Germany—that he too used to attend Sabbath services in a little Berlin Orthodox *shul.*

I do not know—either in Elbogen's case or mine—whether this has anything to do with the profession of teaching Jewish liturgy. It is conceivable that one's acquaintance with the traditional liturgical materials might lead to a love for them. At any rate, in my own case, I used to rationalize my going to the Orthodox German *shul* by saying that "blood is thicker than theology." Perhaps that is simply another way of describing why Dov Sadan, in Buenos Aires, attended the Brody synagogue, and why the author of *Yidn Davenen* was looking, in New York, for the kind of *shul* his grandfather used to attend.

Professor Sadan is, I believe, correct in seeing the element of nostalgia in all of this. I am not so sure, however, that nostalgia is intrinsically a bad thing. Above all, it is important for us to understand that nostalgia is not only the state of mind in which the alienated Jew, or the Jew on his way back to his Jewish heritage, approaches the *Siddur* and the traditional service. Nostalgia is also the mood of the believing Jewish worshipper. Nostalgia is built right into the *Siddur* itself!

How else would you describe a sentiment such as "Return us . . . , and we shall be restored; renew our days as of old"? How else would you describe the mood of many a Psalm which has been incorporated into the traditional liturgy? And what else but nostalgia—at least, until our very own generation—have been the millennial hopes and prayers for the Return to Zion and the Rebuilding of Jerusalem?

Of course, nostalgia can be overdone; and, if it is, it becomes bad. It then merits the criticism which the author of Ecclesiastes levels against it: "Don't say, 'How has it happened that former times were better than these?' For it is not wise of you to ask that question" (Ecclesiastes 7:10). But not all nostalgia is like that.

Perhaps, by reducing the phenomenon to nostalgia, we have not really done full justice to it. I would suggest that the longing for a *community* transcending both space and time, yet immediately accessible by way of family tradition, is as much a factor to be reckoned with as is nostalgia.

And this community of ours, this Jewish people, has rightly been seen by Saadiah Gaon, long ago, as a community only by virtue of its *toroth,* its religious instructions and institutions. Not least among those institutions is the institution of community prayer. It is in the synagogue that we know one another as Jews, that we rehearse our common history and express our common hopes for the future—even as we seek guidance in our present concerns.

I know that what I have just said will sound very *galuthi* (Diaspora-oriented) in the ears of my Israeli friends. But I also know that the Diaspora is not alone in having problems with Jewish identity. It may well be that the Israeli who wants to be a *Jewish* Israeli will, one day, discover that one of the best ways to assert his *Jewish* identity is to stand in prayer with his fellow-Jews, that is, to engage in community prayer.

However, for community prayer to be truly *community* prayer, there will have to be certain features which represent a recognizable constant, linking one worship experience to another. That is why Jewish community prayer would cease to be definable in these terms if today's worship service were to be something totally and entirely different from yesterday's worship service, or last week's, or last year's, or that of a hundred or two thousand years ago.

And thus the fixed liturgy has come about in order to represent the continuum of the worshipping, faith-community. Personally, I do not feel that the "fixed" element of the liturgy has to be quite as fixed and quite as lengthy as it has come to be. Nor am I persuaded that it was *meant* to be quite as fixed or quite as long. I am convinced, for example, that the invention of the printing press has had far more to do with the standardization of the *Siddur*—in all of its various rites—than any particular theoretical aspect of the *halakhah*-making process.

Piyyutim, which, at one time, were left to local option, now, printed black on white on the page in front of you, looked like a Sinaitic mandate not only for the local community, but for whole regions, countries and continents. The printer did that, not the *halakhah!* And that, in some instances, does not only apply to the *piyyutim.*

But how "fixed" is the "fixed" *Siddur* in reality? Perhaps not quite as "fixed" as we sometimes imagine. For example, I have in my possession—and it is not a rare book in America—a prayer book, entitled *Siddur Tif-ereth David.* It is *Nosah Sefarad.* The book was edited in 1951 by Herman A. Segal and published in New York by the Hebrew Publishing Company. As far as I am aware, the Hebrew Publishing Company has never published anything that was not acceptable to the most fastidious Orthodox taste, anything even remotely bordering on *apiqorsut* (heresy).

Consequently, it is not surprising that *Siddur Tif-eret David* contains just about everything: the Song of Songs, and the *raza deshabbat,* and the *athqinu se'udata,* and so on and so on. What *is* surprising in this *Siddur* is the English paraphrase of the Friday night song, *Shalom 'Alekhem.* Here, on page 209, the editor blithely informs us that this paraphrase is "after the German by Leopold Stein."

Now, it is a safe bet that 99 percent of the people using this *Siddur* have never heard of Leopold Stein. Who was Leopold Stein? The answer is that he was none other than one of the leading nineteenth century German Reform rabbis, one, moreover, who was liturgically very creative, and who edited his own Liberal prayer book![1] Leopold Stein superimposed on *Nosah Sefarad,* in the hands of countless *hasidim* welcoming the Sabbath angels? Only in America!

I have, admittedly, taken an extreme example. There are others, less extreme. The *Yehi Ratzon,* recited in the Ashkenazi rite on the Sabbath preceding the New Moon, is an adaptation of Rab's individual prayer; and it entered the Ashkenazi liturgy as a prayer announcing the New Moon less than two centuries ago.

Thus, while the invention of printing gave us the "canonization" of the *Siddur,* that "canonization" has perhaps affected the retention of the old far more than it has affected the admission or the nonadmission of the new. However, the two are, of course, related. With so much of the old, which can no longer be dislodged, there is an understandable reluctance to admit the new which would make the services for worship even longer than they already are.

And there is an additional factor. So many generations have had a hand in shaping the *Siddur* that—with but two exceptions to which I shall revert later— the whole gamut of prayerful response has practically already been covered. Triumph and defeat, joy and sorrow, contrition and confidence, pleading and gratitude, fear and exultation, adoration and quest—they are all in the *Siddur* already! If anything new is now created to supplement what is already there, it would have to prove itself as something clearly superior to what has already been hallowed by tradition.

The exceptions to which I have referred are the Holocaust and the Rebirth of Israel. They *must* find their expression in the *Siddur* of the twentieth century Jew—even though many a medieval *piyyut* or *selihah,* when reread in the light of our own expprience, may serve, in the meantime, to express our feelings about the Holocaust. "In the meantime"—for who knows whether we, in our generation, can really create true prayers?

Max Dienemann, the late Rabbi of Offenbach, saw his synagogue go up in flames in November 1938, and he had to spend some time in a concentration camp. Fortunately, he was ultimately allowed to leave Germany, and, with *Eretz Israel* as his final destination, he found temporary refuge in England. Evidently, it had been Dienemann's intention to compose a *qinah,* a dirge about the destruction of the German synagogues, for, on January 12, 1939, he wrote as follows to an inquiring friend:

Die "Kinoh" werde ich schon einmal machen, aber erst in Palästina. Ich bin noch zu sehr im Hader mit Gott, und man muss mit ihm im Frieden sein, wenn man so etwas schreiben will.[2]

(I am going to get around to composing the *qinah* one of these days, but only in Palestine. I still have too much of a quarrel with God, and one has to be at peace with Him before one can write such a thing.)

Has our generation already stopped quarrelling with God? Are we really at peace with Him now?

But perhaps Dienemann was all wrong. Perhaps there is room for our quarrel with God—precisely in the prayer book. The terrible silence, the interruption of the prayer, which Professor Sadan mentioned as having witnessed is such a "liturgical" quarrelling with God. Others, however, may seek words with which to fill that silence; and the words ought to be provided.

And words ought to be provided to celebrate the Rebirth, to give expression to our gratitude and joy as well as to our hopes and anxieties in connection with the State of Israel.

But who is stopping us? Who is preventing us from uttering those words? To whom, in any case, are we addressing our complaints about the "sealed" prayer book? From whom are we asking permission to open it up again?

The ignorant, who believe that the *Siddur*—in its latest printed edition—was all but revealed by God to Moses on Mount Sinai, will not be swayed by any argument. And those of us who have done research in the evolution of Jewish Liturgy have never regarded the *Siddur* as a "sealed" book in the first place.

If, moreover, we are looking for universal acceptance, for a *Siddur* which would be *kasher lekhol hade'oth* (with the approval of all Jews), then we are certainly on the wrong path, for there never has been any universal acceptance among Jews of *any* single prayer book. Saadiah must have known Amram's prayer book; but he preferred to edit his own. And Maimonides composed a third one—and so throughout the generations. The *mitnaggedim*, to use Professor Sadan's illustration, do not want *veyatzmah porqeneh* in their *Kaddish*, and the Hasidim won't have a *Kaddish* without it!

In the final analysis, it is the people who do the actual praying who have the decisive voice in determining the nature of their *Siddur;* and they will have to learn to live and *daven* without gaining universal acceptance for their particular *nosah*.

One thing, though, seems certain: the traditional *Siddur* is so full of content that any new additions—without corresponding omissions—would make the innovators guilty of inflicting on the people a *tirha detzibbura* ("bother for the community"). Something, in other words, will have to give.

It is here that the real halakhic problem comes to the fore. And it is here that the courageous *morei halakhah,* halakhic decision makers (if our generation is still blessed with such) will have to show the way. Those halakhic decision makers would have to convince the people that no printer, at any time or in any place, can be considered as the ultimate halakhic authority on matters liturgical. It is they, moreover, who, with great scholarship and even greater honesty, will have to determine, on the basis of the classical sources of Rabbinic Judaism, just what the minimum requirements of the "Laws of Prayer" are.

Upon that minimum—which would represent both the link to the past and the common core of prayer for the entire Jewish community—let individual congregations, each according to its own *nosah,* erect a superstructure which would incorporate something of the atmosphere of grandfather's *shul* (whatever may have been its distinctive features) and of the longings and aspirations, the inner struggles and the wrestling for faith, which are the characteristics of the time in which we live.

Our final word. Perhaps those of us who want to "open up" the *Siddur* had better not wait until the halakhic authorities have ruled. In matters liturgical, past halakhic authorities have been in the habit of authorizing what the people had already created through their own efforts and determination. In Heaven's name, let those who want an "open" *Siddur* simply start *davening!*

Notes

1. Cf. Jakob J. Petuchowski, *Prayerbook Reform in Europe* (New York: 1968). Index, s.v. Stein, Leopold.

2. Max Dienemann, *Ein Gedenkbuch* (London: 1946), p. 58.

4
Jewish Prayer in Our Days

A Discussion

Joseph Heinemann

It seems to me that if we think about building a new connection with prayer and the synagogue on the part of those who no longer pray, or who no longer even know what prayer is, then the central issue is not nostalgia. We have a generation that doesn't remember its grandfathers' prayers. Thus, our appeal to that generation, which also includes some genuine "seekers," need not be based on a model that attempts to remind them of what once was in the time of their grandfathers. They need to find a model that speaks to them and stirs them, without reference to any sentimental residue from previous generations. What I am saying is that the sociological pattern has changed, and we are no longer speaking of a generation of rebels but of a generation "which knew not Joseph."

Second, I agree to a great extent with Jakob Petuchowski that if we wish to give the *Siddur* a new look, we need to introduce things which express our own situation, and that it is impossiblee
the enormous and suffocating accumulation of prayers that we have inherited

from the past. In particular, I think of the weekday morning service, to which a person would need to devote a least one hour if he wished to recite it properly and suitably in a quorum, and this hardly any synagogue in the world is prepared for. We can say that this prayer really stultifies itself. Moreover, we ought not to wait for the Rabbis to come along and give their halakhic approval to needful changes. Halakhic rulings of that sort will never be given, and they are also not necessary because this is an area where, in large measure, we may do as we see fit, so long as we do not add to, or subtract from the (eighteen) blessings of the *Amidah*. Everything else is really in our own hands, including the reformulation of several of the eighteen blessings themselves if we feel that it is necessary.

It seems to me that this can be done, if there is a community prepared to do it. The main problem is that no "ultra-orthodox" group is prepared to contemplate such an attempt, at least not here in Israel. Even in synagogues made up of thinking, educated people, a great uproar ensues as soon as someone attempts the smallest change, such as omitting the *Yekum Purkan,* in which we pray for the Exilarch in Babylon! As against this, it would seem that it is possible to do things of this sort in Conservative congregations in the United States, as we have seen in the *Mahzor* of Jules Harlow, which is truly a masterpiece of both expansion and contraction, an example of a kind of plastic surgery which in my opinion, revitalizes the *Mahzor* and its spirit.

Let me illustrate the seriousness of this practical issue. Not long ago, a new *Siddur* entitled *Rinat Yisrael* made its appearance in Israel, published by the Ministry of Education and edited by a public committee of prominent, knowledgeable people. In the first sentences of the Foreword to the *Siddur,* it boasts of "answering the needs of this generation, the first generation of those renewing their independence in our Land." But this claim is not substantiated by the *Siddur* itself. For example, in the long *Ve-Hu Rahum* for Mondays and Thursdays, we read—as in any old-fashioned *Siddur* printed in the Diaspora—"God, see our degradation among the nations and our abomination, like that of an unclean woman. . . . How long shall thy strength remain in captivity?" If this is how a *Siddur* looks which is supposed to "answer the needs of the first generation," we can only conclude that the battle is lost from the beginning, at least among those who see themselves as Jews observant of the tradition and the commandments.

Harold Fisch

I was a bit disturbed by the fact that Dov Sadan placed the emphasis on *piyyutim,* that is, on the tangential aspects of prayer. When I speak of prayer, I think of its central dominant feature, namely, the *Shemoneh Esreh* (eighteen benedictions). It is difficult to see what in that can be considered closed or frozen, what in that can be thought of as becoming antiquated. I understand this complaint with regard to some of the *piyyutim,* but not one of the eighteen blessings as I read them ceases to be relevant at any time or place. Moreover, from a linguistic viewpoint the *Amidah* is directed toward the future and not toward the past. Everything is in the future tense – what we desire to renew and what we want to see from now on. My main reservation with regard to the Conservative and Reform groups is precisely on this point. In the Union prayer book the phrase in the *Musaf* prayer, "we will make and we will offer," is changed to "they used to make and to offer," that is, from future to past tense.

Secondly, I am not certain that what Jakob Petuchowski said about synagogue, communal life, and so on, as central to the preservation of tradition, was correct with regard to those of us living in Israel. It seems to me that if we have a problem in regard to prayer, it is not exactly the problem of the synagogue. It sometimes seems to me that the center of gravity of the religious life, including the life of prayer, has left the synagogue. The synagogue, and even the Jewish community, do not play the same central role in our lives which they once did and which they do in the Diaspora. It is possible that we are on the threshold of revolutionary changes and that we need to think in terms of new spiritual institutions and frameworks.

Akiva Ernst Simon

The only Jewish image of my grandfather which I have in my memory is of when one of his grandchildren was taken to be baptized on the second day of Rosh Hashanah by his son, who had earlier converted to Christianity. Grandfather, who was a member of the same synagogue on Johannesstrasse which Professor Petuchowski has mentioned, did not go to the baptism. He said, "On the second day of Rosh Hashanah I will not go to the baptism of my grandson. I will go to 'temple.' What can a Jew like me – and I am not the only one of my kind – who has no image of a pious grandfather, do about prayer? Solomon Schechter had a saying often quoted: "You cannot serve God with your father's heart." Even if our grandfathers had warm Jewish hearts, it is doubtful whether this would provide an answer or even a partial answer to the cardinal question of our generation.

Large sections of our generation are like the generation of Abraham, though living after the Torah has been given. That is, many people in our generation need to make a new beginning with something which, in itself, is not at all new. This subject was raised by both Professor Sadan and Professor Petuchowski, and I would like to add two comments of my own to this question of novelty and change.

I find it very difficult to pray in the formulae set by the Rabbis. If I were to be sitting in the Chief Rabbinate Council – and I needed to rule on the controversial question, as to whether or not *Hallel* is to be recited on Independence Day with a full blessing, I would propose that one say the blessing, but then recite only half the *Hallel,* in keeping with the midrashic saying about the crossing of the Red Sea, "My creatures are drowning in the sea and you recite a song of praise!"[1] I think that this could easily have valuable religious and educational results. Likewise, I do not go along with the phrase, "Renew our days as of old," in its simple meaning. I do not pray that the days should be restored as they once were. Thus, for example, I do not pray for the restoration of sacrifices, because one who prays for them has to consider the possibility that his prayers might be answered. Even if the risk is small, I do not wish to utter falsehoods before my Creator, requests for things whose coming I would fear. When I say, "renew our days as of old," and we say this quite frequently—I intend to say, without changing the *nosah,* "renew our days as You renewed them in the past." And perhaps one ought to have in mind, "as You made us worthy to renew them in the past."

Yehudah Nini

Historically, liturgical poems were never created from outside, but only by those operating in the context of private or public prayers. Only thus could access be gained to the *Siddur.* Together with this, the *Siddur* was the creation of the community and not of any individual. No *Siddur* put together by an individual or even a committee of scholars could ever enjoy recognition. It must be the product of the experience of the entire community. It would be desirable, perhaps, to broaden the discussion on this point.

As for nostalgia, it is worth remembering that in nostalgia it is the melody rather than the words which count. It is similarly the melody chiefly which binds us to this or that *nosah.* And melody has been somehow lost.

We need to create the collective experience of the melody of prayer, of prayer as a communal experience, whether it is a community which calls itself "religious" or "secular." The foundation of prayer is "Sing to the Lord a new song" (Psalm 96:1) – song, and not the recital or reading of the text alone.

Yehudah Friedlander

A brief personal comment: our problem is not only with omissions, but with additions as well. Once I was almost thrown out of a synagogue for adding one word to the weekday prayers. In the *Yehi Ratson* following the Torah reading on Mondays and Thursdays, in the phrase, "our brothers of the House of Israel who are in trouble and distress, whether in land or at sea," I added the words "or in the air." It led to a local uproar.

As to the matter at hand: if prayer is a substitute for sacrifices, then we know that one was not allowed to offer a blemished animal in the Temple. It was better not to offer a sacrifice at all than to bring one which was blemished. If that is the case, why should it be permissible for us to recite defective prayers, and not search our prayers for possibly disqualifying blemishes? We find in the *halakhah* precise instructions concerning faulty prayers, not only in the matter of the time for prayer or the type of prayer, but even regarding isolated words. For example, the *halakhah* stresses that one is to take care in reciting the phrase *'esev be-sadekha* ("the grass in your field") (Deut. 11:15) in the *Shema,* so that the letter *bet* at the end of *'esev* and that at the beginning of *be-sadkha* do not become merged into one another; or that one is to stress the *z* sound in *le'ma'an tizkeru* ("so that you may remember") (Numbers 15:40) in order that it does not sound like an *s* which would mean something quite different. It thus follows that the *halakhah* is sensitive to the proper recitation of the text of prayer. Despite this, in our synagogues one can find a rich collection of mistakes in practice, beginning with faulty pronunciation and ending in actual errors hallowed through age-long usage, without anyone paying them any attention. One outstanding example: everybody recites, in the Morning Blessings (*Birkhot Ha'Shahar*) the phrase, *Nekavim nekavim, halulim halulim* ("various openings and hollows"). Yet the early manuscripts have shown that the proper reading was *Nekavim nekuvim, halalim halulim* ("pierced openings and hollow spaces"), which seems more exact than the *nosah* we have. We are not halakhic scholars, but it seems to me that one of our first goals should be to correct the text of the prayers. First of all, we need to eliminate those mistakes which have been passed on from one edition of the prayer book to the next, until there is no *Siddur* free of them. This is a task for the halakhic authorities. The layman does not have the necessary authority though he does have the power of implementation. If, for example, we find that a biblical verse is incorrectly quoted in the *Siddur,* then there is obviously something wrong.

As for liturgical poems (*piyyutim*), which are not the main element of prayer, we find something odd. Jews often take greater care with these *piyyutim* than they do with the halakhically significant sections of the service. They rise early for the penitential prayers (*Selihot*) – *piyyutim* whose time or place of composition nobody exactly knows, but then, after an hour of these *Selihot,* they hurry through the more important *Shema* and *Shemoneh Esreh,* with unseemly haste, thus confusing the essential with the less essential.

Yohanan Silman

Excessive stress has been placed here on the national functions fulfilled by prayer, as a guarantor of continuity. At times there was emphasis on family, and not merely on nation. Significantly, we have heard of nostalgia, of the synagogue, suggesting that we are thinking of prayer in a sociological-national sense. My feeling is that a portion of these things were stated from the viewpoint of leaders, whose interest in prayer, as reflected in their words, is in its function of guiding the community, of providing direction and protecting its unity and existence. These are possibly important and necessary interests, but they are definitely external to prayer as such, that is, to the relationship between Man and his Creator. Their concern is with prayer in its historical aspect, rather than with prayer itself.

Since we have spoken about prayer from the viewpoint of continuity and the maintenance of continuity (no matter of whom or of what) it is natural that conservation has been emphasized. In this respect the *Siddur* is closed, since its function, among others, was to reflect or guard some kind of continuity or to revive something which no longer exists and which, through the *Siddur,* we wished to restore to life.

Against this, Abner Weiss raised the question, which in my eyes is central: i.e., to what extent does the *Siddur* express, in practice, the religious needs and interests of *this* generation—if it has such needs and interests at all? It is quite possible that the lack of innovation in prayer is the sign that in fact there are no such interests! The problem is whether the *Siddur* contains within itself a reflection of our spiritual struggle and here I think that the answer is unequivocally negative. Do our prayers relate to the fact that it is difficult for us to pray? It would seem that no such element exists in the *Siddur* and yet it ought to be there, because that is the deepest spiritual concern of our generation. Surely it is both possible and necessary to pray over the fact that it is difficult to pray!

It may be that the ultimate religious ideal, the ideal toward which we ought to aspire, is that of faith, of trust, but we are very far from this. The actual situation of our generation is one of lack of trust, of uncertainty. Perhaps there is a place for a general religious outlook—and prayer cannot be detached from this wider frame—which would boldly recognize our lack of knowledge; which, in place of trust, would stress the danger which even those who perform *mizvot* cannot escape; which would choose as its point of departure the thought that man as man never has the right to assume that he has come to the end of the path, that he has chosen the *nosah* or form or deeds which will indubitably lead him to the goal which he hopes to reach.

Eliezer Berkovits

Our question seems to be: Where are we to find the strength to create new prayers appropriate to our generation, to contemporary man? It is possible that we have forgotten something very important, namely, that creativity does not come from the need for new prayers, but from the quality of Jewish life.

If there is creative power within us, then there will also be prayers to match. The need for new prayers appropriate to the *Zeitgeist* as such will not guarantee creativity. We can learn this by analogy with individuals; an individual who cannot bring himself to pray, will not create new prayers out of this inability.

This is connected with another point which, it seems to me, is fundamental. We have heard a great deal about nostalgia. Jakob Petuchowski pointed out that we even find nostalgia in the *Siddur* itself. I do not myself find nostalgia in the *Siddur*. As Harold Fisch has pointed out, the *Siddur* is not actually a sealed book. For example, the phrase "renew our days as of old," from Lamentations 5:21 is to my mind not a looking backward into history but a turning forward towards the future with the emphasis on the verb, *"renew"*. There is no nostalgia here. To the contrary, we are led to see Judaism as a process continuing through history and to hope for the realization of Jewish goals in history and in the world.

How to talk about the *Siddur* from the viewpoint of history? We sometimes forget that our prayer is primarily communal prayer. The meaning of communal prayer is that we identify in our prayers not only with our own interests, the interests of the generation in which we find ourselves, but also with the interests and goals expressed by the whole historical process. In sanctifying the Name, we pray each time together with all the generations and with all of the Jewish people.

This is, in my opinion, the foundation of Jewish prayer, and for this reason it is based on the classical tradition of our people. The *Siddur* is filled with expressions from the Psalms or the Prophets or the Talmud. For this reason it is possible for us to pray out of a sense of identification with all the generations and of longing for the future of the Jewish people.

There are innovations in the *Siddur,* but we do not feel them as such, because all these innovations which have taken root are based on classical elements. What we most feel therefore is unity.

It is true that the customs are many and varied, but these also have vitality only if they are based upon the common classical sources of our people. For example, I do not pray according to the Sephardic rite, but when I find myself in a Sephardic synagogue I can identify with their *nosah* even though it is different from my own. I can do it because it is based upon the same sources.

Innovations in prayer are lifeless if they are not rooted in our authentic sources. On the other hand, innovations *within* that tradition will not appear to be innovations. I am familiar with new forms of prayer invented in the United States of America and find them boring; and I find myself unable to utter them. It seems to me that anyone with religious feeling will have difficulty with them. As a consequence they are unlikely to survive.

Thus I say: let us innovate by all means, but before all else let us find the creative power within Judaism itself, out of which we will create new prayers. If we find this creative power, which is not just a matter of prayer but a matter of Jewish renewal in general we will find the solution to all our problems. Without it, we will not solve our problem.

Rivkah Katz

I would like to tell a small, true story, which we can perhaps compare in a certain way to the suggestions of some of those speakers who wanted to cut out sections of the *Siddur.*

A man who came from Lithuania to South Africa and lived in Johannesburg, went on wearing his long caftan, or *kapota.* His children, who were born in South Africa, were embarrassed by their father every time he went out into the city wearing this old-fashioned garment. It did not seem right to his young children that their father should wear the same clothes that he wore in Lithuania. Both of the children in the family – they were a brother and a sister – made up their minds, independently of one another that one day they would cut down the long *kapota* and turn it into a jacket, in the fashion of the day. By a strange coincidence, they both hit on the same night to carry out their plan: the son got up at midnight and secretly cut off the bottom of the *kapota,* and in the early hours of the same morning the daughter arose and cut up the part of the garment which remained. The father looked for his *kapota* in the morning and found that there was neither *kapota* nor jacket, but only a very short, ragged-looking vest.

I was reminded of this story upon hearing the suggestions to remove this or another portion of the *Siddur.* Even though as a woman, I am not obligated to recite all of those prayers – I understand from one rabbi that in order to fulfil the *mizvah* it is only necessary for me to recite one of the daily prayers each day – I feel that we must be very cautious in this area, because as the result of too many omissions, the *Siddur* is likely to lose that unique character of which Jakob Petuchowski spoke – that of expressing the whole gamut of human emotions. We are likely to discover that we no longer find these emotions in the *Siddur.*

Yehudah Moriel

It seems to me that at the outset we ought to define what we mean by prayer and what are its preconditions. The definition of the late Rabbi Samson Raphael Hirsch, who derives the verb to pray (*le-hitpalel*) from the root *palal,* to judge, makes sense to me. It is self-judgment, self-examination, self-criticism, and clearly this implies certain criteria.

Here lies the crux of the problem. It is not the *Siddur,* but the source from which it flows, which is stopped up, for no prayer is possible without faith in the full and simple sense. What we are speaking of is wholeness and simplicity, the simple faith which is called forth by the lofty commandment: "You shall be holy, for I, the Lord your God, am holy."

We live today in an anthropocentric world, whose slogan is, "Be holy, because you, human beings, are holy." Even the observant ones among us—if they will be honest with themselves—will admit that this is the real reason for the blocking up of the sources of prayer. For it is only the actual realization of man's immediate confrontation with God (as in the liturgical phrase: "You separated man from the beginning, and taught him to stand before you") that makes human prayer and thus, self-examination and self-criticism, possible. This is the reality on which prayer is based. The sense daily revealed of "I the Lord your God am Holy."

I must ask forgiveness of Professor Simon, whom I know as a teacher, in saying that a man whose world is theocentric, that is, who knows the truth of "for I, the Lord your God, am holy," can make the great sacrifice of praying for the restoration of sacrifices, because we do not have the authority to know what is or is not of contemporary relevance. Are we not perhaps like the story of people sitting down to a table laden with fowl and meat who ask whether there is any place today for prayers relating to animal sacrifices . . . ?

The other matters which have been discussed here are also peripheral. In contrast to Judah Friedlander, I have many times included in my liturgy the prayer for travellers "in the air and on land." And from whom did I first hear this phrase? From a *hasid* with a long beard who prayed in the study-house of the Drohobitsch Rebbe on Tsefaniah Street (an ultra-Orthodox Jerusalem neighborhood), and no one objected to the innovation.

As for the prayer *Yekum Purkan,* and its like. Two years ago I visited the synagogue of the religious kibbutz, *En-Hanaziv,* for the first time, on the festival of Shavuot. They did not recite *Akdamut* (a poem in Aramaic no longer easily understood) before the Torah reading. At first, this was a shock to me, and I was filled with nostalgia for the melody of *Akdamut.* Nevertheless, I myself have attempted and will perhaps succeed in eliminating the reading of *Akdamut* in the synagogue in which I pray. In the end it will certainly be eliminated. It will spread from *En-Hanaziv* to other kibbutzim and to other synagogues.

I do not see any problem whatever regarding the *nosah* of prayer. It has been correctly stated that requirements of the *halakhah* are in this regard extremely minimal. In order to be able to recite the blessings on uttering the morning

Psalms (*Psuke de Zimra*), it is only necessary to actually say the one verse, "You open Your hand, and give food to all that lives" (Psalm 145). If that is so, then there is no problem about including or omitting this or that section. As for *Selihot* and *piyyutim,* we see today that in most of the synagogues in Israel they no longer say them in full. The liturgical poems for the festivals have been completely eliminated, and on Rosh Hashanah, as well they are gradually being cut down. All this takes more than ten years or even fifty years, but it is gradually being done.

One real issue relates to the more fundamental *Shema*—"Hear, O Israel, the Lord is our God, the Lord is One." When I pray as I sometimes do in the talmudical colleges (*yeshivot*), it is not the *piyyutim* or other portions of the prayers which matter, but those few seconds—and seconds are a long time for this purpose—of silence before the *Shema*. This utterance is meant to spring from the depth of the heart where there can be no falsification, deceit, or deception. These people, when they say *Shema Yisrael,* believe in it, and it is as if they are always in the presence of God. Here is the source and here is also—for many—the essential problem.

Moshe Litov

I agree with Dr. Moriel that our essential problem is not the prayer book, but the person praying and his intentions. For that reason, I do not see much good coming out of changing or adding things to the *Siddur*. There are places where a blessing is said for the soldiers in the Israel Defense Forces, and I think that that does add to the service, but I do not see any necessity for making changes in the body of the prayer book. The power of the *Siddur* is in its establishment of a framework for prayer, into which I can put all of my own thoughts and intentions (*kavvanot*). Before the State was established, I recited the phrase "to Jerusalem Your city, return," with one sort of intention, and afterwards I recited it in a different sense. There is even danger in making additions, because one of the virtues of the *Siddur* is that it unites the people. Despite minor variations in *nosah,* every Jew, wherever he may find himself, is able to pray with the collectivity of Israel.

The main problem is how to bring the people back to prayer, how to restore the feeling of prayer, so that they can bring to it those *kavvanot* which are appropriate to them. These *kavvanot* (or unspoken intentions) are the proper area for the innovations needed by each generation. I introduce my *kavvanot* into words which I say and which are identical with the words uttered by my fathers before me.

Gabriel H. Cohn

To this point we have dealt with the problem of why there is no renewal in prayer. Sociological explanations have been offered; Eliezer Berkovits has suggested that there is no atmosphere of creativity, and it has also been claimed that there is no need for any innovations in the actual words of the prayer book. What has been said up to now has dealt only with the written *nosah*. It seems important to point out that prayer is not only words printed in a book. We also need to turn our attention to the entire gamut of things connected to and surrounding prayer, as included in the English word "service."

Actually, as I see it, there is a great deal of innovation in our day realm of "service." True, not much has changed in the *Siddur* itself, but from my experience and from moving about our country here in the Land of Israel, I know that there are many new developments in the atmosphere of prayer and in synagogue practice. I will mention three of these changes.

One relates to the emphasis on certain prayers and the disappearance of others. There are certainly people who do not say the first Aramaic prayer for the leader of the Galut (*Yekum Purkan*), but this is done without the public quarrels which occurred in the past. The prayer is simply left for silent recitation. As against that, other prayers have achieved a special status in the service, for example, the *piyyut, An'im Zemirot,* which in most cases is now led by children, who in this way become participants in the service of worship.

Another innovation, at which Yehudah Nini hinted, is in the matter of melody. It is the melody which creates nostalgia, and not the text, and here a great deal which is new has been introduced. Anyone who knows the synagogue life here in Israel knows that many strikingly new melodies have been introduced, and this has changed the whole atmosphere of the synagogue.

A third innovation, found perhaps less in Israel than in the Diaspora, is in the area of study. I refer to the introduction into the service of explanations and comments by the worshippers themselves. These may take place at the beginning, at the end, or during the service, Thus, prayer does depart from the "closed prayer book" spoken of, and can take on new meanings for different people in different communities.

Notes

1. One view as to why only half the *Hallel* (the great doxology) is said on the final six days of Passover.

Part II

5
The Fixed and the Fluid in Jewish Prayer

Joseph Heinemann

The question to which I address myself is how may we restore to prayer today those principles of renewal that it has almost completely lost during the course of generations? In order to understand the seriousness of the issue and to be aware of the absurdity and paradox inherent in the fact that prayer has, in our days, become transformed into something fixed, routine, and frozen, it is necessary for us to highlight certain aspects of Jewish prayer in its classical, formative period.

The situation in our own day, in which prayer is set, word for word, and any attempt to change even one word leads to sharp and bitter disputes, not only does not reflect the nature of authentic Jewish prayer, but is diametrically opposed to it. In the beginning, the dominant elements in the prayers of Israel were innovation, spontaneity, variety, and creativity. It is true that the Sages developed the institution of fixed prayer, but fixed, obligatory prayer was not at all intended to displace the element of spontaneity. On the contrary, fixed, obligatory prayer was itself, in its day, something new—a specifically Jewish innovation. Judaism originated the idea of prayer as a cultic act in itself, as a valid substitute for other forms of worship and as a service of equal value to the sacrifices in the Temple. This was the revolutionary change.

The ancient world knew of prayer in two separate senses. In one sense it was an outpouring of the heart, the spontaneous expression of the individual who felt, in moments of crisis, the need to turn to his god. This is a universal form of prayer, which exists in every human society. Every man, by virtue of his nature offers prayer, at least in times of spiritual elevation or in times of trouble and need. The other sense, known and practiced, for example, in ancient Babylonia, was prayer as accompaniment to cultic ceremonies in the temples. This form of prayer, by its very nature, did not stand on its own, but was an accompaniment and addition to other cultic acts, particularly animal sacrifices.

In any event, the innovation involved in the institution of fixed, obligatory prayer in Israel was in the fact that prayer became the entire cult itself, without depending upon something else in order to be counted as Divine service. This was the creation of Judaism in the Second Temple period. If, today, this form of prayer is taken for granted in the civilized world, it is only because the two great monotheistic religions, Christianity and, afterwards, Islam, inherited this form of prayer ready-made from Judaism.

Prayer as Divine service does not require any additional ceremony and, in its pure, original form, did not require any special class of cultic functionaries or priests, but was entirely an act of the praying congregation itself. Since all this was transmitted from Judaism to Christianity and Islam as well, we tend to take it for granted. But the truth of the matter is that this type of prayer is actually an innovation, while spontaneous, individual prayer, prayer which springs forth from the heart, prayer that a man utters because he feels the urge to do so—that is the older, "self-evident" form of prayer. At the time that the new form of prayer was created within Judaism, there was no intention to push aside that type of personal, spontaneous prayer known to us from so many chapters of the Psalms, which express the feelings of the individual. No one would want this earlier sort of prayer to be forgotten or eliminated. In practice, from the time that prayer was introduced as a form of communal worship in Judaism, there existed two forms of prayer, and between them there is no contradiction.

Prayer as a substitute for the Temple service belonged to certain times and followed a certain order. It was a routine carried out in the name of the entire Jewish people. Nevertheless, even after obligatory prayer of this kind was instituted, there was nothing to prevent the Jew from praying, in addition, whenever his heart urged him to do so, in a form suitable to his inner feelings. Fixed and obligatory prayers were not intended to limit the personal prayers of the individual at all. On the contrary, set prayer itself left a great deal of room for innovation, variation, and creativity. It is, therefore, all the more strange that the principle of free prayer has so completely disappeared from Judaism in recent centuries, particularly in our own time.

It would be hard to find Jews today who utter personal prayers with any frequency. I do not wish to say that there are not rare moments, special hours in a person's life, during which some short, personal prayer may not be pronounced. But it would seem that personal prayer as a habit is a rare phenomenon. Personal, spontaneous, individual prayer has all but disappeared. Moreover, even the spontaneity provided for within the framework of obligatory prayer has been lost in the course of time. Our prayers today lack those aspects of creativity which made change and innovation possible in the transition from one generation to the next. We are all witnesses to the fact that those few, sad attempts made in our day to introduce new elements into our own prayers—references to the creation of the State of Israel and the like—have not been really successful, and still do not occupy a real place in our prayers.

The Sages, in their day, took it for granted that there was a time for private prayer, namely at the end of the fixed prayers in the synagogue. This element appears in the sources under various names, the best known of which is *tahanunim* (supplications). There is much evidence that, after the conclusion of the congregational prayer, that is, after the reader's repetition of the *Amidah* aloud, each member of the congregation bent forward and supplicated, that is, said his personal prayers. There are many noble examples of these "prayers after prayer" of the great Sages. Some of these prayers, in time, also found their way into the fixed liturgy.

We also know of some less refined and elevated personal prayers which may, perhaps, better exemplify their completely individual nature. It is related in the Talmud (*Bava Metziah,* folio 59b) of a dispute as a result of which a ban (*herem*) was placed on Rabbi Eliezer "the Great" by the High Court, at the head of which sat his brother-in-law, Rabban Gamliel II. After the ban was imposed, Rabbi Eliezer's wife, that is, Rabban Gamliel's sister, took great care never to allow her husband to "fall on his face"—that is, to recite personal prayers after the regular prayers. Why? Because she feared that in this personal prayer he would ask God to take vengeance on Rabban Gamliel, her brother. Even though she watched him like a hawk, the day finally came when she was unable to prevent her husband from uttering his supplication. There are two versions of the story: in one version, she erred and thought that it was the New Moon (when one is not allowed to say *tahanunim*), when, in fact, the New Moon occurred only on the following day; according to the second version, a beggar came to the door, and she had to take care of him while Rabbi Eliezer was completing his regular prayers, thus giving him an opportunity to recite a personal prayer. What happened? No sooner had Rabbi Eliezer begun to pray when a *shofar* blast was heard from the home of Rabban Gamliel, announcing that he had fallen sick and died! What Imma Shalom, Rabbi Eliezer's wife, feared had happened.

It is thus clear, that there was a place for personal prayer both within the framework of individual prayer (the *Amidah*) and at the end of the public prayers. But in the course of time those *tahanunim* which we recite at the conclusion of the *Amidah* of the Morning (*Shaharit*) and Afternoon (*Minhah*) prayers themselves became fixed prayers and were recited according to the set text printed in the *Siddur:* One has yet to see observant Jews daring to substitute a personal *tahanun* of their own for the printed version.

A place for personal prayer was reserved, not only at the end of the obligatory prayers, but even in the main body of those prayers. The Sages not merely allowed, but encouraged the supplicant to introduce some new feature in his prayer, each time and every day. It is related of one sage, Rabbi Abahu, that he said a new blessing every day—something that to us seems very strange for, according to the view of the *posekim,* it is forbidden to recite an "unnecessary" blessing, one that has not been established by the Sages.

The statement of Rabbi Eliezer, "He that makes his prayer a fixed task, that prayer is not supplication," is interpreted in both Talmuds as meaning that it is forbidden for one to recite his prayers as if reading a letter, that is, as if reciting from a printed text. Yet this is precisely what we do three times a day—we read the prayers word for word from the printed text. The truth of the matter is that in the time of the *tannaim* and *amoraim* the prayers were not written; they were considered part of the oral tradition which it was forbidden to write down and "those who write blessings are as if they had burned the Torah scrolls." It was self-evident, not only that one prayed by heart, but that one was forbidden to repeat the identical prayer, word for word, three times daily, every day!

More than this: the Sages, in establishing fixed, obligatory prayers, did not determine the exact text (contrary to what is commonly thought and written in popular books on prayer), but only established a framework: the number of blessings in each prayer, that is, eighteen in the weekday *Amidah,* seven in that for Sabbath and holidays, and so on, and the general content of each blessing, that is, that in one blessing one prays for the rebuilding of Jerusalem and in another one for the ingathering of the exiles. But they did not set, nor did they try to set, a word-for-word version of any blessing or prayer. This was left to the individual worshipper or—to be more precise—to the communal prayer leader (*Sheliah Tsibbur*).

I do not claim that each worshipper was capable of renewing and varying the text every time he prayed, but this was the ideal. For example, it should be possible to say the blessing for the rebuilding of Jerusalem in tens of different ways. I have chosen this example, because it demonstrates that the freedom to create forms was not only theoretical. There are, within the framework of our own prayer book, at least four different versions of the blessing, *Boneh Yerushalayim* ("He who rebuilds Jerusalem"): one in the weekday *Amidah;* another in the Grace after Meals, the third blessing of which is, in terms of content, simply a rewording of *Boneh Yerushalayim;* a third, in the blessings after the *Haftarah,* in a somewhat more poetic form; and a fourth among the seven blessings recited at a wedding (i.e., *Sos tasis*).

May one legitimately claim that these various blessings are merely alternative forms of the same blessing, *Boneh Yerushalayim*? Would it occur to us, for example, that one could recite the version found in the Grace after Meals in the weekday *Amidah*? Yet this is precisely what happened in ancient times. For example, in the version found in the Cairo Genizah, which contains the earliest Palestinian formula, the following version of *Boneh Yerushalayim* appears in the *Amidah:* "Have mercy, Lord our God, upon Israel Your people, and upon Jerusalem Your city, and upon Zion Your dwelling place," and so on. This is the text known to us from the Grace after Meals. Thus, it is clear that this text was not composed specifically for the Grace but might serve just as well for the *Amidah*. The same is true of the blessing following the *Haftarah;* its place might be taken by the parallel blessing found in the *Amidah.* There is in fact evidence that the same version was used in these two different prayer contexts, at least on special occasions. Thus, the Yemenites recite the blessing *Boneh Yerushalayim* following the *Haftarah* for Tisha B'Av in the same form which is used in the *Amidah* for that day, that is, "Comfort, Lord our God, the mourners of Zion and the mourners of Jerusalem," and so on. That version, appropriate to the blessing of the *Amidah,* is also appropriate it seems to the blessings of the *Haftarah.*

We may conclude that each blessing could be formulated in a variety of different ways, as the particular prayer leader felt inclined. It was both possible and desirable to vary the form according to circumstances. Thus it was fitting that *Boneh Yerushalayim* be recited on Tisha B'Av in a manner reflecting the mournfulness of that day's central experience, and conversely under the wedding canopy the same prayer would be recited in a tone of joy and happiness befitting the occasion. But they are the same blessing and their liturgical and halakhic function is the same.

We have thus found that, long after the introduction of fixed or obligatory prayers, and long after the final arrangement of those prayers during the generation of Yavneh, the exact text was left flexible and free, not only because there were as yet no printed *Siddurim,* but because those who founded the prayers did not want to hamper or limit their vitality and dynamism.

Even after specific versions were written and accepted by the vast majority of worshippers and communities, there was still not a complete halt to the dynamic and creative element in these fixed prayers. As soon as prayer had become routinized, the liturgical poem, or *piyyut,* was born—first in Palestine, and then in many other countries. It served to vary the routine, substituting for the one fixed text tens or even hundreds of continually varying ones. The early *piyyut* was not thought of as an addition to the fixed text, but as a substitute for it. For example, in place of the set version for the first blessing of the evening service, the liturgical poets (*payyetanim*) created a special version for the Sabbath evening, another special version for Saturday night, for Rosh Hashanah evening, and so on. The version for Sabbath evening began, "Blessed art Thou, Lord our God, King of the Universe, who completed His work on the seventh day . . . ordaining rest for His people Israel every evening, by His will, rolling light before darkness and darkness before light . . . ," and so on. Here, the regular form of the blessing *maariv aravim* has completely disappeared. For Saturday night, the version begins, "Blessed art Thou . . . who distinguishes between holy and profane," and so on. Only at the conclusion is mention made of the phrase, "He who brings on evening."

By means of *piyyut,* the dynamic, fluid element in prayer was restored. Moreover, the *payyetanim* were not satisfied with the creation of only one or two *piyyutim* to be recited in the *Amidah* for Sabbath morning. One *payyetan,* Yannai, wrote two complete volumes of special poems for the Sabbath morning service, each one of which was tied to the Torah reading for a particular Sabbath. Since the cycle of Torah readings observed in his day in Palestine was triennial, he created more than three hundred different *Amidah* prayers for the Sabbath morning, each one of which replaced the regular text of the *Amidah.*

Thus, there can be no doubt that creativity in prayer existed for a long time, and that this was part and parcel of Jewish communal devotion. This being the case, we must try to understand how it was that matters became turned about so completely. How did it happen that what was supposed to be full of freshness and novelty became, in the end, a stiff and hardened routine?

I do not have a complete solution to this historical riddle, but I can suggest several possible factors. The fixing of the literal, exact text of the prayers, primarily in Babylon, seems to be connected with the loss of command over the Hebrew language. The Jews of the Diaspora did not know enough Hebrew to be able to create prayer forms for themselves. As a result, they had to be provided with a version which they could learn by rote—and these ultimately came to be written down, from the time of Rav Amaram Gaon and onward. Thus the reason for a fixed form of words was the inability to compose freely in Hebrew. At the same time, the Jews of the Diaspora were unwilling to forego the use of Hebrew in their prayers (even though, from a halakhic viewpoint, it is permitted to pray in any language, and whoever does not understand the prayers in the Holy Tongue is allowed to pray in whatever language he speaks and understands). All this led to the establishing of a set version which everyone would be able to repeat by rote and even write down for himself.

Another factor may perhaps be suggested. One finds, in the Babylonian Talmud, a desire to impose order upon all aspects of life, and to set all facets of behavior in an unequivocal halakhic mold. It is possible that, in line with this general tendency, the Jews of Babylonia felt a need to make the area of prayer, too, absolutely fixed (and most of the Diaspora was more influenced by the Babylonian center than by Palestine). The tendency toward fixity was further augmented, in the course of generations, by the tendency of the *posekim,* in turn, to give decisive rulings on all legal questions brought before them. Thus, the later *posekim,* from the *Shulhan Arukh* onward, decided many more details regarding prayer and the exact text of prayer than did the *tannaim* and *amoraim* before them. In their eyes, almost every word of the *Siddur* became a halakhic issue, and accordingly decisions concerning them were given halakhic force.

Other factors, perhaps less important and decisive, such as the *Kabbalah,* worked in the same direction. The Lurianic *Kabbalah,* in particular, introduced the idea that the prayers were composed on the basis of mystical teachings, and that each word, and even the number of words, had a special significance. According to the *Kabbalah,* everything in the *prayer book* has an element of *gematria* (numerology) and mystery. As a result, it is forbidden to alter even the smallest detail. Another factor whose power we ought not to neglect is the effect of the printed text itself. As soon as a person is given a printed book and is told, "pray according to this book," the printed words themselves become sanctified for him. The more he uses it, the less he dares to move even an inch away from the received text or to change even the smallest detail.

Historically speaking, the strong reaction of Orthodox Jewry to the Reform movement during the last 150 years is important. As the Reform movement was concerned, first and foremost, with the synagogue, the form of public worship, and the prayer book, this area became correspondingly sensitive in the Orthodox community. If, in the earlier past, there was still a certain readiness to change, to alter, to add, to remove, to introduce new *piyyutim,* and to remove old ones which no longer found favor with the congregation, from the time that the Reform movement raised the banner of innovation the entire area of prayer has become one in which, "What is new is forbidden by the Torah."

Perhaps we ought to mention one last factor, hints of which one may find in what has already been said. Following the introduction of statutory prayers, even though these were not intended to replace spontaneous and personal prayer, it gradually came to be felt that *real* prayer consisted *only* of what was fixed and obligatory. Organized prayer, with shape and form, where regular blessings were recited, acquired in the end a special distinction. Its role was so central that other prayers, such as formless personal utterances, were thought of by contrast as unimportant. They were good, perhaps, for women, who were not obligated to recite the regular prayers and could thus utter any sort of prayer, even in the vernacular. But this was not, so to speak, befitting to the dignity of the male worshipper. He goes to synagogue and recites properly constituted prayers three times a day. A certain dialectic operated here, which was far from the minds of those who introduced the idea of regular prayer. They did not wish to belittle personal prayer. But their creation—namely, standardized, obligatory prayer—became so strong and influential in the course of time that it and it alone was seen as true prayer, possessing tone and quality and deserving of serious attention.

6
Prayer and *Halakhah*

Joseph Tabory

1

Although the subject to which this chapter is devoted is how the all-encompassing *halakhah* absorbs into itself the world of prayer, I preferred to entitle the chapter "Prayer and *Halakhah*," implying some sort of equality between them and also implying a kind of conflict between the two. The essence of *halakhah* is legal systematization, presenting a complete pattern of life which orders the day-to-day and even minute-to-minute conduct of the individual. It is in this sense that the word *halakhah* has been understood to be derived from the root *halakh* "to go," because it defines the path in which a Jew is to walk.[1] Indeed, it has been suggested that a central theme in many *halakhot* is the idea of circumscription and definition; the law creates order out of chaos and keeps the Jew in the world of order and out of the danger of chaos.[2]

How different is the world of prayer. Prayer has been called by the Rabbis "the service of the heart." Prayer arises from the heart rather than from the mind, from a heart full of emotion which knows no rational restrictions. Jewish prayer has been depicted by Rabbi Joseph B. Soloveitchik, as arising from a heart which beats "rapidly and with an irregular rhythm," a heart which is "wild and savage."[3] How can the world of *halakhah*, the world of law and order, attempt to regulate something which is by its very nature free and wild?[4] It seems that such an attempt would tend to change the essence of prayer and transmute it into "a commandment of men, learned by rote" (Isaiah 29:13).

Nevertheless, *halakhah* by its own nature could not leave any aspect of life unregulated—certainly not such an important and central one as that of prayer. We shall discuss here a few aspects of the endeavour of *halakhah* to grapple with what is still today a central problem of our facing God in prayer: How can we have a regulated, organized prayer which will, at the same time, preserve the freedom of a personal relationship with our Creator?

The inherent conflict between the obligation to pray and the need for prayer to rise independently from the heart is reflected in a discussion that was only fully formulated in the medieval period, although this discussion was, of course, based on an analysis of earlier talmudic texts. Is a Jew commanded by God to pray? The Rabbis interpreted the general biblical injunction to worship God as referring to the specific duty of praying to Him (*Sifrei Devarim* 41). Maimonides took this statement at its face value as meaning that God commanded man to pray to Him, although he here tacitly conceded that the exact details of how and when to pray are not specified by the Torah (*Sefer Hamitzvoth,* Positive Commandment 5; cf. *Hilkhot Tefillah* 1:1). Nachmanides, in his critical remarks to this work, presented formalistic objection to Maimonides by pointing to numerous statements in the Talmud that assert that the obligation to pray is of rabbinic origin. Nachmanides had no intention of denying the importance of prayer. Quite the contrary. He states elsewhere that God had no other purpose in the creation of man but that man should praise his Creator. This is, according to him, the significance of raising one's voice in prayer and of gathering together in the synagogue in order to publicize our praise of God.[5] Nevertheless, there is no biblical commandment to do this, but all its forms have been fixed by the Rabbis. Nachmanides' objections to counting prayer among the biblical commandments are technical, and we feel that he himself was not fully convinced by them. He indeed suggested that Maimonides may have been correct in accepting the rabbinic statement at its face value, but he suggested a new interpretation of that statement. According to Nachmanides, it should rather be explained as requiring a person who prays through his own volition, one who cannot help but call out from his anguish and suffering, to direct his call to God in the belief that He hears our prayers and helps us through prayer.[6] We may suspect therefore that there is really some other or additional reason which underlies the rejection of the concept that God commands man to pray to Him. One may perhaps explain that the philosophical background to this is that true prayer cannot be *constrained,* but can only come forth from the inner recognition of the true believer.[7] It may even be said that prayer is the only true free offering which man has to give to God and the negation of its voluntary character by a *commandment to pray* would deny its true value.⁸

2

Even if we assume that the Ramban is correct in stating that God does not demand of us that we pray to Him, there is clearly a rabbinical injunction to pray. Although the original injunction required only two prayers a day – the evening prayer being considered voluntary – today we accept three prayers a day as obligatory. The halakhic obligation to pray three times a day shows the aspiration of *halakhah* to create an ordered regimen. An ordered regimen tends to stifle extracurricular activities even when their goals coincide with those of the regimen. Is this true also of *halakhah* and prayer? Is one limited to the prayers prescribed by *halakhah* or is there still some element of free offering? Can one offer a new prayer of his own when he feels a need to communicate with God?

For a proper understanding of the question of new and additional prayers it should be pointed out that the only prayer in which one could be considered by *halakhah* as facing God is the one which is known today as *Shemoneh Esreh* (Eighteen Benedictions). This prayer is also known as the *Amidah* ("Standing"), because it is the only prayer of the individual in which he is required to stand. It is this prayer which is meant by the rabbis when they speak of *tefillah* (prayer) because it is prayer par excellence. Therefore early discussions of the possibility of praying to God in addition to the required prayers were limited to this prayer. It is in this sense that Saadyah Gaon says, "Whoever wishes to add a voluntary prayer may pray the Eighteen Benedictions as many times as he wants since there is no other prayer but it."⁹ Rabbi Saadyah's statement is in accordance with the opinion of Rabbi Yochanan who uttered the wish "Would that a person might pray the whole day long."¹⁰ Rabbi Yochanan's wish, as it appears in the Palestinian Talmud and in the *Midrash,* was to be taken literally. He really meant that a person might pray as often as he wished. However, Rabbi Yochanan's saying was not easily reconciled with two statements of Samuel which come after that of Yochanan in the Babylonian Talmud (*Berachot* 21a). In his first statement, Samuel declared that a person who remembered in the middle of his prayer that he had already prayed should stop praying even if he was in the middle of one of the blessings. Samuel's second statement was that a person who had already prayed by himself and now found a quorum praying could join them, but only if he could introduce some novelty into his prayer. In an opinion attributed to Rabbi Hai Gaon, the statements were reconciled by limiting the force of Rabbi Yochanan's statement. The author of the opinion ruled that even Rabbi Yochanan did not permit one to offer additional prayer unless one could introduce some novelty.[11] A less forced reconciliation of these statements is given by Isaac Alfasi. He explains that the two Sages are talking about separate cases: Yochanan permits voluntary prayer when it is clear that it is to be voluntary; Samuel talks of the case in which one meant to pray an obligatory prayer but its nature was changed because he remembers in the middle of it that he had already carried out this obligation. In this case Rabbi Yochanan would agree that one should stop in the middle. The rationale for this, as given by Alfasi, is that prayer is a substitute for sacrifice. Just as obligatory sacrifices cannot be offered voluntarily—so also obligatory prayers. On the other hand, just as there is a place for voluntary sacrifices—so is there room for voluntary prayer.[12] Although Alfasi's explanation seems clear enough, Rabbi Joseph Karo claimed that Alfasi really agrees with Hai Gaon's limitation that an individual may offer a voluntary prayer only if there is in it an element of novelty.[13] The effect of this limitation on voluntary prayer is so great that a commentator was brought to remark that even the evening prayer would be forbidden—since it was originally of voluntary origin—if there were not a specific reference to it in the Bible. Nevertheless, in spite of this restriction, freedom of prayer seems assured—at least in the case in which the individual wishes to add something new to his prayer.

The different ways in which the "something new" or "novelty" was interpreted reflect the various attitudes to spontaneous prayer. Rabbi Sherira Gaon, who was asked what "novelty" was required by Samuel, explained that Samuel's permission to pray a second time in order to pray with the community extended even to *Musaf* of *Shabbat*. In that case, Rabbi Sherira replied, it would be considered sufficient novelty to say, "may it be thy will, O Lord our God, that You will hear the prayer that I prayed before You and that You will restore us to our land and plant us in our border and we will offer to You our obligatory sacrifices."[14] We do not know whether Rabbi Sherira demanded novelty in a true spontaneous prayer but it is clear that even if he did—this demand was no stumbling block in its path. A man could offer the standard prayer freely—as long as he showed in some way that his prayer was a free offering. Entirely different was the attitude of Maimonides who stated that each of the intermediate blessings of the *Amidah* must be formulated anew while retaining the general intent prescribed by the Rabbis.[15] Only the first blessings of praise and the last blessings of thanksgiving may, and must, be retained intact. According to Maimonides, a man could pray freely to God only by creating what was virtually a new composition—which limited drastically the circle of those who could pray spontaneously.

A much more liberal explanation was given by Rabbeinu Asher—although his intention was actually to limit the opportunities for voluntary prayer. Rabbeinu Asher rejected Maimonides' interpretation on the grounds that the talmudic demand for something new was meant to limit the possibilities of voluntary prayer. Maimonides explanation of "something new" was no limitation, for, according to Rabbeinu Asher, anybody was capable of composing a new prayer.[16] Rabbeinu Asher therefore explained that the intention of the Talmud was to limit voluntary prayer to anyone who had a new, unforeseen motivation for petitioning the Almighty. If, for instance, somebody in his family had become sick after he last prayed he could now pray voluntarily in order to add a prayer for the health of the sick man. "Something new" meant, in the opinion of Rabbeinu Asher, not a new composition but a new motivation. In the case of one who did not remember whether he had prayed or not—he could pray without adding anything new at all.[17] The very fact that he was not sure that he had fulfilled his obligation was considered a sufficiently new motivation.

In spite of the liberality of Rabbeinu Asher's opinion, he himself was the source for limiting the possibilities of voluntary prayer. A question was addressed to him about the propriety of Rabbi Masliah's custom of praying twice in the afternoon: once at high noon and a second time toward the evening. In his responsum Rabbeinu Asher says that no one should offer a voluntary prayer unless he was very sure of himself that he would continue with due intentness from the beginning until the very end. If he could not do so, he would be included among those of whom it is said, " 'What need have I of all your sacrifices?' says the Lord" (Isaiah 1:11).[18] In practice, this warning has been so effective that voluntary prayer has virtually been eradicated. Indeed, although Rabbeinu Asher's warning was issued to a person who wished to offer a completely voluntary prayer, it was but a short and natural step to apply it in other cases. Thus, *Shulhan Arukh* permitted one to pray in the case that he did not remember whether he had fulfilled his obligation—in accordance with the above-mentioned opinion of Rabbeinu Asher. But the danger that this might really be a voluntary prayer—in case the person had really prayed but had forgotten it—caused Rabbi Avraham Danziger to declare that in our times one is actually forbidden to pray even in such a case.[19] Others felt that Danziger had gone too far.[20] Nevertheless, the general consensus is that the road to God through voluntary prayer has been closed—de facto if not de jure. Rabbi Yehiel Epstein remarked that he had never seen anyone offer a voluntary prayer.[21]

A more fertile field for innovation lay in the realm of new prayers for various occasions. Since these are not in the halakhic category of prayer, there is no limitation to their introduction. They caught on because the one who used them felt that they helped him in his communion with God and in the outpouring of his heart. Such prayers have been composed throughout the generations. Many of the early ones, composed before the end of the talmudic era, have been incorporated into the prayer book. Some of them have become part of the regular, daily service—such as the blessings recited before the prayer proper, while others appear as prayers for special occasions—such as the prayer recited when going on a journey. These compositions show the hallmark of their origin by their use of standard forms such as blessings, in a manner that does not conform with the rules drawn by the rabbis.[22] The fact that these have been included in the prayer book has not served as a precedent to introduce others. The fear that reciting an unsanctioned blessing may involve one in the crime of taking God's name in vain has created a consensus that one cannot introduce new blessings without talmudic sanction.[23] There have even been attempts to expunge from the prayer book some of the morning blessings which are not mentioned in the Talmud.[24] This fear has created a vicious cycle which has lessened the significance of some of the blessings which are mentioned in the Talmud. Due to this fear, copyists of the Talmud omitted the first part of the blessing which contained the name of God and copied only the final part. They assumed that everyone knew that these blessings were to be recited with the name of God so that there was no reason that they should copy His name unnecessarily.[25] Later generations, trying to adapt their rituals to the Talmud, found these shortened blessings in their text and assumed that they were really to be recited without mentioning the name of God.

The reluctance to mention the name of God when there is any doubt of its halakhic necessity has aroused much controversy about the application of existing blessings to new situations. A well known case is that of *shehechiyanu* on Israel's Independence Day. With all its differences, this is similar to the question of whether one should recite *hagomel* after an airplane trip—since this also is not specified in the Talmud as one of the occasions for reciting this blessing.[26] I would like to bring a personal reminiscence here as a further example of this. When I returned home after serving in an artillery unit in the Litani operation in Lebanon, I recited *hagomel* in the synagogue. A heated discussion arose whether this situation is to be included among those which required this blessing. This discussion was conducted in the same terms as the discussion of the application of *hagomel* to an airplane journey. The different religious positions involved were not openly expressed of course.

Prayers composed in posttalmudic times, by such luminaries as Rabbi Saadyah Gaon and Nachmanides, have avoided these problems by not using halakhic forms. The use of nonhalakhic forms has even sanctioned the return to the prayer book of an item that had been earlier rejected. Rabbi Shlomo Luria recited the Ten Commandments daily in spite of the injunction in the Talmud against this (Babylonian Talmud, *Berachot* 12). He explained that the talmudic injunction refers only to their incorporation into a prayer.[27] As long as one does not resort to halakhic forms of prayer, one may recite whatever texts one wishes. Many posttalmudic prayers have been composed in nonhalakhic forms.

The tradition of such compositions has extended into modern times, with special attention given to those who are not able to get the full benefit from the regular statutory prayers. Many prayers were created in the circles of *hasidim* who were encouraged to pour out their heart to God.[28] Numerous prayers were created for women, in Yiddish, to be recited at every phase of life.[29] These prayers have received partial legitimization—a fact which typifies the dialectics of rejection and acceptance of new prayers. Rabbi Avraham Gombiner ruled that women who say such a prayer have fulfilled at least the biblical commandment to pray.[30] A more far reaching decision is found in the responsa of Rabbi Yitzchok Yaakov Weiss. In reference to the rule that a person may not eat on *Shabbat* morning after prayer until he has made *kiddush,* Rabbi Weiss ruled that even the blessing over the wine is considered prayer.[31]

Most modern prayers that have found acceptance in traditional communities follow nonhalakhic forms. We may count as examples of this form both prayers of the community—such as the prayer for the State of Israel, and prayers of the individual—such as the prayer of a paratrooper before his jump. Opposition to such prayers may bear the guise of halakhic or quasi-halakhic criticism to new prayer as such but its source is generally antagonistic to the things that are behind the new prayer—either the goal that is prayed for or the composers themselves.

Rabbi J. Z. Duschinsky, a late leader of the ultra-Orthodox in Jerusalem, presents an interesting example of this. In one of his responsa he reports that he was asked by "a great rabbi" about the advisability of instituting a new prayer. The historical background of this question is obscured in the responsum but from its date, 1942, one may assume that it was a prayer for the British forces to be victorious over Rommel. Rabbi Duschinsky replied that the men of the Great Assembly who composed our prayers were able to give them an inner content of which we are not fully aware. The outer aspects of the prayer composed by the "great Rabbi" are beyond criticism, but Rabbi Duschinski is unable to judge whether they have an inner content. He concludes, therefore, that we should be satisfied rather with the more traditional prayer, "May He who gives salvation to kings . . . ."[32] Nevertheless, in 1948, Rabbi Duschinski wrote in praise of some Rabbis who instituted an order of prayer for Jerusalem in that year.[33]

An interesting parallel can be drawn from another pole—someone on the other side of the world (in religious views as well as geography). Louis Ginzberg of the Jewish Theological Seminary of New York wrote to Morris Silverman, compiler of an American prayer book, "I am not particularly fond of *making* prayers—they ought to flow from the hearts of inspired poets."[34] Nevertheless, Ginzberg himself composed a prayer for divine aid during the second World War.[35]

Innovations in prayer have been of limited success. Most of those that have been accepted in public prayer are meant more as an expression of communal feelings and mutual goals than an as an expression of communion with God and appeal to Him. The realm of communication with God is left to the standard forms of prayer which have been used throughout the generations. Due to the fact that these prayers are statutory, they represent not only a road to God but also closed gates which prevent the traveller from starting on his journey. As the desire of modern man to travel on the road to God has seemed to lessen, these gates seem to have grown in height. It is to the nature of these gates and the attempts to overcome them that we shall now turn our attention.

3

As long as there is no obligation to pray there is no question about the intentions of the the one who does pray. A person who prays because he feels an inner need to do so prays with all his heart, whether his prayer is one of supplication in a time of trouble or one of thanks to God for His loving-kindness. However, once there is a halakhic obligation to pray and he prays not because of his own emotional need but in order to fulfill a requirement imposed upon him by others—then the question of *kavvanah* becomes one of paramount importance. *Kavvanah* is a difficult word to translate. We shall discuss two aspects of this concept which we shall call intention and attention.[36]

Taking the first aspect, that is, intention: *kavvanah* derives from the Hebrew "direction" or "aim." How does one feel the presence of God so that he can direct his prayers to Him? This problem arises when the average person is obligated to pray at specific times. The truly God-intoxicated person feels the presence of God constantly—as does one who is in severe trouble. According to the popular saying, there are no atheists in the trenches. This is perhaps the real meaning of David's statement, "Evening and morning and noon I pray and sigh" (Psalm 55:18). He does not mean that he sighs only three times a day but rather that he sighs constantly.[37] A man who is constantly involved in the divine activity of studying the Torah—like Rabbi Simeon Bar Yochai—perhaps need not pray at all (*Talmud Bavli, Shabbat* 11a). (As Rabbi Soloveitchik has expressed it, studying the word of God also represents a communion with the divine.[38]) However, the ordinary person, involved in his daily activities, may only rarely, perhaps never, feel the presence of God. *Halakhah* felt that it must call this man to God by requiring him to pray at specific intervals. Thus, a tannaitic statement interprets the words of David as insisting on distinctly separate times of prayer in emulation of Daniel who prayed but three times a day (*Tosefta Berachot* 3:6, ed. S. Lieberman, p. 12).[39] The difficulty inherent in tearing oneself away from one's daily business in order to face God was recognized by Rav Huna who stressed the special importance of the afternoon prayer (*Bavli Berachot* 6b). The Tur explained that the reason for the stress on this prayer is because it comes when a man is absorbed in his affairs.[40] We know only too well how rushed the afternoon prayer can be—when it is not completely forgotten—because so many things are on a person's mind during the day. In this case the Rabbis were faced with a problem of their own creation: How could they create the intention of facing God, a turning of the mind toward Heaven, in one who is totally absorbed in everyday activities and feels no such obligation of his own?

The guides and solutions offered by *halakhah* to the problem of intention emphasize the basic dichotomy between formal law and the essence of religion. While religion is essentially a matter of the heart and mind, law would seem to be capable of regulating only actions and deeds. This is certainly true of secular law which can impose no sanctions on anything which is not objectively provable in a court of law. However, it is not equally true of religious law which can appeal to a man's conscience for sanctions.[41] Secular law is satisfied if a man pays his taxes on time—even if he does so unwillingly—and does not demand that he do so with the idea that he is supporting social projects whose purpose is to help the underprivileged and deprived.[42] Religious law considers the heart and mind as part of its realm and demands their compliance. While the earliest discussion of the importance of intent in fulfillment of commandments is to be found only in the Babylonian Talmud, this discussion is based on hints in tannaitic literature. It has been suggested that one of the fundamental differences between the House of Shammai and the House of Hillel, the background to many of their disagreements, may have been the question of the significance of intent.[43] Therefore, it is not surprising that Jewish law legislated for the mind in specifying that one who prays must have intent of heart (*Tosefta Berakhot* 3:5, p. 12). Rabbi Mana went so far as to say that even if the reading of *Shema* does not require intent—prayer, in the sense of the *Amidah*, that is, the Eighteen Benedictions, does need intent.[44] Rabbi Eliezer went even further in his statement that a man who feels himself unable to pray with *kavvanah* had better not pray.[45]

Nevertheless, *halakhah* recognized the difficulties in legislating for the mind and decreed, with some reservations, that prayer was valid even without *kavvanah*. The main efforts of the *halakhah* toward creating proper *kavvanah* were directed to legislating acts of preparation before prayer. These were to have the effect of rousing the individual to an awareness that he is about to stand in aweful devotion before the Master of the world. This was in accordance with a principle that was formulated much later by the author of *Sefer Hachinuch* that actions have the power to create a state of mind. The relation between actions and intentions is most clearly expressed in the decision of the *Shulhan*

Arukh that though one is required to face the direction of the Holy of Holies in prayer, if one is unable to figure out the correct direction, he is then to direct his heart to his Father who is in heaven (*Orach Chaim* 94).[46] The last attitude is of course not an inferior one but is rather the desired one which can best be reached by external methods.[47] *Halakhah* prefers to prescribe external methods because these are more effective than a simple call to be aware. It is with this in mind that we may understand the prescription of the Tur that one who prays must seek a proper place for prayer, that he must dress properly and see that his own body is properly clean, and that he must prepare his mind for prayer.[48] The final preparation of the body culminates in the requirement to stand in the posture thought proper of a servant who stands before his master (*Orach Chaim* 95). Nothing should be held in one's hands that might interfere with the prayer, and the *Shulhan Arukh* grudgingly permitted holding a *prayer book* (*Orach Chaim* 96, 2).[49] The requirements of the *Shulhan Arukh* are mostly limited to outward behavior, leaving the attainment of the inner awareness to the individual; Rabbi Chaim of Brest-Litovsk went so far as to say that if the individual was not at least aware of standing in the presence of God throughout his prayer—he has not fulfilled the minimal requirement of prayer[50] which was meant to be an inner religious experience.

The second aspect of *kavvanah* is that which we may call "attention"—that is, knowing *what* one is saying. The research of J. Heinemann and others have shown that even when prayer was considered obligatory this obligation did not include strict forms for the prayers. In an intermediary stage, only general rubrics were prescribed such as the idea that one of the requests in prayer must be for the rebuilding of Jerusalem while the actual wording of the request was left to the discretion of the individual. Eventually, the wording of the prayers became definitive and even the number of words in each prayer took on significance. This caused the individual worshipper to have difficulty in feeling a particular relationship to words which had been chosen by others—even when he agreed with the sentiments.[51] The *Posekim* considered this the main problem of prayer and interpreted the statement of the *baraita*, "He who prays should direct his heart to heaven" (*Berakhot* 31a) as meaning that one should pay attention to the meaning of the words he utters (*Tur, Orach Chaim* 98).

Here they revealed the true dialectic tension between the halakhic call to prayer and the recognition that real prayer can arise only from an inner inspiration. The inability to demand proper attention is recognized in the concession that although a person is initially required to pay attention to the meanings of all the sections of prayer, he may pray even if he feels himself unable to concentrate on all the sections—provided he is able to at least concentrate on the meanings of the first sections of *Avot* (Fathers). The strict interpretation of this law implies that if he did not apply even the minimum concentration he must recite his prayers once again.

This is stated flatly by Maimonides (*Hilkhot Tefillah* 10:1) and is accepted by the *Tur*. The *Tur* goes even farther in emphasizing that even if one had *kavvanah* in all the rest of the prayer but omitted the *kavvanah* in *Avot* – one must repeat the whole prayer.[52] However, the *Tur* cancelled the practical importance of his novella by stating that in our times we do not repeat a prayer that has been recited without *kavvanah* because it is most likely that the repetition will have no more *kavvanah* than the first recitation.[53] Here we see the theoretical stress on the importance of *kavvanah* combined with the recognition of the near impossibility in practice: imposing it.

The practical considerations inherent in *halakha* left *halakha* no choice but to insist on the outer forms even when it could not ensure their inner content.[54] This has, in turn, enabled a late European rabbi, Rabbi Zvi Frommer, to claim that *kavvanah* is no more an essential part of prayer than some particular item of the prayer book, such as *ya'ale veyavo*.[55] "Forgetting" *kavvanah* is as insignificant as forgetting any other section of the prayer. However, this has rightly been rejected by others who recognized that though *kavvanah* cannot be forced – it is nevertheless the heart of prayer.[56]

Although *halakhah* seems to be guilty of stressing outward forms and performances to the detriment of true religious feeling which can arise only spontaneously, one must not forget that without the demands of *halakhah* that one keep at least to the outer forms there would rarely be prayer of any type. One might add that even outer forms have significance. Mandatory worship without intention or attention is a higher form of religious awareness than no worship at all.[57] *Halakhah* is not only "a sacred signpost which lights the way to spiritual ascent."[58] It is also the call to man to follow that road. It is then for the traveller to get the most out of his journey.

Notes

1. See Menachem Elon, *Jewish Law – History, Sources, Principles,* vol. 1, in Hebrew (Jerusalem: 1973), p. 143-144, who refers to the literature on the meaning and derivation of this term.

2. Mary Douglas, *Purity and Danger* (London: 1969), chapt. 3, "The Abominations of Leviticus," pp. 41-57. See also Monford Harris, "The Passover Seder: On Entering the Order of History," *Judaism* 25 (1976): 167-174.

3. *Tefillatham shel Yehudim, Maayanot* 8 (Jerusalem: 1964), p. 9.

4. In this respect the *halakhah* has been considered a dialectical synthesis of spontaneity and standardization. See I. Twersky, "Some aspects of the Jewish Attitude Toward the Welfare State," *Tradition* 5 (1963): 144-145, and his further remarks in "The

Shulhan Arukh: Enduring Code of Jewish Law," in *The Jewish Expression,* ed. Judah Goldin (New York: 1970), p. 336 (reprinted from *Judaism* 16 [1967]).

5. "Derashat Torath Hashem Temimah," in *Kol Kitvei Haramban,* vol. I, ed. Ch. D. Chavel (Jerusalem: 1963), pp. 152–153.

6. Rabbi Chaim of Brest-Litovsk has asserted that, according to Ramban, one who prays has the merit of fulfilling a biblical injunction even though he is not commanded to do so (*Hidushei Rabbeinu Haim Halevy, Hilkhot Tefillah* 1:31). This has been strongly questioned by Rabbi Ovadya Yosef (*Yabia Omer,* pt. 3 [Jerusalem: 1960], 8:2). Rabbi Joseph B. Soloveitchik claimed that even Maimonides' prayer arises out of anguish—the daily anguish of human existence (*Reflections of the Rav,* adapted by Abraham Besdin [Jerusalem: 1979], pp. 79–82).

7. This would then be an interesting parallel to another disagreement between the two. Maimonides says that God has *commanded* us to believe in Him while Nachmanides states that this belief, while being the foundation of all the commandments, is not to be counted as a commandment in itself. Interestingly enough, the commandment to love God is considered by Maimonides as an appeal to the mind rather than to the emotion.

8. Cf. William James, *The Varieties of Religious Experience* (Great Britain: 1960), pp. 443–445, quoting Sabatier, who considers *voluntary* (my emphasis, J. T.) prayer as the very essence of religion. Rabbi J. B. Soloveitchik agrees that prayer is the essence of religion, but he asserts that finite man, made of flesh and blood, would be unable to approach God if God had not ordered him to do so ("Thoughts on Prayer" [Hebrew], *Hadarom* 47 [1979]: 87–89). It is God's commandment that strengthens man's backbone so that he can bow down before God.

9. *Siddur Rav Saadja Gaon,* ed. I. Davidson, S. Assaf, B. I. Joel (Jerusalem: 1970 [third printing]), p. 45.

10. *Yerushalmi Berakhot* 1:1 (Venice: 1523), p. 2b (other parallels in the *Yerushalmi* are listed there); *Tanhuma Miketz* 9, ed. Solomon Buber, p. 196.

11. Quoted in the commentary of *Talmidei Rabbeinu Yonah* on the *Alfasi* to *Berakhot,* ed. Wilna, p. 12b. This ruling appears also in the commentary of Rabbeinu Hananel (*Otzar Hageonim, Berakhot* III, p. 20–21), although his explanation of the talmudic passage differs. He accepts the fact that Rav Yochanan disagrees with Samuel but the ruling is in Samuel's favor. However, Samuel admits that one may pray voluntarily if one introduces something new. This ruling is probably not of Rav Hai's as a responsum of his is found in *Shaarei Teshuvah* (no. 96, quoted in *Otzar Hageonim, Berakhot* I, p. 50) in which his opinion is identical to that of Alfasi, which we shall discuss below.

12. Alfasi on *Berakhot,* ed. Wilna, p. 12b. Alfasi may be dependent on the responsum of Rav Hai quoted in the prior note. A corollary of this rationale is that a community, which is not permitted to offer voluntary sacrifices, may not institute voluntary prayer. However, many rabbinical authorities disagreed. See Y. Tchepansky, *Rabbeinu Ephraim,* in Hebrew (Jerusalem: 1976), pp. 340–341.

13. "Beit Yosef" to *Tur Orach Chaim* 107.

14. *Shaarei Teshuvah* 89 and elsewhere. The responsum is quoted in *Otzar Hageonim* to Berachot, I p. 52. Rabbi Sherira's explanation is probably based on the statement of Rabbi Yosi in the *Yerushalmi* (*Berakhot,* end of chap. 4, 8c) as this responsum appears in a collection of Rabbi Sherira's responsa in which the *Yerushalmi* is frequently quoted (*Teshuvot Hageonim,* ed. Abraham Harkavi [Berlin: 1887], no. 263). See also S. A. Poznanski, *Inyanim Shonim Hanog'im Litekufat Hageonim* (Warsaw: 1909), p. 82. However, R. Yosi's statement appears as the answer to a somewhat different problem and its application here is, apparently, an innovation of R. Sherira.

15. *Yad Hachazakah, Hilkhot Tefillah* 1:9. However, Maimonides adds that even if he introduced an innovation in only one blessing it is sufficient to show that it is a voluntary prayer and not an obligatory one.

16. Quoted by his son in *Tur Orach Chaim* 107. This opinion is not found in any of Rabbeinu Asher's extant writings. Does his animadversion show the quality of his society or does it anticipate his own explanation of "something new"? Rabbi Joseph Karo, in his notes to the *Tur,* pointed out that many simple people would be at a loss to compose something new.

17. *Hilchot Harosh, Berakhot* 3:15. Rabbeinu Asher is here following a line adopted by the Tosafot. They pointed out that Rabbi Yochanan's statement appears in the Babylonian Talmud in connection with a specific situation. The Talmud states that a person who does not remember whether he has prayed his obligatory prayer may do so—in the light of Rabbi Yochanan's statement. In their attempt to reconcile Rabbi Yochanan's wish with the statements of Samuel, the Tosafot declared that Rabbi Yochanan's wish was limited to the case where one did not remember if he had prayed or not. Rabbeinu Asher added the rationale to this: Rabbi Yochanan agrees on the need for novelty; this novelty need not be a new prayer or even a new motivation for prayer is sufficient.

18. *She'eloth Uteshuvoth Harosh* (Wilna: 1885), 4:13; cf. 4:9.

19. *Chayei Adam* 27:17.

20. Yehiel Michal Epstein, *Aruch Hashulchan,* 107:13; Chaim Chizkiah Medini, *Or Li,* responsa (Izmir: 1844), no. 20.

21. Epstein, *Aruch Hashulchan,* 107:12.

22. J. Heinemann, *Prayer in the Period of the Tannaim and the Amora'im,* tr. from Hebrew by Richard S. Sarason (Berlin: 1977), p. 156 ff.

23. *Encyclopedia Talmudica* (Hebrew), vol. 4 (Jerusalem: 1956), p. 313.

24. *Encyclopedia Talmudica,* loc. cit. For a study of the vicissitudes of one of these blessings see Zvi Groner, "A Benediction that Was Forgotten and Revived," in Hebrew, *Bar-Ilan Annual* 14-15 (1977): 94-97.

25. Cf. Yaakov Emden, *She'elath Yabez,* pt. I, 81; Rabbi Moshe Feinstein, *Igrot Moshe, Hoshen Mishpat* (New York: 1964), pp. 245-246.

26. Feinstein, *Igrot Moshe,* pp. 251-252.

27. *Teshuvot Maharshal,* no. 64.

28. See Bezalel Landau, "Prayer in Hassidic Literature," in Hebrew, *Mahanayim* 40 (1960): 155-156.

29. M. Waxman, *A History of Jewish Literature,* vol. 2 (New York: 1960), pp. 641-642; Shmuel Haggai, "Hadim'ah Hazakkah shel Hatehinnah," *Mahanayim* 40 (1960): 113-120.

30. Magen Avraham to *Orach Chaim,* 107:2. Cf. Chaim Chizkiah Medini, *Or Li,* no. 8, who questions the opinion of Rabbi Gombiner since these prayers do not fit the standards of prayer.

31. *Minhat Yitzchak,* pt. 4, 28:3. An abstract of the responsum appears in G. Ellinson, *Woman and the Mitzvot,* in Hebrew, (Jerusalem: 1974), p. 37.

32. Joseph Zvi Duschinsky, *She'elot Uteshuvot Maharitz,* (Jerusalem: 1975), no. 47.

33. Ibid., no. 48.

34. Eli Ginzberg, *Keeper of the Law; Louis Ginzberg* (New York: 1966), p. 311. See also *Hadoar* 24:39 (28 *Tishri* 5706) for his and his colleagues' reaction to Mordecai Kaplan's prayer book.

35. *Keeper of the Law,* p. 312.

36. S. Rosenberg gives the sources for this division and adds a third aspect of *kavvanah* that we will not discuss here.

37. For further examples of this see A. M. Honeyman, "Merismus in Biblical Literature," *Journal of Biblical Literature* 71 (1952): 11-18.

38. *Reflections of the Rav,* pp. 71-72. In another context Rabbi Soloveitchik has elaborated on the similarity between prayer and Torah study that "unite in one redemptive experience" ("Redemption, Prayer, Talmud Torah," *Tradition* 17:2 [Spring 1978]: 70).

39. S. Lieberman, in his comments to this passage (*Tosefta Ki-fshutah,* vol. 1 [New York: 1955], p. 29), points out that the passage permits one to spend the whole day in prayer provided that the prayer is divided up into three separate sections.

40. *Tur Orach Chaim,* 221. The Tur apparently thought that the afternoon prayer should be offered early in the afternoon. The Beis Yosef points out that the Tur's father, the Rosh, was apparently of the same opinion (commentary to *Orach Chaim,* 223). However, the popular custom seems to have followed the opinions of the Gaonim that the afternoon prayer was said late in the afternoon which enabled them to combine it with the evening prayer. For a discussion of the legal and sociological aspects of their combination see Jacob Katz, "Alterations in the time of the Evening Service: An Example of the Interrelationship between Religious Custom, Halacha and their Social Background" (Hebrew), *Zion* 35 (1970), 35-60.

41. In this vein Moshe Silberg has pointed out that secular law is oriented to the judge and the court while the *halakhah* is oriented to the individual (*Principia Talmudica* 8 [Hebrew] [Jerusalem: Faculty of Law of the Hebrew University Legal Studies, 1964], p. 52). M. Elon discusses the sanction of the conscience in Jewish law in his above cited work, pp. 173-180.

42. I. Twersky shows the significance of this in philanthropic acts in "Some Aspects of the Jewish Attitude toward the Welfare State" (see above, n. 4).

43. Y. D. Gilat, "Intent and Act in Tannaitic Teaching" (Hebrew), *Bar-Ilan* 4-5 (1967): 104-116.

44. P. T. *Berakhot* 25, 5a according to the reading in the Geniza MS. See L. Ginzberg, *A Commentary on the Palestinian Talmud* (Hebrew), vol. 1 (New York: 1941), p. 357; E. E. Urbach, *The Sages: Their Concepts and Beliefs*, tr. I. Abrahams (Jerusalem: 1975), p. 395.

45. B. T. *Berakhot* 30b. From the context in the Talmud the statement seems to be an early one. Although the author is not specifically identified as Rabbi Eliezer ben Hyrcanos, his statement is certainly consistent with the latter's approach to prayer. See Y. D. Gilat, *The Teachings of R. Eliezer Ben Hyrcanos and Their Position in the History of the Halakhah*, in Hebrew (Tel Aviv: 1968), pp. 83-84. The absence of statements by R. Eliezer on liturgical matters has been noted by J. Neusner as being consistent with R. Eliezer's opinion that a fixed liturgy is not to be followed ("The Formation of Rabbinic Judaism," in *Aufstieg und Niedergang der romischen Welt*, II 19,2 [Berlin and New York: 1979], p. 29).

46. Saul Lieberman (*Tosefta Ki-fshutah*, pt. I [NY: 1955], pp. 43-44) points out that the fact that the Tosefta refers to "his Father who is in Heaven" in the same context in which the *Mishnah* refers to "The Holy of Holies" shows that the latter reference is really a toponomy for He whose Presence is felt in the Holy of Holies.

47. See Lieberman (*Tosefta*, p. 44), who shows that the turning of the heart may also have been taken literally.

48. *Tur Orach Chaim* 90. I have changed the order of the requirements as they appear in the printed editions of the *Tur* to fit in with the order of their exposition in the following chapters. Preparation of the mind is dealt with in the last place in chapter 98. Further external devices as aids in arousing *kavvanah* such as: using a prayer book; praying quickly(!); and others, have been suggested by more recent rabbis. See a list with bibliography in Ovadya Yosef, *Yabia Omer*, pt. 3, 10:4.

49. See Louis Ginzberg, *Geonica* I (repr. New York: 1968), p. 120, on the introduction of prayer books.

50. *Hiddushei Rabbeinu Haim Halevy, Hilchot Tefillah* 4:1. A similar idea is found in the dictum of Ramban, quoted by the Beis Yosef and glossed by the Ramo in *Yoreh Deah* 335:4, that one who has visited the sick and not prayed for him has not fulfilled his obligation.

51. We shall not discuss here those cases in which the sentiments were no longer felt appropriate due to historical changes such as the call to eliminate the prayer for the Babylonian Exilarch or the more recent demand to change the form of mourning for the fall of Jerusalem. See Joseph Heinemann, "Changes in the Prayer and in Synagogue Practice," in *Steps* (Jerusalem: The Movement for Torah Judaism, 5731), pp. 37-43.

52. *Tur Orach Chaim* 101. The Tur's novella changes the whole impact of the talmudic statement. Originally it tended to lessen the demand for *kavvanah*, but according to the Tur's explanation it created a total demand for *kavvanah* – albeit limited to *avot*.

53. *Tur*, loc. cit. This modification was not included in the *Shulhan Arukh* of Rabbi Yosef Karo who instead included the stricter novella of the Tur. However, Rabbi Moses Isserless added this last modification in his glossary to the *Shulhan Arukh*, ad loc.

54. This is again reflected in the insistence of modern decisors on the use of Hebrew for prayer (see *Mishnah Berurah* 101:13 and the "Beur Halakhah") even though earlier decisors permitted the use of other languages if Hebrew was not understood. However, the insistence on Hebrew was rather part of the reaction against reform. See Joseph Heinemann's review of Jakob J. Petuchowski, *Prayerbook Reform in Europe,* in *Tarbiz* 39 (5270): 218–221.

55. Cf. *Eretz Tzvi* (Responsa) (Lublin: 1939), no. 22. Rabbi Z. Frommer stressed the importance of prayer with a congregation since such prayer is accepted even without intention. This has the effect of changing the significance of prayer from being a communion with God to being an expression of the community of Israel. In many Jewish communities outside of Israel this has become the main meaning of the synagogue.

56. Rabbi Ovadya Yosef, *Yabia Omer,* pt. 3. *Orach Chaim* 10:4.

57. Cf. Aaron Lichtenstein, "R. Joseph Soloveitchik," in *Great Jewish Thinkers of the Twentieth Century,* ed. Simon Noveck, (1963), p. 294.

58. Ruth Birnbaum, "The Man of Dialogue and the Man of Halakha," *Judaism* 26 (1977): 52.

7
Prayer and Jewish Thought: Approaches and Problems (A Survey)

Shalom Rosenberg

Methodological Foreword

The Categories

Due to the quantity and wide range of material on the subject of prayer, we cannot undertake a general discussion of it without first establishing some scheme of systematization. Few attempts have been made in this area. Professor Joseph Heinemann, in the foreword to his book, *Prayer in the Time of the Tannaim and Amoraim*,[1] mentions the attempt of A. Spanier[2] in the 1930s to divide prayer into various formal, external categories such as praise, petition, doxology, and so on. Another approach which Heinemann mentions is the philological-historical and relates primarily to "historical questions concerning the development of the *nosah* and a systematic attempt to reconstruct its original form."³ Heinemann himself takes form-criticism as his method, the starting point for his classification of prayers being dependent upon linguistic forms and other stylistic signs, which in turn leads to the important and fruitful division among prayers in terms of locale, that is, prayers belonging to the Temple, the synagogue, the study house, individuals, and so forth.

For one who sets out to write the history of prayer and its beginnings, there is no doubt that Heinemann's approach is correct. However, when we turn to the philosophical questions involved, these formal categories lose their relevance. In the course of the years, with the crystallization of fixed prayers and of the *Siddur,* distinctions arising out of the different origins of prayers has become blurred, and in their place other distinctions, which in turn create new categories, have begun to emerge. From the viewpoint of a student of thought, the most significant categories are those which allow for a clear and fruitful systematization of different positions, and in particular to an understanding of the interrelationships of different parts of the prayers. The problems involved in such an inquiry are not the same as those of Heinemann, but they are parallel to them. We have, therefore, attempted to create a typological system, despite the danger that in doing so we may lose sight of the accepted divisions of schools and trends.

Oral Worship

The construction of our typological system necessitates a broadening of the meaning of the term "prayer" which, in strict halakhic usage, refers to the *Amidah* alone. The discussion of prayer, as a rule, involves not only prayer in this limited sense, but the recital of the *Shema,* the various blessings, and the reading of the Torah as well, each of which belong to distinct, separate halakhic categories. The great thinkers of the Middle Ages were aware, as we shall see below,⁴ that though, through this broader usage, important halakhic distinctions might be overlooked, it is possible even halakhically to speak of prayer in this broad sense. For prayer includes not only speech-acts, but other actions as well, such as standing, bowing, wrapping oneself in the *tallit,* the use of song and melody, and even, perhaps, weeping and dancing.

The language of prayer thus includes not only words but, as it were, a whole dictionary of gestures, ceremonies and symbols. To relate to prayer in its fullness requires a clear recognition and understanding of these additional elements, which are fully provided for in the *halakhah.* All these forms of expression belong to a common category, which we may term worship in and through language.

Our discussion is based on the basic intuition that prayer parallels language. Charles Morris divided the science of language or signs—semiology—into three levels: syntax, semantics, and pragmatics. In syntax one is concerned with the form, the relationship of symbols (in our case, words) to one another. In semantics one is concerned, in addition, with the meaning of symbols, that is, the relationship between symbol and object. Here we reach the level of meaning. In pragmatics one deals with a system of usage, that is, the totality of relationships among the words, their meanings, and the man who uses them.

We may transfer this model to the study of prayer, adding to these three levels a fourth, the changing historical dimension.

The first level is that of form analysis of the prayers, which has been done quite competently by Heinemann in his study.

On the second level, that of prayer as a semantic system, the emphasis is placed on the theology behind the prayers: the *Siddur* as a totality of beliefs, hopes, and duties.[5]

The third level involves the relationship between the praying man and his prayer: the function which prayer fulfills in human life, its place in a general system of thought or philosophy.

On the basis of this analysis, and following the semiotic model, one may say that the main thrust of the controversy surrounding the Reform movement in the 19th century focussed on the first level, that of the formal setting, that is, the external aspects of prayer, such as the physical arrangement of the synagogue or the language of prayer. In a later stage, the conflict moved to the semantic level, to such theological problems entailed in the text of the prayer book as the return to Zion and the rebuilding of the Temple.[6] Contemporary discussions of prayer are simply new variations of the struggle on these two planes. Examples of this are: in the semantic area, the changes, additions and deletions suggested as a result of the rise of the State of Israel, the liberation of Jerusalem, and so on; in the formal area, improvements in the arrangements for prayer, the standardizing of the *nosah,* participation of women, and so on. It is interesting to note that discussions in both these areas completely ignore the essential aspect of prayer, viz. man's relationship to it, despite the fact that here is the decisive question which will determine the future of prayer.[7]

The discussion of formal and semantic aspects is not the exclusive heritage of the modern period. It has accompanied prayer from its earliest days, beginning with the prohibition of saying *modim modim* in the Talmud and the struggle over the recitation of *piyyutim* in Geonic times.[8] But beyond these explicit debates there was also a struggle within Jewish thought between different conceptions in the third area, namely, that involving the nature and meaning of prayer. This realm involves not the theology *in* the *Siddur,* but rather the theology *of* the *Siddur* and *of* the act of prayer. What is it that makes it possible or necessary for a man to pray?

In light of these methodological comments, we shall address ourselves here to two primary areas:

1. The types of approach to prayer within different schools of Jewish thought.
2. The problems of prayer in the modern age.

In our typology of approaches to prayer, we will describe six positions which seem to represent the main options. The first and most basic position is what we may term "simple" or naive; following that, we will discuss three approaches characteristic of kabbalistic and philosophical thought—that is, the theurgic, the mystical, and the didactic; finally, we will discuss two approaches within contemporary thought, the existential and the institutional, and the synthesis between them.

In light of these different directions or positions, we will discuss, in the second section, the problems of prayer for modern man. Here, three paradoxes are involved: the cosmological, the theological, and the anthropological. On these we shall focus attention.

Approaches

Simple Prayer

One may distinguish between biblical thought and perhaps aggadic thought, on the one hand, and later thought, with its mystical and philosophical streams, on the other with the help of the notion of reflexivity. Nonideological thought "thinks," but it does not render an account to itself of this thinking. It is unreflective. Against this, ideological thought comments upon itself, sees itself as a known object. "It is necessary to know that there is knowledge, and to ask about this knowledge, in order for philosophical knowledge to exist."[9] Conscious knowledge makes knowledge itself a problem for philosophical clarification.

Here, we find ourselves at a methodological parting of the ways. In classical Jewish thought (by this I mean both medieval Jewish philosophy and *Kabbalah*), the study of prayer means the analysis of the place of prayer within a particular system of thought, according to the testimony of the thinker himself. Such study requires the construction of a theoretical framework by means of which one will arrive at ideas implicit in the sources, that is, the biblical and rabbinic literature.

Simple prayer, as we shall henceforth call nonideological prayer, is the starting point of our discussion. Here the mai n problems involved are those of defining the boundaries between it and creations similar to it. How are we to distinguish between monotheistic prayer and pagan prayer or magical oaths? What are its implications for the idea of God?[10]

We shall discuss below the problematical relationship between prayer and magic, postponing till the end of the paper the discussion of other theological implications connected to our idea of the "whom" to which prayers are addressed.

Theurgic Prayer

Is prayer a magical act? The dangers of such an approach are obvious, in light of the existence of magical prayers in almost every period. Magical prayers, whose composers attributed them to *tannaim* or *amoraim,* are known to us from the very earliest times, and there are even magical imitations of well-known prayers.[11]

The danger of seeing prayer as a magical act was one of the challenges to both kabbalistic and philosophical thought. This problem is particularly critical in the Neoplatonic tradition. In these sources, one finds a confusion of ideas taken from Plato and Plotinus and their students, and from the magical traditions of late antiquity. While this problem exists with regard to all the *mitzvot,* it has special force in regard to prayer.[12]

It is extremely difficult to define the border between prayer and magic. While it is generally possible to distinguish between prayer and the use of a magical formulae, it is difficult to isolate the distinction between them in principle. In the relevant literature, this distinction is drawn in one of three ways:

1. The difference between prayer and magic is inherent in the different relationship to the text of prayer. While the power and effectiveness of magic is dependent upon the correctness of the formula and its precise execution—that is, the words or actions which express it—the main element of prayer is the human intention involved.

2. Magic operates automatically, while prayer is not *necessarily* answered. The will of God is the bridge between prayer and its answer, and this will is not subject to any causal law. The pseudo-scientific approach which characterizes magic is transformed in prayer to a pseudo-personal one. Of these two approaches, the former typifies the stance of medieval Jewish thought, while the latter that of Jewish thought in more recent generations.

While the first approach is valid with regard to kabbalistic thought as well, this seeming resemblance forces us to seek an additional distinction between kabbalistic and magical forms of prayer. The distinction proposed is based on neither the structure of prayer nor the mechanics involved in it, but on its goal. It is as follows:

3. The purpose of kabbalistic prayer, or *mizvot* or Divine service in general, is theurgical and not magical. Magic serves man; the purpose of theurgy is "to sustain the harmonious and smooth functioning of the Divine powers."[13] In theurgy, man turns himself into an instrument of the Divine plan; the service is not for mundane needs but for "the needs of the Almighty."

We shall now examine the implications of each of these three distinctions.

Intention

An outstanding articulation of the importance of intention and of the unique problematic involved in prayer is found in the *Hovot Ha-levavot* ("Duties of the Heart") of R. Bahye ibn Pakuda. Bahye divides the commandments into "duties of the heart" and "duties of the limbs." Within this division, prayer occupies an inbetween place. By its nature, prayer is a combination of both—act and intent:[14]

> Every deed which is for God must fall into one of three categories: first, those which are exclusively duties of the heart; second, those which are duties of the heart and the limbs together, such as prayer, study of Torah, and praise and thanks to God. . . . . And know that the words of prayer are like the outer shell . . . and prayer is like the body, while the concentration upon it is like the spirit.

The main element separating prayer from magic is the fact that religious acts are worthless unless they are done with the devotion of the heart.[15] Rabbi Yehudah Halevi expresses this idea in requiring of man two things, which he sees as the foundations of Torah: "One, to believe that the Torah is from God; and two, that it be accepted with a faithful heart by the community" (*Kuzari* 3:23).

There are many halakhic sources which view intention (*kavvanah*) as the central foundation of prayer. However, one ought to point out the multiplicity of meaning this concept has in talmudic sources. In addition to the meaning this term has in common with other *mizvot*—namely, the *intention* to do one's duty—*kavvanah* in prayer has three further primary meanings:

1. Understanding of the text of the prayer: "First of all, he ought to think about the meaning of the words with all the strength of his mind and his understanding."[16] Or else "One who prays must concentrate his heart on the meaning of the words which he utters with his lips, for even were he to speak

before a mortal king he would organize his words and concentrate upon them carefully."[17] or Finally "*kavvanah*—refers to the concentration of the heart upon the act of praying."[18]

2. Awareness of the situation of man in prayer: "He must first bear in mind that he is standing before the Creator of his spirit and his soul."[19] Or, in the definition of Maimonides, "He should see himself as standing before the Divine Presence."[20]

3. The inner transformation of man as a consequence of prayer, which is "the service of the heart": "Thus, the essence of prayer is the purification and refinement of the heart and the cleansing of the mind, for this is the beloved service of the heart."[21]

Medieval philosophers stressed particularly the third meaning of *kavvanah*, to the point of denying the value of any other type of prayer. "Prayer without intention is like a body without a soul."[22] In general, one may say that the meaning of *kavvanah* in any intellectual system was a function of the entire system and its relation to prayer. Maimonides defined *kavvanah* in a way which combined the second and third meanings: "What is *kavvanah?* That he clear his mind of all other thoughts and see himself as if standing before the Divine Presence . . . and he should not treat his prayer as one does who is carrying a burden, who casts it off and then goes on his way. . . ." (*Laws of Prayer,* 4:16).

In a comment which has become classic, Rabbi Chaim of Brest-Litovsk stated that the crucial point in this statement of Maimonides' is that *kavvanah* is not an addition to prayer, but that *kavvanah* is the essence of prayer, that which defines it.[23] These comments, in turn, receive a philosophical interpretation in the teachings of Rabbi Joseph B. Soloveitchik. The distinction between *kavvanah* in its second and its third meaning is explained by him as follows: in the one case, *kavvanah* expresses a limited intention towards a specific act, while in prayer man is obligated to "direct his whole self toward God."[24] In other words, the covenantal encounter with God and the speaking with Him are the essence of prayer, while the concrete act of reciting certain texts is the means of praying, rather than the prayer itself.

Necessity and Freedom

Ernst Simon, writing on prayer, draws the boundary line between prayer proper and magic by invoking the notion of compulsion. In magic, man attempts to force God to do his will, but success would mean the transformation of God into an idol, and of religion into idolatry.[25] Prayer, on the other hand, is the attempt to express the relationship of creatureliness, the absolute dependence of man upon God. This view, related as it is to Yehezkel Kaufmann's concept of monotheism, has a provenance in modern as well as classical Jewish thought. A clear expression of it is given by Rabbi Judah Loew of Prague:

> "The sacrifices of the wicked are an abomination to God, but the prayer of the upright is His will" (Proverbs 15:8). King Solomon wishes to say here with regard to the worship of the Almighty, that God does not desire a particular act of worship because he benefits from it, because if that were so it would make no difference to him whether the act were performed by the righteous or by the wicked. But this is not so, for as it is said, "the sacrifices of the wicked are an abomination"; from which it follows that worship does not benefit God, but man alone. . . . Thus, "the sacrifices of the wicked are an abomination," for God does not desire to benefit the wicked, but only the prayer of the upright is His desire.[26]

Magic and Theurgy[27]

The theurgic function of prayer is expressed in the works of the kabbalists and those influenced by them. We ought to emphasize that it is only possible to understand this type of prayer against the background of a particular world view, according to which man's acts exercise an influence upon cosmic history—and—if the cosmos is not separated from the Divine realm—upon the "needs of the Almighty" Himself. Human action causes a flow of plenitude and the "unification of the Holy One, blessed be He, and the Shekhinah."[28] In a well-known passage, the *Zohar* portrays the effect of prayer as a series of four *tikkunim,* or repairs, which are performed simultaneously.

The first *tikkun*—the repairing of oneself, to attain perfection.
The second *tikkun*—the repair of this world.
The third *tikkun*—the repair of the upper world and the hosts of heaven.
The fourth *tikkun*—the repair of the Holy Name, with the secret of the holy Chariots, and the secret of all the worlds, above and below—a full and proper repair.[29]

The repair of the upper worlds and of the Holy Name are characteristic of theurgic prayer. The repair of the worlds is performed by the ascension of the prayer,[30] which breaks through the heavens until it reaches the highest level and performs a "unification." An unimpeded ascent of this kind depends upon intention. A defective prayer is likely to be caught by the forces of impurity, but a successful ascent brings down a flow of plenitude from on high.

The true intention of prayer is then, according to the theurgic understanding, not a request for the needs of man, but man's self-transformation into a vessel for the repair of the world.

Mystical Prayer

A different position from that of the theurgist is the mystical, which is also part of the kabbalistic tradition. An expression of this difference is found in the following passage from the *Zohar,* which describes two levels of prayer:[31]

> "For the children of Israel are My servants . . ." (Leviticus 25:55). It is a commandment to serve God with all kinds of worship, both inside and outside the Temple, in all of those acts called "service": through prayer, through the fulfillment of the *mizvot* of the Torah, for all is called "service," like a servant who looks after his master to do whatever he needs. . . .
> Israel are called by God by these two names: servants . . . and sons. . . .
> In the service with which man serves God, there is one which requires both functions, that of a servant and of a son, so that the Holy One, blessed be He, is glorified by him. . . .
> And what is that "service"? It is that of prayer, in which he must be both servant and son, to be included in these upper levels: to serve and to order his prayer in the mystery of servant-ness, to perform the service of repairing the worlds; and to attach his will to the secrets of wisdom, and to cling to his master in the upper secret-places as is needful.
> A son always cleaves to his father without any separation, for there is no one who can stop him, while a servant does the service of his master and arranges the repair of the worlds.
> He who is both of these at one time, in one conjunction—this is the man who brings about the mystery of all faith in one unity, without any separation, and joins everything together.

Before us are two levels: the service of the servant and that of the son. The *Zohar* connects these levels respectively to the *Sefirah* of *Malkhut* (Kingship) which is the aspect of servanthood, and to that of *Tiferet* (Splendor), which is Israel, the aspect of sonship. Yet these attributes represent two differing outlooks on the nature of prayer. One is the type of the service of the servant; it is prayer which brings about the repair of the world even though the servant is unaware of its full significance. The other is the prayer of the son: *devekut,* clinging, attachment to God—that is, Mystical Prayer, in the full sense. Only one who attains to this sort of prayer is capable of "repairing" the upper worlds, and even the Holy Name itself.

This conception of *kavvanah* differs from the theurgic conception, and we may describe it in general terms as mystical prayer,[32] although this is a general heading, and one that includes many different and varied kinds of prayer. Before we attempt to describe the various types, let us stress that, fundamentally, mystical prayer has existed in Judaism for thousands of years, maintaining a continuity in spite of changing forms.[33]

In *Merkabah* and *Hekhalot* mysticism, prayer had the ecstatic function of elevating man up to heaven. Instead of bearing their usual semantic values, the words of prayer were seen as holy names, emotionally charged, and able to arouse the visionary to his mystical journey, providing him with technical aid.

The motifs of mystical ascent to heaven were retained in the occult doctrines of *Haside Ashkenaz* (German pietists of the early Middle Ages),[34] but side by side with them there also developed a tendency to see in prayer a meditative act,[35] which was made possible by the learning of secret signs. German Hasidism brought about a reinterpretation of texts by means of added meanings and *kavvanot,* through various means of interpreting letters, particularly that of numerology.[36] These activities greatly contributed towards the crystallization of the text of the *Siddur* and its careful preservation.[37]

In the *Kabbalah* of Provence and Gerona, we find visions which are similar in their nature to those of the Merkabah mystics, but with more stress on the connection of man to the upper regions within the world of the *Sefirot*.[38] The most important means of expressing this teaching was found by these schools in the theory of *devekut* – "devotion," or "clinging."

Thus, we hear in the name of Rabbi Isaac the Blind: "Our teacher, the pious one, said that the main service of the enlightened ones and those who know His Name is, 'to Him shall you cleave.' This is a great principle of the Torah with regard to prayer and the recitation of blessings: that he should faithfully set his mind as though cleaving to the Source on high."[39] This cleaving or clinging took different forms: "The clinging of thought," "the clinging of the will," "the clinging of the soul," and so on. "The clinging of thought" is described as the contemplation of the *Sefirot* and when this reaches the *Sefirah* of *Hokhmah* (Wisdom) "the separation between human thought and Divine Thought is erased for a moment."[40] "Clinging of the will" refers to the negation of the individual will and "clinging of the soul" is another process, a sort of cutting off of the connection between the soul and the body, and a momentary absence of separation from the supernal source.[41]

Lurianic *Kabbalah* gave a new push to the mystical interpretation of prayers, particularly with respect to the doctrine of *tikkun.* "Repair" was accomplished by means of *yihudim* – "acts of union." In place of concentration upon the correct *Sefirah* came concentration upon the correct Divine Name. The words of prayer again became transformed into a type of instrumentality for elevating man to the upper worlds.[42]

Of all of the different stages of Jewish mysticism, Hasidism is outstanding for the central role which it gave to prayer. To understand the unique nature of hasidic mystical prayer, we must return momentarily to the distinction we drew earlier between mystic and theurgic prayer. An interesting example of the phenomenological difference between them, despite the common kabbalistic source, may be found in their attitude towards the prayer text. Theurgic prayer brought about a symbolic reinterpretation of the text, while mystical prayer sometimes brought about its disintegration. In both cases, the normal semantic units lost their value, but where in theurgic prayer new semantic units with symbolic meanings were formed, in mystical prayer the emphasis was transferred almost completely to nonsemantic units, (e.g. letters) which became a medium by which to reach a higher level. Thus, for example, the Baal Shem Tov is credited with the statement, "As astronomers are able to see the stars on a clear day by means of their instruments, so we have instruments with which to see the upper realms and attributes. These are the letters."[43]

The set *nosah* of prayer serves mystical prayer as a sort of vehicle for supernatural experience "in which in one instant, in a flash of vision, he goes beyond time."[44] From that point on, the speech and the thought become separate, as is expressed in the saying of the Baal Shem Tov: "When I cause my thoughts to cling to the Holy One, blessed be He, I allow my mouth to speak what it will."[45] The Maggid of Mezeritch explains this by means of the assertion that the speech is within the thought, but "in deep concealment."[46] Thus, the highest level of prayer is attained when mouth and heart are not necessarily at one with one another. Words are only the apparent substance of prayer.[47]

Our discussion up to this point also sheds new light on the distinction between *hasidim* and *mitnagdim,* with respect to prayer. The distinction between the mystical and theurgic approaches, both of which spring from the *Kabbalah,* contributes to our understanding of the distinction between these two movements, despite the fact that both of them drew on the sources of the *Kabbalah* and used its terminology. While these two trends, in their pure form, are merely the abstractions of scholarship, the existence of the different emphases is perfectly clear.

The thought of the *mitnagdim,* which also influenced the teachings of the *yeshivot,* (rabbinical academies), is characterized by a double direction: an emphasis on the theurgic aspect of *mizvot,* including prayer, and the tenet that this aspect requires nothing more than the simple straightforward fulfillment of the *mizvot.*

These two points, in addition to quite a few mystical ideas, are articulated in the work *Nefesh Hahayim,* by Rabbi Hayyim ben Isaac of Volozhin: "The idea of blessings and prayers to God signifies a real multiplying and increase. For it is His will, for reasons hidden within Him, that by means of our prayers and blessings we should repair and unify the upper worlds and forces so that they be fit to receive the holiness of the upper light."[48] The theurgic goal is the essential intention of prayer. ". . . Its entire intention is to add power in the realm of holiness. In the same way as a soldier forgets all of his own needs and concerns and willingly risks his life for the king's honour . . . so it is appropriate that the upright man place all of his concentration and purity of thought into prayer so as to add power to the upper worlds. . . . The essence of *kavvanah* requires that it serves the needs of what is above."[49]

The common denominator of these two mystical approaches is that in each of them prayer loses its primary, simple meaning. The Maggid of Dubno described this by means of a parable: "A fire started in one house in a town. If the people of the town are united and each one hurries, not to save his own property, but to put out the blaze, then it is not difficult to do so. But if each applies himself to saving his own house, then the blaze grows and spreads to destroy everything, and no one is safe."[50] In a similar manner, the Maggid of Mezeritch taught: "A man ought not to pray for his own needs, but should pray that the *Shekhinah,* the Divine Presence, be redeemed from exile, for the *Zohar* calls those who pray for their own needs and not for the *Shekhinah* 'Arrogant, barking dogs.' "[51]

From the standpoint of the mystic, regular prayer is an act with overtones of impropriety. "It is stated in the writings of the *Ari,* Rabbi Isaac Luria, that if a man does not concentrate upon the intentions of prayer according to the true path (i.e., *Kabbalah*) then the more intensely he prays the more he is guilty of begging a reward from his master."[52] Petitionary prayer in the usual sense is seen as "begging a reward from one's master," and thus, paradoxically, the more one concentrates on the literal meaning of the words, the more distasteful to God is one's prayer. The fact that prayer is formulated by the Rabbis in petitionary form does not detract from the sharpness of this paradox. "Even though they wrote in the prayer book, 'Inscribe us for a sufficient livelihood,' 'Inscribe us for forgiveness,' etc., which would make it seem that the entire petition is for the satisfaction of material needs, and that being so, the more one concentrates on prayer in this sense, the more one is 'begging for bread.' "[53]

Didactic Prayer

While the field of operation of theurgic prayer was the world outside of man, that of mystical prayer was the soul of man itself. The latter, as it were, internalized the former. Philosophical thought, which also saw the main locale of prayer as the soul of man, saw its primary purpose as didactic. This approach included two related but distinct motifs, to which we shall refer, in the interests of brevity, as "instructional" and "educative."

The view of prayer as "instruction" makes the text of the *Siddur* the heart of prayer, and our encounter with it the essential point of confrontation and concentration. On the other hand, the view of prayer as "educative" and as tending toward the formation of personality places the emphasis on the act of prayer itself and its consequences.

Both of these approaches are found in medieval Jewish philosophy. According to the one, the *mizvot* are reminders of various ideas, while according to the other they are a path towards *devekut* or devotion – a clinging to God, in the sense that this was understood in classical Jewish philosophy.

Expressions of the first approach are to be found in the rationalistic and Aristotelian stream. Thus, Gersonides (14th century) calls for philosophical study of the prayer text, and this despite the lurking danger of praying merely from habit.

> A man does not bother to examine in depth that which he is used to, nor to ask the question, "Why was this made in such and such a manner? . . ." For you see, with regard to the prayers which the Men of the Great Assembly set out for us, that we recite them constantly as a routine but fail to understand their secret. One of the reasons why many of our Sages err in these matters is because they give little thought to the meaning intended. Similarly, you will find many other things in our perfect Torah which, because we are so used to them, we are satisfied to merely read without trying to understand their intent.[54]

A strong expression of the second point of view – that is, the educational value of prayer – is found in Rabbi Yehudah Halevi, who saw in prayer an instrument for the education and elevation of the soul.[55] This approach occupies a central place in the thought of Rabbi Hasdai Crescas, as well. Crescas sees in prayer, as in other commandments, a means of arousing man "to the heights of arousal and to bring man to the love of God and to cleave to Him, even though we are far away in actuality."[56] This approach was further developed by Rabbi Joseph Albo in the wake of Crescas. In his view, prayer is intended primarily to prepare and to receive the supernal influence. That is, it is not a transcendent act – a generating of heavenly influence, as in *Kabbalah,* but an immanent process of generating a "new spirit" within man, which qualifies him to receive the transcendent influx.[57]

The view of prayer as determining or influencing the personality is found in various streams of more modern Jewish thought. We will quote two examples of this, one from the teachings of Rabbi Samson Raphael Hirsch (nineteenth century), the other from certain writings of the *Musar* movement in the same period.

Judaism, according to Hirsch, sees all of life as service of God. From this, it follows that the unique status of prayer requires explanation. The peculiar and characteristic meaning of prayer, as against that of the *mizvot,* results from the different areas in which they work. While the *mizvot* are part of the active life of man in the world,[58] prayer acts on man himself. Man attains his perfection by means of a rapid change in the course of his thoughts and emotions; "The root meaning of the verb *hitpalel,* from which is derived the noun *tefillah,* prayer, is to 'test oneself' and to 'judge oneself'. . . . The one who prays thus leaves the circle of active life in order to make a true and just judgment of himself . . . to see the judgment of God and of the world upon his actions . . . in order that he may dedicate himself anew to the active life."[59]

The view of prayer as shaping the soul is also found in the literature of *Musar,* particularly in that of the last generations. Thus, in the foreward to the *Siddur 'Ishe Yisrael* by R. Yitshak Malzan, one of the disciples of Rabbi Yisrael Salanter, we read:[60]

> Generally, one ought to look at the *kavvanah* of prayer from two angles: 1. To arrive, to the best of our ability, at the intention of those who set out the prayers according to their words and expressions. . . . 2. The main intent of prayer is to uplift the soul . . . as Rabbenu Yonah wrote in his commentary to the Talmud (*Berakhot,* chap. 5) on the statement, '. . . so that they may direct their hearts towards heaven': 'The intent is not that they should concentrate on the recitation of the prayers as such, but that they should intend to make their hearts whole.' "

The two motifs mentioned by the editor of this *Siddur* correspond, in a general way, to motifs found in the philosophical literature as a whole.

This brief passage does not represent the entire *Musar* movement, of course, but it is very typical, and makes it possible for us to understand other texts, which make use of a seemingly mystical terminology.

Rabbi Eliyahu Dessler, for example, writes[61] of prayer as bringing man towards a cleaving to God, but "a *devekut* which is above his own natural level, for through it there is opened before man the possibility of reaching higher than the potential of his own understanding." In prayer there is "a point wherein the worlds touch one another." There is room here for a mystical interpretation, but the basic experience is meditative.[62]

Existentialist Prayer

As against these approaches, we may mention another, characteristic of many streams in modern Jewish thought, which, for the sake of brevity, we shall call the existentialist approach to prayer. Although it includes many streams and nuances within itself, among which there is considerable conflict, we may speak of a certain common denominator, in the understanding of prayer as dialogue. Prayer is neither an activity in the world nor one within man alone, but a dialogue between man and God, "as if he speaks to Him face to face,"[63] or "like a man who whispers into his neighbor's ear."[64] As Joshua Heschel has said,[65] it is possible to express the essence of prayer in this sense through the rabbinic saying, "Know before whom you stand" (*Berakhot* 28b), in which the emphasis is on the "whom" rather than the "what." The "I" prays neither to a power nor to a process, nor even to a set of values. Prayer has one and only one unique meaning: the act of standing before a "Thou" who is at least as real as the "I" who prays.

This dialogic aspect of prayer is found within the other approaches as well, but there it is more peripheral and hidden. For example, within the philosophical approach one may find alternative interpretations. To take a modern example, Rabbi Samson Raphael Hirsch expounds the various blessings of the *Amidah* by means of a paraphrase, one passage of which follows:

> *Avot* [The Patriarchs—the first of the Eighteen Benedictions] . . . You have acquired knowledge of God, whose glory fills the universe . . . that He is the God of your fathers and the God of your people. As He appeared to you in His Name in the life of your ancestors, . . . likewise He does deeds of kindness and creates everything with His great love . . . and the children's children shall base their lives on the lives of their ancestors . . . because He is the one who teaches and raises them . . . and because of this, great is your desire to dedicate yourself to His service.[66]

In this passage, whatever its exegetical value may be, the most striking feature is the transformation which has occurred in the identity of the "thou", which is no longer God, but the praying subject.

A good expression of the decisive difference between these two forms of address, written with a sensitive understanding of the immanent categories of prayer, was given toward the end of the Middle Ages by a commentator who understood well the philosophical approach, namely, Rabbi Yitshak Aramah. An examination of two differing forms of address enables Aramah to draw a distinction between prayer and *Keri'at Shema:*

This is the reason why they said that one who read *Shema* but without making it audible to his own ears did not fulfill his obligation: because this recitation is the opposite of prayer. Prayer is speech with God. Thus, he need merely shape the words with his lips and God will hear and answer him, for He hears the utterance of the heart. Accordingly, our Rabbis said, 'Whoever raises his voice during prayer is one of little faith' (*Berakhot* 24b). . . . However, those passages which come to teach and instruct us regarding the roots of our faith and how to behave must be recited aloud, so as to be heard by our ears, as is written, 'Hear, O Israel, the Lord is our God, the Lord is one' (Deut. 6:4), because he addresses himself in the name of God throughout this passage.[67]

Mystical prayer is also different, in principle, from dialogic prayer, although in a paradoxical way it also contributed to its development. Dialogic prayer is based on a straightforward interpretation of the halakhic sources, as well as the personal experience of generations of those who prayed. In particular, the influence of Hasidism stands out. Above, we described hasidic prayer as drawing upon the theurgic, and leading forward to the mystical type of prayer. For our purpose, another characteristic is important here: through making prayer central to the religious life of the Jew, it created the existential prayer, placing it in a kind of dialectical opposition to the mystical.[68]

What are the characteristics of existential prayer? As against both the theurgic and mystical modes, one may say that in it man stands before God in all of his smallness and creatureliness, and with all of his needs and requests. Theurgic prayer saw prayer as a Divine need; mystical prayer agreed that, in the final analysis, man prays on behalf of his own needs, but his requests for material goods are basically trivial in comparison to the true request which a man ought to make, that is, for a closeness to God. Within the mystical stance one is likely to find the desire for the "great resignation"[69] from the ordinary concerns of life.

An additional distinction between the existential and the mystical posture relates to the consciousness of the individual who is praying. The existential posture, by definition, implies that man utilizes his normal psychic abilities during the course of his prayer. Against that, mysticism sees prayer, ideally, as occurring in a changed state of consciousness. (This characterization is common to all the varieties of mysticism, despite the variety of "theoretical" interpretations of this phenomenon.)

To a large extent, one may identify the existential approach with the "normal mysticism" of which Max Kadushin speaks.[70] This "normality" is expressed in the fact that the mystical experience which is spoken of by him is one which may be realized by the average individual. Admittedly, in one place Kadushin poses a slightly different model, in which the existentialist stance is seen as "miming" the mystical experience, that is, in behaving as if some sort of personal revelation were, in fact, occurring.[71] This model, too, has elements of truth, which derive particular significance from the fact that the two approaches – the mystical and the existential – frequently use the same terminology. Nevertheless, there is a basic phenomenological difference between them: the existentialist experience does not express itself in paranormal psychological events, but in normal experience, only that instead of man, God is the object or addressee of the experience.

The view of prayer as dialogue is central to the thought of Rabbi Joseph B. Soloveitchik.

> Prayer likewise is unimaginable without man standing before and addressing himself to God in a manner reminiscent of the prophet's dialogue with God. The cosmic drama, notwithstanding its grandeur and splendor, no matter how distinctly it reflects the image of the Creator and no matter how beautifully it tells His glory, cannot provoke man to prayer. Of course it may arouse an adoring-ecstatic mood in man; it may even inspire him to raise his voice in a song of praise and thanksgiving. Nevertheless, ecstatic adoration, even if expressed in a hymn, is not prayer. The latter transcends the bounds of a merely formal liturgy and must not be reduced to the external-technical aspects of prayer such as praise, thanksgiving or even petition. Prayer is basically an awareness of man finding himself in the presence of and addressing himself to his Maker, and prayer has one connotation only: to stand before God.[72]

Prophecy and prayer are different phases of the same dialogue, in which it is only the order which is different: in prophecy the initiative comes from God, while in prayer, from man.

The view of prayer as dialogue is found in a great deal of modern Jewish thought. The connection between revelation and prophecy is found as well in the thought of Franz Rosenzweig, who sees in prayer the response of the soul to revelation.[73] But the uniqueness of Rabbi Soloveitchik's position is in his emphasis on the community as the subject of the conversation. This is the theme of the following section.

Institutionalized Prayer

It is impossible to relate to prayer within the framework of Jewish thought without touching upon the subject of communal prayer, which is one of the original creations of Judaism and which, in its turn, influenced the other monotheistic religions. Public worship is at the heart of prayer in Judaism. Its strength comes from the community, but the community is also the source of many of its problems.

The public character of prayer finds expression in its linguistic formulations. Prayer is normally formulated in the plural, at the price of the deliberate distortion of many biblical expressions. However, Jewish prayer is collective prayer not only in the semantic sense, but also in the technical sense, as expressed in its structure and in many halakhic rulings relating to prayer, such as the obligation to pray with the community or at least "at the time that the community is engaged in worship."[74]

From a historical viewpoint, communal prayer passed through various stages of development. There were two directions of change: on the one hand, a weakening of the collective element in order to allow room for personal devotions; on the other hand, the transfer of some of the functions to the cantor, who beccme more and more independent. These two contradictory directions point to the basic problem created by the very existence of communal prayer, the problem of the tension between the spontaneity of the individual and the "fixity" of public prayer. From the point of view of the individual, communal prayer will always seem to have a fixed character, however wide may be the freedom granted to the community to introduce novelties.

This tension may be exemplified from an innocent passage found in an ethical will left by a father to his son. In a warning in his book, *Yesh Nohalin,* Rabbi Abraham ben Shabtai Sheftel Hurvitz writes:[75] "You oughtn't to think even of words of Torah during the prayers, even though both of them are holy, for our Rabbis say, 'One time for Torah, and another time for prayer.' "[76] On the other hand, he writes: "You always ought to have a book near at hand in the synagogue, such as a *Tur* or *Mishnah,* so that when the cantor sings *Kaddish* or *Kedushah* or one of the other passages which they are inclined to stretch out, then you may look at that book—not to study it out loud, for that would be forbidden as an interruption in the order of the service—but to read it silently, as casual study. Then you will have Torah and prayer together in one place, and it will be well with you. Only be careful that this practice does not detract from your service of prayer, for concerning this our Sages said, 'One time for Torah, another time for prayer.' "[77]

How we may ask is communal prayer explained in Jewish thought? The classic source is found in the thought of Rabbi Yehudah Halevi, who paved the way for those who followed him in the statement that the community brings about the completion and correction of the prayer of the individual. Halevi's statement hints at the fact that individual prayer is, in principle, egoistic, and that only within the community do the various individual prayers achieve harmony. Communal prayer is composed of varying and differing aspects, "so that one completes what is lacking in another, unwittingly or sinfully, and out of it all may come a complete and whole prayer, in perfect devotion."[78]

However, the central motif in communal prayer is found, without doubt, in the idea that its totality is more than simply the harmonious sum of all the individual prayers. In communal prayer, the praying subject is the Community of Israel and, according to this view, the *minyan* (prayer quorum of ten) constitutes a group representing the entire people[79] – which seeks expression in the form and content of its prayers. The synagogue becomes the home of the community of Israel, a spiritual center of the people and the place of service of the community.

This interpretation of communal prayer provides an additional source of tension. The community itself is subject to the tension subsisting between the problems of the present and the fixity of the past, as expressed by the "freezing" of events and things in the *Siddur*. Both the tensions belonging to the individual and those of the community ultimately find their release in the dynamics of prayer. The relationship between the individual and his society finds expression in a constant process of transformation in which, on the one hand, the prayers of the individual are transformed into prayers of the community,[80] and, on the other, communal prayer exercises a decisive influence on the shaping of the prayers of the individual.

One sees this tension between past and present in a striking way in the many disputes concerning prayer in the period following the establishment of the State of Israel.[81] Here, too, the influence worked in both directions. On the one hand, the new generation created new lamentations or attempted to "sing a new song"; however, the acceptance of the heritage of the past, as crystallized in the *Siddur*, formed a collective personality for the entire people, cutting across geographical boundaries, and joining together vast tracts of history. The very archaism of the prayers has a weight of its own, so that the mention of the "remnant of their scribes" or of the *yeshivot* of Babylonia that no longer exist become part of our collective being and historical memory. In the words of David Flusser, it is precisely the "continuity of the praying generations which converts prayer into a trans-historical structure."[82]

Here, Rabbi Soloveitchik's important insight, which sidesteps the prayer of the individual and offers instead an existentialist interpretation of the prayer of the community, comes into play.

There is a fundamental danger related to communal prayer; and that is the risk of seeing it as a mode of divine service which has an essentially societal function, as in Durkheim's interpretation. This danger is translated into practice in the fact that, from an institutional viewpoint, synagogues serve purposes other than prayer, and that these purposes often become primary.

According to Soloveitchik, all this is based on a misunderstanding, grounded in the failure to distinguish between community in two different senses. The praying community is different from ordinary society which is based on mutual advantage and the division of labor; the former is the covenantal community. Institutionalized prayer must be the dialogic prayer of the covenantal community.

It is possible to describe modern thought as being divided into two approaches; on the one hand, there is the philosophic approach, which sees in prayer a means for bringing man to perfection, and on the other hand, there is the institutional approach, which sees in prayer a function of the community and the nation. Is prayer a monologue, or is it, perhaps, a social activity? Or, to quote the biting words of Joshua Heschel: "Is prayer an expression of religious solipsism or religious behaviorism? Of auto-suggestion or of tradition?" In the dialogic prayer of the community, there is an attempt to overcome this dilemma.

The recognition of the central place of communal prayer in Judaism raises the problem of the Holocaust in all its sharpness. The problem of the individual whose prayers are unanswered, of the man who stands before the paradox of faith and despair, is a part of prayer as old as man himself. The Holocaust intensified the reality of this paradox, not only for the individual, but for the community too. The overcoming of this paradox would mean, as in the words of the Talmud,[83] the restoration of the crown of prayer as of old, and the finding of the strength of faith to cry out, as after the destruction of the Temple: "These are His mighty acts and these are His terrible deeds."

Prayer in the Modern World—Paradoxes and Paths

No phenomenon expresses the essence of religion more than prayer. Despite this, prayer always had a problematical philosophical character. We will discuss below three paradoxes, in which the idea of prayer is entangled: cosmological, theological, and anthropological.

The Cosmological Paradox

The central problem involving prayer in classical Jewish thought was cosmological. Its fullest expression is found, to my mind, in the *Sefer Ha-iKarim* of Rabbi Joseph Albo. Among the many questions raised there,[84] we will discuss one central one, presented in the following passage:

> That which led people to doubt the efficacy of prayer is similar to that which led them to abandon the knowledge of God—namely, that one

cannot avoid one of two possibilities: either that God decrees good for a given person, or that he does not decree this. In the one case, it follows that prayer is superfluous and, in the other, it is of no help in changing God's will.[85]

In other words, the question is that of the relationship of prayer to Divine Providence. If man's fate is determined by the principle of "special providence," what is the use of prayer? Albo rightly sees in this question a continuation of the talmudic discussion about the power of prayer to negate evil decrees (Tractate *Rosh Hashanah* 17a).[86] Albo's famous reply is that, in a paradoxical way, prayer itself is one of the factors in the operation of Providence. The relationship of prayer to Divine decree parallels the relationship of human effort and talents to the laws of nature. In light of this parallel, Albo formulates a metaphor which has become classic: "It would follow from their words that Divine decrees apply only when the one who is subject to them is in a given situation, but if his situation should change, so would the decree. For this reason, they said that a change in name or a change of one's deeds can change the decree." Prayer, according to this, is one of the means of changing man and turning him into another person, to whom the decree will not then apply.

Another formulation of the paradox in classical Jewish thought places prayer not against the decree of "special Providence" but against the determinism implied in "general Providence."

This problem was formulated by the rabbis in connection with the concept of "vain prayer." One may not pray for what is absurd: "One who prays for things past utters a vain prayer." (Tractate *Berakhot* 54a) A question is raised concerning those events in the future whose character has already been determined, for example, "His wife was pregnant, and he prays that his wife should be delivered of a male child.' " Such a case, the *Mishnah* rules, is a vain prayer, and the Babylonian Talmud elaborates (*Mishnah,* 60a) that such a prayer is permissible only in a borderline case of undetermined outcome or in a case where it is at least possible that the outcome is still uncertain.

The response of Rav Yosef there, however, introduces the possibility of another solution: "Rav Yosef replied: 'And afterward she bore a daughter' (Genesis 30:21). What is meant by 'afterward'? Rav said: 'After Leah passed judgement on herself, the fetus was changed into a daughter, as it says, "And she called her name Dinah." ' The reply given here to Rav Yosef, "One does not draw arguments from miraculous occurrences," implies that behind Rav Yosef's question stands a prayer which asks for "miraculous deeds" and which would deny the laws of nature. Such an opinion is explicitly stated in the Jerusalem Talmud, which allows one to pray for a particular sex for the child until the moment that the woman actually begins to give birth:

"The School of Yannai taught, 'Our *Mishnah* speaks of one who crouches over the birthstool, but until then he may pray, as is said, 'We are like clay in the hands of the artisan.' Rabbi said in the name of the School of Yannai, 'Dinah's fetus was originally male, but after Rachel prayed it was made female'" (*Berakhot* 9:5).[87]

An additional formulation of this paradox is found in a *baraitha* in the Babylonian Talmud (Tractate *Bava Metziah* 42a):

> Our rabbis taught: When he goes to measure his threshing floor, he says, "May it be Thy will, O Lord our God, that You send blessing on the works of our hands." Once he began to measure, he says, "Blessed is He who sent blessing on this threshing floor." If he measured and afterward prayed, this is a vain prayer, for blessing is not found on that which is already measured or counted, but only in that which is yet hidden from the eye, as it is said, "God will command His blessing for you in your barn." (Deuteronomy 28:8) with a play on the words *samui* (hidden) and *asam* (barn).

According to the first passage quoted (from the Babylonian Talmud), a petitionary prayer is only possible in a case of ontological indeterminism. Against this, the above *baraitha* (relating to the threshing floor) permits us to pray even in a case of epistemological indeterminism: that is, when we don't yet know the nature of a certain reality, even though it has already been determined. Everything happens as if we were praying for a retroactive change in reality, or as if our prayers in the present were received by God in the past, when the indeterminism still existed . . . that is, perhaps even before the creation of the world.

These three meanings of the paradox point to three options open to modern man in approaching the problem of prayer:

1. The belief in the existence of gaps in the general laws of determinism, which exist in man or even in physical nature outside of him.
2. The belief that petitionary prayer means, for scientific man, the hope for a miracle.
3. The belief in the possibility of harmony between the natural cosmos and the religious world of man. This belief may take on a different character for different thinkers.

Beyond these three options is another possibility, which would strip petitionary prayer of its literal meaning and reinterpret it in a radical way. Such a position has been proposed by contemporary thinkers of various streams, from

Franz Rosenzweig to Isaiah Leibovitz. A hint of this revolutionary reinterpretation may even be found in the words of the Sages, in a motif which has returned again and again in various shapes and forms and in different periods. This approach holds that prayer only seems to be a means of attaining worldly needs. But in fact, the Sages have reversed this direction, and our prayers relate to needs which become essentially occasions for attaining closeness to God. The human order, which appears natural, reflects an opposite and antecedent ontological order: "Why were the matriarchs barren? Because God desired their prayers."[88]

Following this reversal of the meaning of petitionary prayer, rooted though it is in classical Jewish thought, the posture of simple prayer becomes problematical. F. Heiler, the author of a classic work on prayer, sees in the words of Emmanuel Kant an illustration of the philosophical criticism of "simple" prayer. According to Kant, petitionary prayer is an absurd and arrogant delusion whereby man distracts God and, as it were, diverts Him from the path of divine Wisdom, in order to gain for himself some petty, temporary advantage.[89] A strikingly similar point was made in the same period in the hasidic study house of the Maggid of Mezeritch, though with a subtle difference from the Kantian formulation:

> A parable is told of a king who ruled over several countries, both near and far. They all obeyed the commands of the king and feared him, and they were constantly attentive to his desires. For this reason, the king turned his heart towards them and protected them from all enemies and harm, so that they could be free to obey him. And the king turned aside from all of his other concerns and from his enjoyments and pleasures, and all of his thoughts were taken up with what was best for these states and their needs and how to protect them, and he constantly pondered wise thoughts about their guidance. . . . One day, a poor, unfortunate, sick and wretched man came from a faraway land, and cried out in the king's courtyard about another person who had crossed him and caused him harm. When the king heard the cries of that man, he treated them as null and void in his pure and clear thoughts. He sent his servant to find out what it was all about, but the man ignored the servant and continued shouting, "O, my lord, the king, save me!" And the king was forced to leave the great and elevated thoughts with which he was constantly occupied in order to attend to the case of this man who had cried out "robbery," even though the robbery of which he complained didn't even amount to a penny. For it was the king's habitual way to hear both great and small, so that they should know that justice was done in the land. And this should not be deemed otherwise than a great indignity for the king, for he had to leave

his plans for the kingdom and his pure thoughts to hear the cry of this fool, even though this leper was unworthy that the king should even look in his face, let alone that he should come be allowed to enter into the king's palace and state his complaint before the great and mighty king—surely this was a great descension.

And the meaning of the parable is self-evident. For when there is no law below, the Holy One, blessed be He, makes judgment up above, and is forced to attend to the small, material things of this world. And even though He watches, all of His creatures and all of creation, with a watchful eye, this concern which comes about in response to the cries of lowly man makes it clearly evident that He is, so to speak, forced to attend to them—and this is called a descent. . . . But when there is judgment below . . . He is not forced to descend—that is, to attend to the petty, material things—and then His honor is greatly upheld."[90]

In this hasidic parable, in contrast to Kant, there is meaning to petitionary prayer, even though it is a harassment to God. It is not the ideal, but rather the last resort for one who hopes for change in the world, and in this lies its simplicity and naivety. The idea that naive prayer is accepted and that its outcome might be reflected in the outer world no doubt involves a profound paradox for contemporary man. He was brought up in a scientific worldview which presumes to offer a full and comprehensive explanation of all phenomena and yet in spite of this he is bidden to stand in prayer. It is the paradox of the man who, in spite of knowing the laws of meteorology, stands and prays to God to "cause the wind to blow and the rain to come down."

The Theological Paradox

Is prayer possible without an anthropocentric image of the One who hears prayer? In prayer, one "speaks to God as if to a ruling king who is liable to a change of heart, as one speaks to a father who might be prepared to give in if we press him, or to a kind hearted man of means who might become even more kind and generous in response to suggestion."[91] This is the classical formulation of the theological paradox. An even sharper expression of this contradiction is implicit in the crisis of religious language in our day. Are praise and thanksgiving any easier for us, theologically, than request and petition? Do they not also constitute a human language?

This question is not new in Jewish thought. It is central in the thought of Maimonides, and its source is in rabbinic teachings. Rabbi A. I. Kook relates to this question by means of a radical and paradoxical interpretation of the following talmudic dictum: "Rabbi Simlai expounded: Let a person first recite the praises of the Holy One, blessed be He, and afterwards pray. From whence do we know this? From Moses, as is said, 'And I prayed unto God at that time, Lord God, You have started to show Your servant Your greatness and Your mighty hand,' and then he added, 'Let me pass over and see the good land' (Deuteronomy 3:23–25)" (*Berakhot* 32a). The requirement according to which prayer is preceded by praise, seems, at first glance, a sort of bribe. Its true purpose, however, according to Rabbi Kook, is different. Prayer is request and beseeching. It is preceded by praise, so as to express the paradox that man prays to God despite the fact that He is beyond human influence. "Prayer must be clean of any thought of changing the Divine Will or of acting against the laws of God."[92] Prayer is formulated in anthropocentric language, but the praise which precedes constitutes a kind of theological caveat, warning us against possible error.

The question as to whether praise is possible is part of a far more general question regarding theological language as a whole: how are we to relate to it? Mysticism, which placed prayer at the top of its scale of values, took exception to the view that it was only concerned with temporal needs—that is, they rejected the view of prayer as directly petitionary. On the other hand, in twentieth century thought and its encounters with prayer, we find a paradoxically different emphasis. The existentialist stream has given new force to the notion of prayer as petition. At the same time the analytical and positivistic streams have raised new problems regarding the theological language of "praise." What does it mean and how does it mean?

We have already mentioned the way in which this theological problem is articulated in Maimonides' *Guide to the Perplexed*. Parallel expressions of this difficulty are to be found in other works of Jewish thought and, following them, in the *Siddur* itself! The *Shir Hakavod* (Hymn of Glory) opens with a direct expression of the paradox:

I tell of Your praise, but I have not seen You.
I imagine You, I describe You, but I have not known You.

Despite the fact that God is above the understanding of the human heart and beyond the grasp of the human eye, we continue to pray, to utter sweet songs and to weave poems as an expression of the longing of the soul for God. And when our poet, at the conclusion of the above hymn, says, "May the song of the poor man be dear in Your eyes," this refers, not to the man poor in material things who brings his song in place of sacrifices and incense, but to every man, poor of tongue in that he possesses only human language. This is inadequate and yet it is the only language available to us for the purpose of theological expression.

The most consistent conclusion to be drawn from this crisis of language is found in the thought of Professor Yeshayahu Leibovitz. According to him, not only is the language of praise a human language, but the attempt to speak about God is itself a human attempt which can never free itself from the bondage of human categories, and any attempts to construct a theology at all are therefore either misguided or arrogant. In this theology-less Torah, prayer acquires a new meaning. It is the sign of our "standing before God."

Professor Gershom Scholem has drawn our attention to the fact that the distinction between prayer and other *mizvot* is such that we may understand prayer as a separate category, which creates opportunities for meditation and mystical experience.[93] Leibovitz's stance negates this distinction, to a great extent. Prayer is simply a commandment, one more specific item in the overall framework of the *mizvot* and similar in its major characteristics to all the others. Leibovitz could have overcome the paradox more satisfactorily if he had relinquished the claim of a total similarity between prayer and other commandments. For while the *mizvot* may be similar to one another from a formal viewpoint, and prayer is in this sense like other *mizvot* — there are essential differences among them from the viewpoint of content. We will attempt to articulate these differences by means of a new use of the classic distinction in halakhic thought between obligations related to individuals and obligations related to objects.

There are *mizvot* which relate to specific actions, which are the purpose of the *mizvah;* against these, there are other *mizvot* which set goals for man and obligate him to reach a certain state. Even within the framework of a theology-less Torah, the *mizvah* of prayer doubtless does not imply a purely mechanical act, i.e. the mere enunciating and discharging of the words of certain texts. Such a conversion of printed signs into sounds could be performed — were the *halakhah* to permit this — by a prayer-machine. Its meaning is rather the creation of a certain state: that of the praying soul. The clarification of this state then solves the theological paradox. Prayer establishes an "I-Thou" relationship to God, without necessitating the acceptance of any particular theology or of the concept of a personal God. Our problem thereby ceases to be a theological one, and becomes that of the content of the *mizvah*. The meaning of the verse, "I set God constantly before me," comes like the obligation to engage in dialogic prayer even in a world without theology.

Religious language, the language of man, comes neither to describe an outer reality nor to express an inner world, but to develop the inner world by relating it to various, perhaps even to all, the areas of life and, by choosing experiences and emotions from all of them, to build the fundamental religious experience of man. It is precisely the connection of prayer with the language of man, with real life, which contributes to the formation of the inner world.

The fact that religious language is not a philosophical language attains its full significance through this solution. The logicians of the Middle Ages based their religious language upon the theory of the signification of names. The greater part of the theory of Divine attributes may be summed up as a conflict among three differing concepts of the nature of names: those who saw the names of God as equivocal names or homonyms, those who saw them as univocal names, and those who saw them as analogical or ambiguous names, the concept expressing the relationship of the attribute or name to its usage in daily speech. Negative theology argues its position on the basis of the claim that names appear in religious language as homonyms of the Divine Name, while those who believed in the possibility of positive theology saw the attributes being used either in terms of their plain meaning (univocal names) or as some sort of analogy (ambiguous names).

This radical theory of names was intended to make artificial or translated names comprehensible. Translated names are technical terms, borrowed or transferred from one area to another when, in this translation or transferral, the thread of meaning connecting the two areas is broken. The intransitive, transitive, and reflexive verbs, for instance, have nothing to do with human standing, going out, and returning, despite the accidental analogy which led to their creation. The use of metaphors, on the other hand, always requires a return to the original meaning of the word, from which we are asked to draw various associations. Religious language is based specifically on metaphors.

Maimonides expressed this idea several times in the *Guide* – for example, in his explanation of such *mizvot* as the laws of the Temple (3:45) and in his explanation of the use of religious language in biblical and rabbinic literature (1:46–49). This religious language is not part of his theory of attributes, but an instrument of educating man to form his basic religious experiences. These experiences focus upon three basic relationships, all of which are woven into the prayers, and all of which are taken from ordinary human experience: son–father; servant–king; wife–husband. The essential relationship to "our father in heaven" opens wide vistas, rich in social and mystical associations, which religious language does not so much describe, but rather brings it about.

The Anthropological Paradox

Rav Kook was well aware of the challenges presented to theology, not by logical positivism, but by the tradition of Kantian philosophy. Nevertheless, he saw the necessity for the development of a religious philosophy, through his faith in the existence of some sort of parallel between the human models which we create and that reality which is beyond our grasp. But despite this, the starting point for Rav Kook's understanding of prayer, as the religious phenomenon, was not theological but anthropological.

One half of the anthropological dilemma is the outcome of the revolutionary change in the understanding of man's role in the cosmos. Man has ceased to be the center of the world, and his theurgic abilities are disputed by the average modern person.[94] This new reality subjects prayer, or at least one common understanding of it, to a conceptual revolution and to the need to explain itself anew, in a manner removed from theurgic concepts and closer to an existential understanding of prayer.[95] The other side of this dilemma takes the form of a double challenge: on the one side there is the mystic, who sees prayer as an expression of egotism and the subjection of God to the petty will of man; and on the other side there is the Promethean, who sees in prayer an expression of human submission to an all-powerful God and the negation of the self. The rebellion of the latter finds its strongest expression in Nietzsche, and appears in some forms of modern psychology, which defines submission to God as a form of neurosis.

The anthropological paradox, arising out of the the dilemma of man who is jealous of God, is the essential source of the religious difficulties of modern man, who sees in his own autonomy his essence and his being. Many solutions have been proposed during the twentieth century, the central motif being the idea that prayer is not, in fact, an outer compulsion, but the expression of an inner need, by means of which man builds his personality. In a very general and simplistic way, one may say that a more positive view has begun to replace the notion of religion as an illness or neurosis and prayer as one of its symptoms. In the course of this century, the more positive psychological function of prayer began to be understood, as part of a more general, basic change in the attitude toward religion.[96]

In a certain way, the approach toward prayer as the fulfillment of a deep and basic human need was already expressed by Yehudah Halevi in comparing prayer to food, which is certainly a fundamental need of man.[97] Such an interpretation may be carried further in various directions. Halevi himself claimed that the various blessings over food, and so on, themselves add a certain foretaste to our pleasure.[98] A second line of thought would flirt with the approach of psychosomatic medicine. The righteous man lives by his faith and is healed and heals others. If telepathy is not an illusion, then it is also possible that prayer is not a violation of the laws of nature, but is subject to other, hidden laws of causality which we do not yet recognize.[99] Leibovitz is sharply critical of any such interpretations. His thought relates to prayer as "a specifically religious institution, something which religion demands and requires, and not a release for our desires or a confirmation of our metaphysical leanings."[100]

In a manner that ought not to surprise us at this stage of the discussion, Leibovitz analyzes the ordinary semantic meaning of prayer. "The text of prayer is the ritual-ceremonial form that has been established for the act of worship by which man serves God."[101] The psalms of praise and the requests for one's needs were established on the basis of "psychological" or historical reasons, but any other form could have been of equal value. The semantic content of prayer constitutes a "specific ritual and ceremonial," and thus one oughtn't to seek *kavvanah* as *attention* to content, but as "the *intention* to thereby serve God."[102] Leibovitz not only explains prayer in light of this conception but points out a struggle between two conflicting conceptions of prayer in the sources themselves: "A prayer of a poor man, when he is faint and pours out his heart before God" (Psalm 102:1) and "A man should wake up in the morning like a lion to do the service of his Creator" (*Shulhan Arukh, Orach Chaim* 1:1). The first approach, according to him, while doubtless including elements of all of the approaches mentioned above, sees in prayer primarily the fulfillment of a psychic function. Petitionary prayer may be understood, generally, as "an act which man does for himself, for the fulfillment of his needs—and in this respect there is no difference between physical, intellectual or spiritual needs."[103] "Pouring out one's heart" is like any other act which man does "for his pleasure and for the satisfaction of his spiritual needs—like poetry, music, art and cinema."[104] While it is a cathartic act of self-elevation, it is without any religious meaning whatsoever.

Despite the biting tone of Leibovitz's criticisms, they are paralleled in classical Jewish thought. Particularly interesting is the approach of one of the first representatives of the Aristotelian stream in Jewish philosophy, Rabbi Abraham ibn Daud. He sees in prayer only a minimal kernel of the service required of each man. "Let not the servant think that in praying morning and evening he will reach his final goal. For in truth, though he receives a reward for his performance of this *mizvah,* he still needs to fulfill the *mizvah* of, 'and Him shall you serve.' "[105] The meaning of service (*avodah*) in Hebrew is "constant effort," and the meaning here is that man should constantly have God before him. This needs to be done even during the daily round of life, so that man "should attribute his success . . . to Him" and relate his failures or "the bad things which happen to him" to his remoteness from God and his consequently being "without a guard to watch over him." Service of God is "the constant involvement of the mind with God," and *devekut,* clinging to God, is nothing other than this service. "After Scripture said, 'You shall fear God and serve Him,' it said 'and cleave to Him' (Deuteronomy 10:20), and this is to add zeal and constancy of service to it."

Surprisingly, we are told here that attributing the events of daily life to God is not so much an expression of faith in Divine Providence as it is an additional means of cleaving to God, as this is understood here: a constant standing in the presence of God.

To use the generalities we established above, both ibn Daud and Leibovitz, each within the context of his own worldview, submit to the first two paradoxes. The world operates according to its usual manner, whether this be the order of Aristotle or that of Einstein. Prayer does not have reference to theological truths belonging to other areas — whether such areas are accessible to us, as ibn Daud held, or whether they are more or less inaccessible, as held by Leibovitz.

The essence of prayer, in their view, is expressed in nonsubmission to the third paradox. In fact, the greatest demand made upon man is to take upon himself the yoke of the service of God, expecting nothing in return. The sharpest expression of this, to my mind, is in the fact that the concept "clinging," which is understood by most approaches as the final goal of prayer and Divine service, is explained by Ibn Daud as a way of refining the nature of prayer — it is constant service. The central question of prayer, then, is found in this paradox. J. B. Soloveitchik expressed it in his own way by pointing out the contrast between two fundamental human types, one of whom sees his ideal as the conquest of the world around him; the other gives expression to his humanity through submitting to the rulership of the One who stands above him. "When man triumphs over nature he acquires glory; when he is overpowered by the Creator of nature he achieves redemption."[106]

Prayer as Yearning

The conclusion to which religious existentialism tends is non-surrender to the anthropological paradox. Against this there is the mystical alternative, whose outstanding modern spokesman was Rabbi Abraham Isaac Kook. It denies the existence of any opposition between prayer and the basic ideals of modern man, expressed in their longings for autonomy. Such longings may signify man's jealousy of God, but in Rav Kook's mode of mystical thought, jealousy of God is absurd, for there is in truth no place empty of Him. Or, less sharply stated, "the soul is a portion of God above" and "the part longs for the whole."[107] Parallel to this ontological fact is a psychological reality: that prayer is not a norm imposed from without but a channel for the expression of inner longings, found in both man and the entire creation. "All of existence longs for the source of its life, every plant and shrub, every grain of sand and clod of earth, the smallest creatures and every growing thing, the skies above and the holy Seraphim, all parts of each thing and every whole — everything murmurs, longs and yearns for the joy of the wholeness of their Source above."[108]

Rav Kook sees in prayer an expression of the longings of the soul for its source. In popular imagery, prayer is understood as a musical instrument, through which the soul expresses its desire. In fixed, institutionalized prayer this image is reversed: the man who prays becomes the instrument on which is played the song whose notes are written in the *Siddur* and whose composer is the Community of Israel. The praying community is an orchestra, a choir. Between these two extremes there is a third possibility, expressed in the thought of A. J. Heschel, to whom the act of prayer is an act of resonance, in which a note from one instrument strikes an echoing chord in us. This idea of resonance is expressed in the approach of Rav Kook.

In conformity with this concept, Rav Kook interprets the following talmudic text.[109] "Rabbi Eliezer said, 'He who makes his prayer a fixed thing, his prayer is not true prayer.' What is meant by 'fixed'? Rabbi Yaakov bar Adi said in the name of Rabbi Oshaya, 'Whoever makes his prayer like a burden.' " Rav Kook explains that one ought not to understand prayer as a burden, that is, a fixed external obligation, because then prayer "rather than renewing the strength of the soul, will make it more weary." Prayer is not an external duty, but an "inner feeling," which bursts forth and is then channeled into words.

In this way, there is also a harmonization of the existential and mystical approaches to prayer. Prayer is "the uplifting of the will and its revelation."[110] In this uplifting, the human will "ascends to its highest reach, unites with the general will, with the light of the life of the universe." This cleaving of the personal will to the cosmic, general will means, in mystical terms, the negation of individuality and of the personal will. But Rav Kook's approach is different. Within the general will are "included all wishes." The will of a private person and his requests constitute part of the general will. According to this, "the life of the will brings about the fulfillment of the request, through the fact that the general will represents the individual in his most blessed individuality."

These final comments on the "most blessed individuality" come to stress that, if personal prayer is blemished by egotism, it is still essentially positive only that care must be taken that the private needs are singularly "blessed." To pose the private will as being then in contradiction to the general universal will is absurd, for "the will of no creature is separate from the general Divine will, which is revealed in the light of all life and in every creature." So that in this instance it is the the mystical stance, which sees in all reality the revelation of God, that brings Jewish thought to the positive valuation of the individual will and of reality.[111]

In the continuation of this approach, prayer is seen as the act of adjustment between the private will and the general will, in which the private will is not negated but clarified as "an expression of the will as directed towards the divine."[112] This is a primary definition. In order to understand it precisely one ought to stress that prayer does not form a link or connection to the "general will," but only reveals it.[113] One might, perhaps, express the mutual relationship between the two sides in the language of *Mishnah* (*Avot* 2:4). "Do His will as if it were your will," is the first level, after which one reaches the level at which "He will do your will as if it were His own."

As against the approach of Maimonides, which is echoed in Leibovitz and which sees prayer a as the performance of a *mizvah,* Rav Kook presents an approach similar to that of Nahmanides, seeing prayer as "mercy," that is, a call to divine grace, the fulfillment of a need. But the understanding of prayer as need doesn't necessarily imply cheap utilitarian and hedonistic interpretations. It is sustained by the belief that the *mizvah* corresponds to reality, and the soul of man carries the fingerprints of creation. The assumption of a relationship between need and *mizvah* is not vulgar hedonism, but an expression of the hope that the world is built on mercy. Even modern man, the conqueror of outer space, needs prayer.

> How great in value is the prayer of the righteous! How much ought the civilized world to be thirsty for pure prayer! How much do progress and modernity need to clear away the obstacles which lie in the path of prayer, so that its hidden radiance may shine out and be enjoyed! And this shall surely come.[114]

Sources for Chapter 7

Agus, J. B. "The Meaning of Prayer." In *Great Jewish Ideas,* ed. A. E. Millgram. B'nai B'rith Great Book Series. 1964, pp. 219–236 [MPR].
Baelz, P. R. *Prayer and Providence.* London: 1968 [PPR].
Bar-Sha'ul, E. *Mizvah va-Lev.* Tel Aviv: 1956 [MTL].
Berkovits, E. "Prayer." In *Studies in Torah Judaism.* New York: 1969 [PRA].
——. *Major Themes in Modern Philosophies of Judaism.* New York: 1974 [MTH].
Blidstein, G. J. "The Limits of Prayer: A Rabbinic Discussion." In J. J. Petuchowski, ed., *Understanding Jewish Prayer.* New York: 1972, pp. 112–120 (originally appeared in *Judaism,* Spring 1966) [TLP].
Burkhill, T. A. *God and Reality in Modern Thought.* New York: 1963 [GRM].
Cohen, H. *Dat ha-Tevunah mi-Mekorot ha-Yahadut.* Jerusalem: 1972 [DTM].
Cohen, Y. "Al ha-Tefillah be-Yom ha-Azma'ut." *De'ot* 39 (Spring 1970): 262 [TBA].
Dan, Y. *Torat ha-Sod Shel Hasidut Ashkenaz.* Jerusalem: 1968 [THS].
Eisemann, Moshe ha-Levi. *Iyyunim bi-Tefillah.* New York: 1974 [IBT].

My thanks go to the late Professors S. Pines and M. Schwartz and to Professors P. Mendes-Flohr, Y. Libes, M. Halamish, E. Atkis, and Rabbi P. Laderman for their many useful suggestions and comments. They each have a share of credit for this work; the errors, however, are all mine.

Emden, Rabbi Y. *Siddur Beit Ya'akov.* Jerusalem: 1968 [SBY].
Enelow, H. G. "Kawwana: the Struggle for Inwardness in Judaism." In *Jewish Studies in Honor of Kaufmann Kohler.* Berlin: 1913, pp. 82–107 [KAW].
Flusser, D. *"Beit ha-Knesset ke-Musag be-Dat Yisrael." De'ot* 29 (Spring 1965): 164–168 [BHM].
——. *"Ha-Tefillah Omanut Avoteinu." De'ot* 11 (1960): 45–48 [HOA].
Gordis, R. "A Jewish Prayer Book for the Modern Age." *Conservative Judaism* 2:1 (October 1945): 1–20 [JPB].
——. *The Ladder of Prayer.* New York: 1956 [TLP].
Goster, T. H. "Modernising the Jewish Prayer Book." *Commentary,* April 1954 [MJP].
Gottlieb, E. *"Mashma'utah Shel ha-Tefillah ba-Kabbalah."* In *Mehkarim be-Sifrut ha-Kabbalah,* ed. Yosef Haker. Tel Aviv: 1976, pp. 38–55 (also in the present volume) [TBK].
Greenberg, M. *Biblical Prose Prayer: A Window to the Popular Religion of Ancient Israel.* Berkley: 1983 [BPP].
——. *Harza'ot Al ha-Tefillah ba-Mikra.* Jerusalem: 1981 [HAT].
Greenberg, S. *The Jewish Prayer Book: Its Ideas and Values.* New York: 1957 [JPB].
Heiler, F. *Das Gebet.* Published in English as *Prayer: A Study in the History and Psychology of Religion.* Transl. S. McComb. New York: 1958 [PST].
Heinemann, Yizhak. *Ta'amei ha-Mizvot be-Sifrut Yisrael.* Vols. I, II. Jerusalem: 1966 [THB].
——. *Rabbi Yehudah Halevi ha-Ish ve-Hogeh ha-De'ot, Knesset.* Vol. VII, pp. 261–279 [HVH].
Heinemann, Yosef. *Ha-Tefillah bi-Tekufat ha-Tanna'im veha-Amora'im.* 2d ed. Jerusalem: 1966 [HBH].
——. *"Hiddush Penei ha-Tefillah." De'ot* 11 (1960): 42–43 [HPH].
Heschel, A. J. "The Spirit of Jewish Prayer." *Proceedings of the Rabbinical Assembly of America* 17 (1953): 151–215 [TSJ].
——. *Man's Quest for God.* New York: 1954 [MQG].
Hirsch, Rabbi S. R. *Horev.* Transl. M. Z. Aharonson. Vilna: 1902 [HRB].
——. *Tefillat Shemonah Esreh ve-Korban ha-Tamid.* Tel Aviv: 1961 [TSE].
Idelsohn, A. Z. *Jewish Liturgy and its Development.* New York: 1932 [JLD].
Jacobs, L. *Jewish Prayer.* London: 1956 [JPR].
——. "Prayer." *Judaism* 18 (1969): 210–215 [PRA].
Kadushin, M. *Organic Thinking: A Study in Rabbinic Thought.* New York: 1938 [ORT].
——. *Worship and Ethics: A Study in Rabbinic Judaism.* Evanston, IL: 1964 [WOR].
Karl, Z. *Mehkarim be-Toledot ha-Tefillah.* Tel Aviv: 1950 [MTT].
Kohler, K. *Jewish Theology Systematically and Historically Considered.* New York: 1968 [JTH].
Kohn, E. "Prayer and the Modern Jew." *Proceedings of the Rabbinical Assembly of America* 17 (1953): 179–181 [PMJ].
Kook, Rabbi A. Y. H. *Olat Re'iyah.* Jerusalem: 1963 [ORY].
——. *Orot haKodesh.* Jerusalem [ORK].
Lamm, N. *Faith and Doubt.* New York: 1971 [FAD].

Leibovitz, Y. *Yahadut, Am Yehudi u-Medinat Yisrael.* Jerusalem and Tel Aviv: 1976 [YAM].
Peli, P. *"Ha-Berakhah-Petah li-Tefillah." Petahim* 2:16 (*Adar* 1961): 31–38 [BPL].
Petuchowski, J. J. "Can Modern Man Pray." *CCAR Yearbook* 77 (1967): 168 [CMM].
——. *Prayerbook Reform in Europe.* New York: 1968 [PRE].
Phillips, D. I. *The Concept of Prayer.* London: 1965 [CPR].
Rapel, D. *Ha-Tefillah.* Jerusalem: 1968 [HTF].
Rhymes, D. *Prayer in the Secular City.* London: 1967 [PSC].
Rider, D. *"be-Inyan Tefillah Nekhonah." De'ot* 30 (Fall 1966): 286–287 [ITN].
Schatz, R. *Ha-Hasidut ke-Mistikah.* Jerusalem: 1975 [HKM].
Scholem, G. *Kabala.* Jerusalem: 1974 [KAB].
Simon, E. "On the Meaning of Prayer." In *Tradition and Contemporary Experience,* ed. A. Jospe. 1970, pp. 269–279 [OMP].
Sobelman, Y. *"Al ha-Tefillah." De'ot* 30 (Fall 1966): 284–286 [AHT].
Soloveitchik, Rabbi Y. D. *Ish ha-Emunah.* Jerusalem: 1988 [AHE].
Spanier, A. *Zur Formengeschichte des altjüdischen Gebets* MGWJ LXXVIII (1934): 438–447 [ZFA].
Tal S. *"Be-Olamah Shel Tefillah." De'ot* 29 (Spring 1965): 172–178 [OST].
Tishbi, Y. *Mishnat ha-Zohar.* Vol. I. Jerusalem: 1957 [MHZ].
Urbach, E. *Hazal-Pirkei Emunot ve-De'ot.* Jerusalem: 1976 [HZL].
Weiss, J. "The Kavvanot of Prayer in Early Hasidism." *JJS* 9 (1958): 163–192 [KHS].
Weiss, Y. *Mehkarim be-Hasidut Breslav.* Ed. M. Faikaz. Jerusalem: 1975 [MBR].
Wolff, A. A. *Die Stimmen der ältesten gläubwürdigsten Rabine über die Pijutim.* Leipzig: 1857 [DSA].
Yaron, Z. *Mishnato Shel haRav Kook.* Jerusalem: 1974 [MSK].

Notes

Letters refer to sources for this chapter listed previously.

1. Heinemann, HBH (Hebrew), p. 9f.
2. See Spanier, ZFA. A fuller list of articles by A. Spanier may be found in Heinemann, HBH (Hebrew), p. 197.
3. Heineman, HBH (Hebrew), p. 10.
4. For example, R. Yitshak Aramah.
5. On the methodological problems involved in this research, see Urbach, HZL (Hebrew), p. 2.
6. On these questions, see Petuchowski, PRE.
7. See Heschel's response to the debate concerning prayer in his TSJ, pp. 212–215, and his comment on the fact that the greater part of the discussion was devoted to questions that might be considered extraneous: "Man lives not by decorum alone," ibid, p. 212. One may argue that the division into levels and the analysis that follows is not free of ideological bias on the part of this researcher, but the same may be said of any scientific study of this type.
8. Compare Ibn Ezra to Ecclesiastes 5:1 and sources collected in Wolff, DSA.

9. Nathan Rotenstreich, *'Al Tehumah shel ha-Filosofia* (Jerusalem: 1969), p. 14. Professor Gershom Scholem has often stressed the importance of this distinction for the history of Jewish thought. See his *Ha-Kabalah be-Provence* (Jerusalem: 1962/1963), p. 8f. Scholem stresses the transformation of thought into ideology in response to apologetic needs, both within and without.

10. For the development of prayer in the Bible, see Moshe Greenberg, HAT (Hebrew), who also discusses the methodological problems confronting the biblical scholar in this area.

11. Scholem, KAB, p. 185.

12. See Yitshak Heinemann, THB (Hebrew), p. 60f.

13. Tishbi, MHZ (Hebrew), p. 434. In a similar manner, Buber distinguishes between hasidic pansacramentalism and primitive pansacramentalism, as "between the concept of 'unification' and magical action." Magic is the act of a subject upon an object, while unification is directed "not to itself, but to God." (*Be-pardes ha-hasidut*, in Hebrew [Tel-Aviv: 1944/1945, p. 89). See also Baruch Kurtsweil, *le-Hukhah ha-Mevukhah ha-Ruhanit shel Dorenu* (Ramat Gan: 1975/1976), p. 79f.

14. See *Sha'ar Heshbon ha-nefesh* and compare to *Sha'ar yihud ha-ma'aseh*. For a general discussion of the problem of *kavvanah*, see Enelow, KAW.

15. Y. Heinemann, THB (Hebrew), p. 61.

16. See R. Jacob Emden, SBY (Hebrew), foreword, p. 6.

17. *Tur Shulhan Arukh, Orach Chaim* 98.

18. Bar-Shaul, MTL (Hebrew), p. 114.

19. Emden, ibid.

20. Maimonides, *Hilchot Tefillah*, chap. 4.

21. Emden, ibid.

22. *Hovot Ha-levavot, Sha'ar* 8, sec. 3, 9.

23. See *Hidushe Rabenu Hayim Halevi, Tefillah* 4:1. In *Hilchot Shofar*, Maimonides states that one who blew the *shofar* unintentionally did not fulfill his obligation, while in *Hilchot Hamets u-Matsah* 6:3 he states that one who was forced to eat *mazah* on the first night of Passover did fulfill his obligation. In *Hilchot Tefillah* 4:15, he states that one who prayed without *kavvanah* did not fulfill the *mizvah*. R. Hayim reconciles these different positions by positing the existence of three differing kinds of *kavvanah*. See Sobelman, AHT (Hebrew).

24. J. B. Soloveitchik, AHE, pp. 35–37, and the footnote there.

25. See Simon, OMP, p. 270f.

26. *Netivot Olam*, Netiv Ha-avodah, chap. 1. In the Zhitomir edition, 1887, p. 19a.

27. After completing this chapter, I came across the article of the late E. Gottlieb, TBK, which is found in this volume. His conclusions seem, in principle, to confirm the distinction made here between theurgic prayer and mystical prayer. Of particular interest are his remarks concerning the connection between the teachings of R. Chaim of Volozhin and the works of R. Meir ibn Gabbai, which applies this distinction to the kabbalistic significance of prayer in the eighteenth and nineteenth century, which we discussed above.

28. See on this Tishbi, MHZ, pt. 2: *Avodat Ha-kodesh*, p. 429f.

29. The Hebrew translation is taken from Tishbi, MHZ (Hebrew), p. 261.
30. See the list of sources in Tishbi, MHZ (Hebrew), p. 261f.
31. *Zohar,* pt. 3, 111b–112a. The Hebrew is from Tishbi, MHZ, pt. 2, p. 360.
32. E. Gottleib, TBK (Hebrew). See note 27 above.
33. This survey is primarily based upon the work of G. Scholem, especially KAB.
34. Scholem, KAB, p. 38.
35. See Scholem, KAB, p. 32.
36. Ibid., p. 339.
37. German Pietism enriched the *Siddur* with prayers and *piyyutim* of various sorts. Some of them were a type of continuation of the Hekhalot hymns, that is, descriptions of the hymns of angels of different degrees. Others were influenced by the early Hebrew translations of the works of R. Saadiah Gaon and introduced philosophical elements, as in the *Shir Ha-kavod* and *Shire Ha-yihud.* Generally speaking, these prayers were not intended for the public but for a select elite and only entered the *Siddur* in a late period. See Scholem, KAB, pp. 38–41. On the general theology of the German pietists compare Joseph Dan, THS (Hebrew), p. 369.
38. Ibid., p. 369.
39. Commentary to Song of Songs by R. Ezra, 8: Tishbi, MHZ (Hebrew), p. 288.
40. Tishbi, MHZ (Hebrew), p. 289, See footnote 69 there.
41. See Tishbi, MHZ (Hebrew), pt. 2, p. 292, on this.
42. Scholem, KAB, p. 177. Lurianic *Kabbalah* exerted a decisive influence upon prayer, unlike the earlier *Kabbalah,* through the addition of new prayers, and through the system of *kavvanot,* whose outstanding representative was the school of the Yemenite kabbalist R. Shalom Sharabi. Its indirect influences, such as its effect upon the change of the *nosah* of prayer in Hasidism, were no less important.
43. *Orah la-hayim,* R. Abraham Hayim ben Gedalyah of Zlotshov, (Jerusalem: 1959–1960), p. 98a. See Rivkah Schatz, HKM (Hebrew), p. 97.
44. See Schatz, HKM (Hebrew), p. 103.
45. *Magid devarav le-Yaakov,* 2, 71. See Schatz, HKM, 108.
46. *Or Torah,* 78b, Schatz, HKM, 107.
47. After a phrase of Professor R. Schatz, HKM, p. 91.
48. *Nefesh Ha-hayim* 1824, sec. 2, chap. 4 (Shanghai: $^{1943}/_{1944}$), p. 51.
49. *Nefesh Ha-hayim,* 2:11, Shanghai ed., pp. 57–58.
50. See *Siddur Ishe Yisrael,* p. 395, and see there R. Yisrael Salanter's objections to this prayer.
51. *Magid devarav le-ya'akov,* 3, 74; Schatz, HKM, p. 81.
52. See R. Zev Wolf of Zhitomir, *Or ha-Meir,* 1798, p. 7a. Quoted in Weiss, KHS, p. 164 n. 2a.
53. Ibid., 34b.
54. Gersonides' Commentary on the Torah, end of *Ahare Mot,* Venice ed., 160, 3, and see Y. Heinemann, THB (Hebrew), pt. 1, 100.
55. *Kuzari* 3:11, and see Heinemann, HVH (Hebrew), p. 271.
56. *Or Hashem,* Vienna ed., 57a f., and see Heinemann, THB (Hebrew), 107f.

57. This idea is found in the explanation of sacrifices in Halevi and Ibn Ezra. See Heinemann, THB, p. 137, and 61, 66.

58. Hirsch, HRB (Hebrew), p. 271.

59. Hirsch, HRB (Hebrew), 272.

60. *Siddur Ishe Yisrael*, p. 5.

61. *Mikhtav me-eliyahu,* vol. 3 (Bnai Barak: 1973/1974), p. 62f.

62. M. Kadushin saw in the blessings of the prayers a sort of response to a meditative experience, parallel to blessings generally, which are a response to an empirical experience. See the first chapters of his book, WOR.

63. For the source of this expression see the remark of Pinchas Peli, BPL (Hebrew), p. 36 n. 32.

64. Talmud Yerushalmi, *Berakhot,* chap. 9, 101.

65. See Heschel, TSJ. Compare the naturalistic, Reconstructionist stance of Eugene Kohn, PMJ. On the dilemma existing between naturalism and supernaturalism see Louis Jacobs, PRA and P. R. Baelz, PPR.

66. Hirsch, p. 283.

67. *Akedat Yitshak, sha'ar* 58.

68. J. Weiss distinguished in this manner between mystical Hasidism and Hasidism of faith. While it may be that some of his conclusions are overly generalized, the basic distinction between contemplation and ecstasy, on the one hand, and conversation with one's Creator, characteristic of Bretslav Hasidism, on the other, is correct. There is no doubt that mystical motifs exist in the writings of R. Nahman, but the transition from "extinguishing consciousness" and suppressing personal identity to an "I-Thou" relationship stands out. See Weiss, MBR (Hebrew), p. 93f. Thus, from the outset we find existential motifs in Hasidism, opposed to the generally accepted mystical interpretation. Compare Schatz, HKM, p. 86f, on differing traditions in the name of the Great Maggid.

69. See Schatz, HKM, p. 78.

70. Kadushin, ORT, pp. 237-240.

71. This, in my opinion, is the main thesis of Kadushin in WOR.

72. Soloveitchik, AHE, p. 35.

73. See Hugo Bergman, in various writings.

74. *Shulhan Arukh Orach Chaim* 90:9, 16.

75. R. Abraham Hurvitz (1550-1615), student of the RaMA, father of the *ShLaH*. See H. H. Ben-Sasson's article on him in *Encyclopaedia Judaica* 8:985-986.

76. Amsterdam (1701), p. 5a.

77. Ibid., 16b, and see the comments of the son of the author there.

78. *Kuzari* 3:19, and see Bar-Shaul, MTL (Hebrew), p. 120, which compares these comments to the *Zohar* (Genesis 167b).

79. The connection between the *minyan*-community and the People of Israel is witnessed by the phrases "upon us and upon all Israel," and so on. See on this David Flusser, BHM (Hebrew).

80. For example, the custom of R. Hanina and R. Yanai, who dressed in their Sabbath clothes and said, "Come and go out to greet the Sabbath queen" or "Come,

bride; come, bride" (*Shabbat* 119a), the prayer of Rav, which became the prayer for Rosh Hodesh (*Berakhot* 16b), and the prayers of Rava and of Mar the son of Rabina (ibid).

81. On changes of prayers for reasons connected with Israeliness, see the journals *Amudim*, of the Religious Kibbutz Movement, and *De'ot* passion. On the care that one is to take not to change the prayer text without clear halakhic sources, see Y. Cohen, TBA (Hebrew).

82. See Flusser, HOA (Hebrew), p. 46.

83. *Yoma* 69b.

84. Among other subjects, Albo deals with the principle according to which one is to pray to God alone (4:16-17).

85. *Sefer Ha-ikarim* 4:18.

86. On prayer and Divine decree see Blidstein, TLP, and compare Urbach HZL, p. 252, and Soloveitchik, AHE, pp. 42-43, note.

87. I have heard an oral tradition in the name of Rav Kook on the importance of the differences between the Bavli and the Yerushalmi on these matters. A similar analysis is found in Blidstein, TLP. A view seeing Rav Yosef as requiring prayer for miracles is found in the *Tsalah* of R. Yehezkel Landau.

88. *Tanhuma*, Toldot, 9. See Y. Heinemann, THB, p. 152 n. 57, and his HVH (Hebrew), p. 83; (and not 183 as misprinted in THB). See also Bar-Shaul, MTL, p. 99.

89. Heiler, PST, p. 89, and see Berkovits, PRA, introduction.

90. *Likute Yekarim*, 7a, quoted in Schatz, HKM, pp. 81-82.

91. Kook, ORY (Hebrew), p. 14. On prayer in the teaching of Rav Kook, see Yaron, MSK (Hebrew), p. 62 and especially n. 13.

92. Kook, ORY, p. 14.

93. Scholem, KAB, p. 176.

94. See also Gordis, TLP, p. 10f.

95. On a possibility of this sort see Lamm, FAD, p. 156-157. Professor Lamm raises the possibility of a reinterpretation of R. Hayim of Volozhin's views of theurgy, according to which man does not influence the cosmos and the mystical worlds beyond it, but only the dialogue with God.

96. Peli stressed this in BPL (Hebrew), p. 37f.

97. A modern return to this motif may be found in Burkill, GRM, p. 214-215 and Jacobs, PRA, p. 215. Prayer is intended to guard our spiritual wakefulness so that we may continue to feel the mysterium tremendum.

98. *Kuzari* 3:13, and see Peli's article, BPL (Hebrew).

99. Gordis, TLP, p. 20f.

100. Leibovitz, YAM (Hebrew), p. 386.

101. Leibovitz, YAM (Hebrew), p. 386.

102. Leibovitz gives an example of this explanation by means of a passage from the *NaTsIV* (YAM, p. 390). This passage belongs to an approaah influenced by the *Kabbalah*, which we described above as "theurgic" and contrasted with petitionary prayer. It is interesting to note that despite the necessary criticism, there is a possibility

of calling this a "Leibovitzian reading," which illustrates how deeply many aspects of Leibovitz's thought are rooted in classical Jewish thought.

103. Leibovitz, YAM, p. 385.
104. Leibovitz, YAM, p. 388.
105. *Emunah Ramah,* Weil ed. (Frankfort: 1852), p. 100.
106. Soloveitchik, AHE, pp. 24–25.
107. Bar-Shaul, MTL, p. 109, and see the continuation of his discussion there.
108. Foreword to Kook, ORV (Hebrew). As in other areas, there is an interesting parallelism, which is far from being identical, between Kook's approach and that of Hermann Cohen. "Prayer is longing. The longing in prayer for God is the search for God, which wishes to remain forever in search, for the finding of its goal is not the object but only the 'closeness to God.' But this closeness is always love, always longing, always action: it is never an intellectual relationship alone. . . . " See H. Cohen, DTM (Hebrew), p. 399, and see Berkovits, MTH, pp. 35–36, on the "dialogic monologue."
109. Kook, ORY, p. 16.
110. Kook, ORK (Hebrew), pt. 3, p. 50.
111. For views against this motif see in R. Schatz, HKM, p. 82: "One oughtn't to pray for one's physical needs . . . one should not desire that 'He do your will,' for that is obviously an act of self-interest" (*Or Ha-emet,* Hosiyatan [$^{1918}/_{919}$], p. 1b).
112. Kook, ORV, pt. 3, p. 49.
113. Ibid., p. 53.
114. Ibid., p. 49.

8
Prayer in the Thought of Yehudah Halevi

Eliezer Schweid

I would like to begin with two comments pertaining to our discussion. The first relates to the distinction which has been drawn between the scholarly analysis of a given approach to prayer and the urgent wrestling with the problem of prayer as such, as it presents itself to us today. This distinction, while possible, seems to me neither necessary nor useful. It is preferable to begin with the presentation of several characteristic approaches from the past and then to proceed to those questions which trouble Jews today. Thus I shall not engage in a precise, scholarly description of Halevi's system of thought, but rather suggest how that system can become a starting point for a discussion of prayer as such. To my mind, this is the only justification for talking about the thought of Halevi in a framework such as ours.

My second comment relates to the need to determine the proper point of departure. Rabbi Adin Steinsaltz has argued that it is impossible to deal with prayer as an isolated subject. One must first discuss faith. But in order to do that, one must in turn discuss that which precedes faith, for otherwise one evades the issue (as I think Rabbi Steinsaltz himself does). Prayer is one of the components of a religious way of life. In order to understand it, one must first define the basic assumptions of that way of life, and then show how prayer fits into them.

The theory of Halevi—highly relevant to our purpose—relates to prayer as a component of the religious way of life. In his discussion in the *Kuzari* he opens, as he does throughout the book, with the words of the king. Interestingly, the king's question is not concerned directly with prayer, but with the behaviour and way of life of the *hasid*, the pious man, in our time. The *haber*, or Jewish sage, describes the way of life of the contemporary *hasid*, and in the course of his answer it becomes clear that prayer is the center about which everything else revolves. In order to understand this center, one must see the entirety in which it is set, and to do this one needs to say something about the religious world view of Rabbi Yehudah Halevi in general. As our space is limited and the subject is vast, I will briefly set out in summary form those axioms which are essential to the understanding of his thought.

The first premise: Halevi attempts to discuss every subject by directly weighing our experience of it. And he always seeks that experience which is most appropriate to the subject at hand. The unique experience that characterizes faith is prophecy. This central assumption is expressed in the literary framework of the *Kuzari*. The king does not set out to investigate faith out of intellectual curiosity, but because of a specific experience, namely, his dream. It became clear to him that only someone who could answer his questions out of authentic religious experience, and not in a speculative fashion, could teach him the true path in the service of God.

The second premise: in accordance with the accepted medieval ontology, human experience teaches that the world is an organic unity, in which each lower layer constitutes the basis for those above it, while each higher layer is the completion of those below. We perceive the strata of mineral, vegetable, animal, and human existence through our senses. On the basis of this general experience and by way of analogy, we may conclude that all existing things have a cause which generates them, sustains them, and guides them; and that there are spiritual agencies which mediate between physical bodies and their ultimate cause, namely, God. This understanding of the world is one to which the Philosopher testifies on the basis of ordinary human experience. Halevi accepts this picture but, on the basis of prophetic experience, adds an additional level between man and the spiritual agencies. (He also suggests that perhaps we can say different things about the spiritual beings themselves than those said by the Philosopher.) The prophets then (or more precisely, the Jewish people, all of whom have a portion in the prophetic gift) constitute a level of reality separate from that of man as such. As man is distinguished from the animal, so is the prophet distinguished and separated from the rest of humanity. If man is distinguished from the beast by his intellect, then the prophet is separated from other men by the "Divine element" within him, that is, by his ability to confront spiritual agencies and the deity in the same direct, unmediated manner as ordinary men confront the world of material objects.

The third premise: everything in the universe exists on its own level, but its existence there is contingent upon a certain activity which is focused on the level above them. So long as they are attracted toward the level above themselves and attempt to become like it, they maintain themselves at their proper level, and this activity is in fact their service to the Creator. From this viewpoint, the worship of the Creator is a cosmic matter. It is not a matter of man alone; rather, the entire created universe serves its Creator through the very act by which it maintains itself on its own level, because this activity draws the creatures to imitate what is above them and thereby seek their perfection. But together with this, one ought to remember that the earthly, bodily creatures, including man, are also drawn downward; everything which exists in the world, including man, contains within itself the various levels of being which are below it. These levels all have their bounds and limitations. The result is a kind of fatigue which comes about through the constant attempt at self-transcendence and self-perfection, and this fatigue leads to a certain weakening and backsliding. For this reason, no achievement is guaranteed, and a constant battle is waged between the positive impulse leading upward and the negative impulse dragging downward.

Clearly, all this shows the influence of Plato. Earthly creatures are less than they were intended to be in their original form because of their immersion in matter, and all of their activities are thus a movement of restoration. They must constantly attempt to restore themselves to their original state, which they have lost and are constantly losing because of their physical nature. However, Halevi adds another dimension to that of Plato—and this is a structural element in his thought. According to him, the upward striving is not only an act of return to some original state but also an ascent. This is so because, in his view—and this ought to be strongly stressed—the various levels of existence are not totally separated from one another but are interconnected. Thus, the perfection of each level is significant for the levels below it, particularly with regard to the position of the prophet within the Jewish people and of the Jewish people within humanity generally. The perfection of the Jewish people as a people of prophecy has significance for all human beings, because through the Jewish people other people partake in prophetic wholeness. If the nations of the world cling to the Jewish people in the same way as the Jewish people cling to their prophets, then the wholeness of the people Israel would be reflected in all mankind, who would then live on their level with the same perfection that Israel lives on its level. This is possible because as we have pointed out, the perfecting of one level spreads out and penetrates those beneath it.

From this, it follows that the restorative activity in Halevi's understanding, is twofold. On the one hand, it is expressed in the effort of the lower being to elevate itself and to imitate that which is above it—and this is its service, through which it attains its original form. On the other hand, there is an emanation or influx from above, which enters into that which is prepared to receive it, in the same way as light enters one whose eye is open to it. In Halevi's words: Divine Providence watches for that which is prepared for it, in order to affect it. Indeed, this principle traverses all the levels of existence. Whenever an appropriate act of preparation is performed by the receiver, he receives something extra and is lifted higher than he was previously. This occurrence is part of his intrinsic nature. It is impossible that that which is prepared below should not become the recipient of transcendent influence, for this influence exists and operates at all times.

A fourth assumption: on all levels of reality the individual being or item has no separate existence. They represent some collectivity, and, apart from that, they cannot be what they are, because their own individuality is merely their negative limitation. It follows that perfection of being is always related to organic wholeness. This needs to be emphasized, because it explains the importance Halevi attaches to communal prayer and, in general, to life within the community. Thus, whilst an individual might pray against another person, the community as a whole will never direct prayer against the interest of one of its members. But, more particularly, the individual is never complete except in relation to the wholeness of a community. His wholeness as an individual is contingent upon his participation in the community: thus, when he stands before God, he must do so with the community. This approach has a very concrete implication, for the act of standing within the community means conforming to certain norms, which the community determines for its members so that they may be what they are intended to be. In community, each individual must fulfill the task unique to himself within the general framework. Society means organism. The individual has no separate life, but he does have a special place within the social organism. This is the case in communal life generally and, as we shall see, specifically in regard to prayer.

An additional assumption connected to the above is that God, the Creator, is present in the entire universe, and that the entire universe, in all its levels, is present to Him. Yehudah Halevi occasionally speaks of God or Divinity as the soul of the entire creation, in the same way as the soul is present in the body—not in the sense that it is identical with the body, but that it is present in it and spread throughout it in order to guide it—in this way is God present in the entire body, in the entire world, in the entire universe, and even though He is not perceived by the senses, the heart feels His presence.

There is a final assumption, which I would like to mention as introduction to Halevi's specific doctrine of prayer: namely, that the perfection of the people of Israel, that which belongs to its proper level, is the perfection of prophecy. Prophecy is, by its nature, an experience of being in the presence of God. What makes the prophet unique is not his knowledge, although, of course, he knows a great deal and must have intellectual wholeness. What is special to him is the experience of being in the presence of God. If there is one thing which the prophet alone can teach others it is not theology or metaphysics but the way in which man can experience that presence, in accordance with his strength and his situation. Such presence is attained in accordance with certain preparatory conditions—bodily, social, and ritual. The way of the Torah, which is anchored in prophecy, is intended to bring the Jewish individual toward a prophetic, or at least a quasi-prophetic, experience. This is the primary purpose of the *mizvot*. This goal was first reached by individuals, and afterward by an entire people. In the millennium perhaps all mankind will attain it, each one according to his level, for the hierarchy will be preserved even then. In any event, the *mizvot* are acts which are learned through the prophetic experience. Man cannot learn them by means of reason or speculation, just as man cannot by means of reason learn that a given substance can provide the cure for a particular disease. We learn of the efficacy of a given cure by experience alone, and in the same way we learn of the value of a given form of worship—and the relevant experience for this sort of learning is prophecy. However, it ought to be stressed that the prophetic command by itself is only a direction toward preparation, and completeness is not attained by merely fulfilling the *mizvah*. Only by fulfilling them with the proper kind of intention do we receive Divine inspiration and this is what is meant by experiencing the presence of God.

And now turning to the question of prayer itself, I would like to refer once again to the literary context in which it is discussed in the *Kuzari*. From the outset, Halevi introduces prayer as a substitute: the King of the Khazars, who already knows something about the Torah and Jewish history, asks, "What is the way of the *hasid* (pious man) today?" He already knows that there is a difference between the Jewish way of life today and that which was followed when the Temple stood in Jerusalem and prophets still functioned (prophecy being contingent upon the Temple and the Land of Israel). Had the book been written during the period of the Temple, it would have described the service in the Temple, the sacrifices, and so on; but being written in the current era, it deals with prayer. Thus, from the outset, one is speaking of the way of life of the pious man in exile, with particular stress upon a well-known fact, but one of critical importance in the thought of Halevi: that is, that prayer is a reflection of something else, more authentic than itself. It is an image, and perhaps even an image of an image, because it reflects the worship in the Temple, which in turn reflects the prophetic experience.

What follows from this is that prayer is similar to prophecy, which, as we shall recall, is the experience of unmitigated presence before God. Prayer recreates and reflects the conditions of revelation. In praying, one attempts to elevate oneself to the state of being in the presence of God and in so doing sees in the inner eye of his imagination, which is the instrument of prophetic experience, those events of theophany known to us from the Torah. The implication is that one follows in the footsteps of those who have gone before and who experienced revelation directly. If one may adapt an aesthetic theory here, prayer is an art in the Aristotelian sense, namely, *mimesis*. One who prays imitates known occasions of revelation and thus lives them anew, according to his level and ability.

In this context, I would like to comment briefly on something which ought to be treated as a separate subject, namely, prayer in the poetic works of Rabbi Yehudah Halevi. Halevi was a master of prayer in the additional sense that he wrote prayers of his own and made a significant contribution to the prayer book. Does this not perhaps contradict what was said earlier? Not necessarily. An examination of the liturgical writings of Halevi will reveal that he is faithful to his basic insight—that prayer follows in the footsteps of revelatory experience. Yet this does not rule out individual creativity in prayer. Such originality resides in the mode of expression, and that mode is unique to each and every prayer.

A second conclusion which follows from the premises listed above is that prayer is a restorative process. This is expressed in a metaphor Halevi uses in order to explain prayer (and for him metaphor is a basic and fundamental matter and not merely a matter of decorative phraseology). Thus he compares the *mizvot* to medicines and prayer, to a meal: prayer is to the soul what a meal is to the body. A meal restores the powers of the body which have waned during the day's work; the body descends below its desired level, it becomes weakened, and food restores it to its original strength. Prayer does the same for the soul. The soul becomes distanced from its original state during the course of its daily concerns. It weakens and submits to the impulses and pressures of the body instead of overcoming them. Prayer, like food, restores the soul to its original state—one in which the will exercises full control over the body. The higher powers to which the soul is attached are then able to experience the Divine Presence. Man needs to make an effort to be in this state, and prayer is the means.

We have pointed out two aspects of the original state of the soul: its relationship to the body and its relationship to higher powers. These two aspects find expression in the restorative activity of prayer. The first, immediate effect of prayer is the restoration of spiritual vigor by the renewal of the dominion of the soul over the powers of the body. The personality that has disintegrated and lost control over itself begins the restorative process by calling itself to inner discipline. Halevi depicts the state of prayer, in its beginning, as an act of taking over command anew. We ought to pay attention here to the way in which the dialogue proceeds: the *Haber* does not directly answer the king's query about the behavior of the pious man but seemingly avoids the question with an ironic answer; yet this evasion itself contains the beginnings of an answer. The irony accentuates this. The practice of the pious man, he says, is like that of a king. Just as it is the task of the king to maintain discipline, so that the entire state may act as one body, so the pious man about to embark upon prayer is like a ruler summoning his troops and giving them orders. He first examines carefully whether all are in fact obedient to him, whether all of his urges and physical powers are directed toward one end. Then, once the body and soul are in harmony, he can lift his entire personality to a higher plane, that of presence before God.

It is clear, then, that the prayer-state involves a dialectic tension. From the outset, it is a state of intense alertness of soul. For prayer, in Halevi, is not passive meditation—on the contrary, the personality at prayer is intensely active. Nevertheless, the entire goal of this activity is obedience. The soul summons itself and all the powers subject to it to obey the will of the Almighty, and this obedience prepares the soul for an infusion of power, which is not controlled by man but is a gift of grace descending upon him from above. The emanation of the Divine element into the soul of the praying subject is the presence sought in prayer.

Since prayer is a state which demands concentration of all the forces of the personality, it becomes in a sense the purpose of life; and here we return to our opening comment. The devout person or *hasid* directs and prepares himself in all his doings for the hour of prayer, which is the heart of his day. More than this: he must focus all his acts toward prayer even when he is not directly engaged in it. In the blessings, in particular, there is a kind of preparation for prayer, to which Halevi attaches special importance. In the act of reciting a blessing for benefits received, the *hasid* trains himself to turn to his Creator in gratitude for all the gifts which he has enjoyed. All of the *mizvot* must be performed out of the intention to obey and through obedience to gain the Divine Presence. Prayer is unique only in that it represents a pure concentration of this intention.

Up to this point, we have described prayer as an act of restoration. However, it is not only that. The movement of return to the original state leads toward an even higher level. This is a phenomenon characteristic of Halevi's thought, which we mentioned above in the third premise, namely, that he adds one further dimension to the Platonic formula. He does not see authentic reality as given and complete, without room for change or addition, but as an ever-advancing horizon of development, ascent—that is, a process beyond mere restoration—both in the realm of history, and of personal biography. History, from the creation until the time of the Messiah, is a history of progress leading toward a higher perfection.

In the path of the individual, as well, there is not only a return to an original state, but an attempt to reach a higher state of completeness. A man becomes complete through the training of the self in prayer. This is also expressed in the way of life of the faithful. This is depicted not as a cycle, but as an ascending spiral. The prayers of the weekday ascend toward those of the Sabbath; the Sabbath prayers ascend toward the New Moon; the prayers of the New Moon point up toward the Festival prayers; and the prayers of all the festivals are climaxed in the service of the Day of Atonement, which symbolizes complete redemption. This is a cycle in which man ascends from one level to the next, until he reaches the pinnacle of Divine presence in the service of the holiest day of all.

The final point to be stressed is that prayer, in the understanding of Rabbi Yehudah Halevi, is a communal act, and it is only within community that prayer finds its proper setting. If Halevi's position were to be that prayer is a function separate from the rest of a man's life, one might then go on to argue that private acts of prayer possess a certain completeness. But Halevi explicitly denies this in the beginning of the third section of his book where he criticizes the practice of Christian and Moslem ascetics, who isolate themselves in deserts and on mountaintops to devote all of their time to prayer. At first glance, one who devotes all of his life to prayer would seem to be a very great saint, since Halevi holds that prayer must be the choicest act of a man's day. What, then, could be better than that a man should be occupied with the choicest activity all the time? But Halevi, in commenting on these ascetics, says that their involvement in prayer, and the new prayers which they formulate, are a powerful experience only at the beginning, and that afterward all that remains is mortification of the flesh and weariness of the spirit. Dedication to prayer alone accomplishes nothing. Far from drawing one near to the Divine Presence, it removes one from that presence. The reason for this follows from his general outlook: in the same way as the individual does not stand by himself but is part of a community, so prayer does not exist in isolation but is part of an entire way of life; and an entire way of life is only possible when an individual lives within a community. In the same way as his life is incomplete outside of community, so also is his prayer. We have already spoken of the theoretical basis for this.

The *Kuzari* also contains analyses of certain specific prayers and the commentaries on them, but as far as I can tell these do not add much to the understanding of his essential approach. Halevi's original contribution to the understanding of prayer is in his account of the process of preparation unique to it, and in his explanation of the religious importance of the relevant halakhic regulations. In this area he adds to the understanding of prayer as an encounter with God through recapturing the ideal prophetic experience. All the acts of our lives to which prayer gives expression are to be concentrated toward attaining this supreme level. Of course, one may only offer Halevi's model as one among several possible models, but it seems to be important, and, even though it is expounded against the background of medieval theology, its importance is not confined to the Middle Ages. With a change of terminology, Halevi could be describing one of the possible approaches to prayer for our own day also.

9
Prayer in the Thought of Maimonides

Marvin Fox

Every serious student of the thought of Maimonides, particularly of his *Guide of the Perplexed,* is aware of the special problems that are posed by the apparently contradictory positions he advances in that book. In his introduction to the *Guide,* Maimonides takes special pains to prepare his readers for the arduous task of studying his book. He tells us explicitly about the contradictions which we may expect to find, and he provides the perceptive reader with some methodological tools for dealing with them. Despite his cautions and his help, students of Maimonides are far from having solved all the problems of interpreting the *Guide* and resolving those same contradictions.

One of the areas in which these contradictions emerge in a particularly striking way is in Maimonides' treatment of prayer. In this chapter I propose to examine his views concerning prayer, as they are set forth in the *Guide* and in his earlier writings. I shall attempt to explicate his doctrine and to give an account of the way in which he brings together differing, and even opposing, views with respect to the nature of prayer and its philosophical and theological foundations.

An initial reading of the relevant sources in the corpus of Maimonides leads to the conclusion that he advances two different and apparently inconsistent views about prayer. One seems to be conventional, simple, and in accord with popular uncritical religious sentiment. In this account God is seen as master of the world. He is at one and the same time a stern judge and loving father. His majesty merits and evokes our praise. His kindness and compassion merit and evoke our thanks. And in our awareness of our total dependence on Him, we turn to Him in plea and supplication for our needs. He hears (or knows, if we want to avoid the anthropomorphism) our prayers and responds to them favorably or not as our merit warrants and His judgment determines. Moreover, even though we lack merit, He may choose nevertheless to respond to our supplications. As a loving and compassionate father, he knows our faults, yet He may choose to change his stern decree in response to our prayers.

The opposed view emerges from Maimonides' philosophical understanding of the nature of God and His relationship to man and the world. From his philosophical perspective all conventional notions of prayer seem deeply problematic. From within the philosophical understanding it may still be possible to provide for expressions of thanks to God, but there is little place left for either praise of God or supplication for His help. Praise seems to be impossible, since according to the philosophical doctrine, there is nothing we can say about God that does not detract from His glory. This is a reflection of the limits of human language, and as such is also a reflection of the limits of our intellectual capacity. Maimonides has established through an elaborate set of arguments that we can have no knowledge of God that can properly be expressed in the language of positive attributes. To think or speak of God using positive predicates and intending them literally is a major philosophical error. Insofar as we can think or speak about Him correctly at all, it can only be through negative attributes.[1] From this perspective, every positive statement about God turns out to be false or meaningless. Having set forth the elements of the theory of negative attributes, Maimonides urges us:

> Desire then wholeheartedly that you should know by demonstration some additional thing to be negated, but do not desire to negate merely in words. For on every occasion on which it becomes clear to you by means of a demonstration that a thing whose existence is thought to pertain to Him, may He be exalted, should rather be negated with reference to Him, you undoubtedly come nearer to Him by one degree. . . . On the other hand, the predication of affirmative attributes of Him, may He be exalted, is very dangerous.

It seems then that it is not possible for us truly to praise God in prayer. Whatever we might say in our paeans of praise that is phrased in the language of affirmative attributes will certainly be wrong, if not downright insulting as we shall soon see.

The problem is even more aggravated with respect to prayers of supplication. It would appear that the very presuppositions of all petitionary prayer are not only unsound, but, in Maimonides' view, border on the heretical. Petitionary prayer presupposes that there is some meaningful sense in which it can be affirmed that God hears us when we address Him, and that He takes account of our petition. If our prayer is successful, God is affected by our petitions in such a way that He changes His intentions with respect to us. If we fail to move Him, then He rejects our petition. The classical model for such prayer may be found in the supplications of Moses, some of which are answered and some of which are denied. When he pleads for a change in the Divine decree that prevents him from entering the land of Israel, Moses employs every device to play on God's sympathy. Yet he fails to move Him, and his petition is denied. In fact, it is denied with a show of irritation. "But the Lord was wrathful with me on your account and would not listen to me. The Lord said to me, 'Enough! Never speak to Me of this matter again! . . . for you shall not go across yonder Jordan.' "[2] On the other hand, when he pleads for the people of Israel after the golden calf episode he succeeds. God condemns the people for their faithlessness and says, "Now, let Me be, that My anger may blaze forth against them and that I may destroy them. . . ."[3] God announces His fixed intention, yet the *Midrash* sees in His words, *haniha li* "Let me be," an invitation to Moses to plead for the people.[4] He implores God with a variety of petitionary arguments and pleas and his prayer is accepted. "And the Lord renounced the punishment He had planned to bring upon His people."[5] The Talmud goes so far as to suggest that the prayers of the righteous not only have the power of changing the Divine intentions, but that God so desires the prayers of men that He casts them into circumstances where they will be forced to turn to Him for help. In one especially striking formulation, our *Sages* ask, "Why were our ancestors childless?" and they answer, "Because the Holy One, blessed be He, longs for the prayer of the righteous." The passage continues with the following observation: "Why is the prayer of the righteous compared to a pitchfork? Just as a pitchfork turns the grain from one position to another, so does the prayer of the righteous turn the disposition of the Holy One, blessed be He, from the attribute of anger to the attribute of mercy."[6]

Any literal reading of these texts (and they are, after all, typical rather than exceptional) involves affirmations about God which Maimonides rejected vigorously. First, it would suggest, if not force us to affirm, God's corporeality. More important, since this problem might be dealt with by an allegorical reading of the texts, it forces us to postulate the very kind of relationship between God and man that Maimonides explicitly denies. Even worse, it leads to the conclusion that God is subject to change, a direct contradiction of a fundamental principle of the Maimunistic theology. And worst of all, it makes God subject to affections since He is moved by man's efforts, and this is very nearly an ultimate heresy in the Rambam's opinion. Despite these difficulties, there are texts in the corpus of Maimonides which treat petitionary prayer in a straightforward way, expressing no hesitation and feeling no difficulty in the notion that God hears and responds to prayer. On the other hand, there are also passages, especially in the *Guide of the Perplexed*, but not only there, which make such a conception of prayer seriously suspect, if not totally untenable. It is to these diverse texts that we must address ourselves in order to arrive at some clear idea of what Maimonides had to say about this subject.

In his essentially halakhic writings the conventional notions prevail with very little exception. Here, where Maimonides functions as classical Jewish teacher and jurist, his task is to codify and explicate the law. Since it is beyond all question that the law includes, among its fixed duties, statutory forms and occasions of prayer, as well as other acts of worship which are connected with prayer, he has no choice but to acknowledge the obligation and to set forth its rules and patterns in detail. In so doing, Maimonides usually adopts a purely traditional tone in which he advises his readers to seek God's help for the fulfillment of their needs. He does not limit such petitions to ordinary human needs, but even with respect to the ultimate religious quest (as Maimonides understands it), namely, the intellectual apprehension of God, he still urges that we seek Divine help and turn to God in prayer. This is explicitly stated in his *Commentary on the Mishnah* when he says that one who seeks to know fully the secret teachings of Scripture should turn to God in prayer and ask His help in penetrating to the esoteric doctrine.

> For this end [i.e., the knowledge of esoteric doctrine] it is not sufficient for a man to devote himself with all his effort to the study of the Torah, but he must direct his heart to God and pray to Him and plead with Him to grant him this special knowledge and to help him by revealing to him Che secrets which are hidden in Scripture.

This, he says, is what David did when he prayed, "Open Thou mine eyes that I may behold wondrous things out of Thy law."[7]

The view that Rambam holds consistently in his *Mishnah* commentary is that the essential meaning of *tefillah* is petition *(bakasha)*. Thus, in explaining the prayers which precede and follow the study of Torah, Maimonides notes, that they are called *tefillah* "in accordance with the root meaning of the word, namely, that petition is what we understand by *tefillah*."[8] For the most part this is identified with ordinary petitionary prayer in which we ask for our basic human needs. It is significant that, as we have seen, this common conception of prayer as petition is extended to include petitions for knowledge of God's secret lore. However, generally in the *Commentary on the Mishnah* he simply records thh usual obligations for petitionary prayer as they emerge from his explication of the relevant mishnaic texts. So far as I can determine there is no place in this commentary where he raises directly any question of a theological sort about the problem of petitionary prayer. It goes without saying that, in this context, he also affirms the propriety of prayers of praise and thanks and records our duty to offer them. The unquestioned assumption is that God hears our supplications and that when we merit it in His eyes He accepts our petitions and grants our requests.[9]

There are only three discussions in the *Commentary on the Mishnah* which might possibly be taken as reflecting some restrictions on the conventional notions of prayer, and not one of these is decisive. In commenting on the principle that we are obligated to praise God for the evil things that happen to us just as we praise Him for the good (*Berakhot* IX, 5), Maimonides explains as follows.

Because of the limits of our perspective, we never know the full significance or consequences of any event; therefore we should always assume that it is ultimately for our good, despite the fact that at the moment it may appear to be disastrous. Confident that God does only what is good, we can praise Him in faith and trust, assured that in the end we shall come to see that today's apparent catastrophe is tomorrow's blessing. If this is the case, it might seem to follow that all petitionary prayer is improper, since one is asking God to change present circumstances. If we trust Him and are certain that whatever He causes to happen must be for the good, then why is it ever right to question His judgment through prayers for improved circumstances?

In response we must note the fact that there is nothing original in Maimonides' interpretation of this *Mishnah*. It is simply a summary paraphrase of what is offered in the *Gemara* (cf. *Berakhot* 60b). There the various modes of explaining this principle of law are captured in the single aphorism, "All that God does is only for the good." Just as our Sages saw no inherent contradiction between this confident trust in God under all circumstances and the requirements of petitionary prayer, so does Maimonides seem to find no difficulty here. It is right that he should not, since it is clear enough that accepting in good faith whatever God causes to happen need not preclude the hope and prayer that He might help us achieve our ends in ways which are less painful.

In his comment on *M. Pesahim* IV, 10 (which he identifies as a *Tosefta*), Maimonides presents us with a second occasion that might be construed as opposed to petitionary prayer. We are told there that among the deeds for which Hezekiah was praised was *ganaz sefer refuot*, he removed from public use certain books containing formulas for healing diseases. In his comment, Maimonides refers to an interpretation he heard that commends Hezekiah because people using medical knowledge, rather than prayer, to heal themselves, show their lack of faith in God. In language of unmitigated ferocity, Maimonides attacks the idiocy of such a view. Prayer, he says, is not intended to be a substitute for human effort. We not only may but must use all available knowledge for the benefit of man. There is here, he says, no defect of faith at all. On the contrary, we show our faith by thanking God for having made known to us the ways of healing. Again, there is here no rejection of petitionary prayer, but only an attack on what he takes to be wholly unsound and dangerous views. There is no inconsistency whatsoever between making the maximum effort to help ourselves, while seeking Divine blessing on our efforts and Divine aid for that which lies beyond our own capacities.

The third instance in the *Commentary on the Mishnah* that might be construed as a possible rejection of conventional prayer is in the text oo the fifth of Maimonides' thirteen principles of faith. What he stresses here is that only God must be worshipped, but none beside Him may be worshipped. In the development of this principle he speaks only of praise and *avodah*, but says nothing about petition. It seems to me that one would have to strain very hard and in a tendentious way to conclude from the omission of any reference to petitionary prayer here that Maimonides is subtly indicating his rejection of it. I raise the issue only because the contemporary mode of reading Maimonides lays so much stress on the esoteric character of his writing that it is easy to imagine that some interpreter might read this kind of point into the Fifth Principle. While I accept the general view that Maimonides was anything but a straightforward writer of ordinary expository prose, I see no ground for seeking anything hidden in this text. It is clearly labelled as an attack on idolatry, and it is reasonable that it should restrict itself to those aspects of worship which are relevant to the rejection of idolatry.

To the extent that the *Mishneh Torah* is a law code, it reflects standard talmudic teaching and does not differ significantly in its treatment of prayer from what we find in the *Commentary on the Mishnah*. Here, too, Maimonides sets forth and codifies the accepted laws of prayer and reflects the accepted attitudes toward the nature of prayer and its effectiveness. There are, of course, numerous passages in which he specifies the obligation to pray regularly and in which he explicates the rabbinic teachings concerning the three varieties of prayer, that is, praise, petition, and thanks. As one would expect, the statutory times for prayer and the required forms are all set forth in detail, just as the special occasions for worship are also codified. With respect to praise, he follows the official teaching which limits praise to the specific forms and language instituted and approved by the Rabbis. A typical example is his statement concerning the prohibition of the *Mishnah* (*Berakhot* 5:3) against praying in the form of "to a bird's nest do thy mercies extend" in which he reproduces the tenor of the talmudic discussion. Here he concludes, as does the Talmud, that one should limit his praise of God to the specific language used by Moses. Anything more is improper and becomes denigration rather than praise.[10] Given his philosophic conviction that all praise which expresses itself in terms of positive attributes is necessarily in error, it is only reasonable that Maimonides should simply follow this rabbinic ruling in his code.[11]

In his discussions of supplication and petitionary prayer Maimonides again codifies the law and expresses no doubt whatsoever about the principle that God hears and responds to our prayers. In fact, there are cases where His favorable response seems to be assured. Thus, following explicit talmudic sources, Maimonides teaches that

> for a community [in contrast with an individual] whenever its members repent and offer supplications with sincere hearts, they are answered, as it is said, "For what great nation is there that hath God so nigh unto them, as the Lord our God, whensoever we call to Him."[12]

This is not an isolated instance but reflects a doctrine which occurs a number of times in the *Mishneh Torah* and in a variety of contexts. Not only is the supplication of a righteous community heard and answered directly, but such is also the case with respect to the petitions of certain individuals. For example, "Whoever feeds the poor and the orphaned at his table—if he calls out to God, He answers him, for it is written, 'Then shalt thou call, and the Lord will answer.'"[13] It seems clear that this kind of prayer is understood as affecting God's judgments and His actions with respect to given men or communities. Whatever may have been God's original intention, He sometimes changes His plan in response to these prayers. This is explicitly stated by Maimonides when he sets forth the conditions for judging the authenticity of a supposed prophet. We expect his predictions to come true, but not necessarily. For, if they are predictions of punishment, calamity, or doom, it may be that the intended victims repented and prayed which caused God to regret His earlier intention and to change it.[14]

Such a conventional treatment of prayer seems to run directly contrary to the philosophical principles with which Maimonides opened his Code. Early in the first book, where he sets out the basic elements of a sound understanding of God, Maimonides states forcefully that God does not change because there is nothing either in the world or in Him which can cause change in Him. There is in Him neither "passion nor frivolity; neither joy nor melancholy; . . . it is said, 'I am the Lord, I change not.' If God was sometimes angry and sometimes rejoiced, He would be changing."[15] We can interpret all the prophetic statements about God's feelings and His active responses to the ways in which those feelings are caused by men in nonliteral ways. In fact, Maimonides insists that we must read them in this way only. What then happens to any literal significance to petitionary prayer? Whatever possible purpose it might serve, it can hardly continue to be understood literally as a way in which man affects God by arousing His sympathy or compassion. The model of the merciful father is helpful only so long as we can take seriously the analogy between the heavenly and the earthly father. Once we are forced to admit that they do not resemble each other in any regard, and that God is absolutely unchangeable and subject to no affections, the analogy breaks down completely. At this point it seems impossible to bring together conventional popular notions concerning the nature of prayer and the sophisticated philosophical notion of the nature of God that Maimonides holds to be a foundation of the Jewish religion. Provisionally, we can perhaps do little more to resolve what appears to be an unresolvable tension in his thought, than to suggest that he talks on one level as halakhist and on another as philosopher-theologian, although, as we shall see, this does not seem to be a satisfactory solution.

The problems, as well as some direction toward a solution, emerge most fully when we turn to a study of the treatment of prayer in the *Guide of the Perplexed*. The major philosophic themes which can guide us to an understanding of Maimonides' theory of prayer, include, in particular, his views concerning the nature of God, our knowledge of God, providence, true worship, and the proper end of man. These views are, at best, adumbrated in the *Mishneh Torah* while they are given full, if obscure, treatment in the *Guide*. To the extent that any solution of the problems in the *Mishneh Torah* is possible, it will depend on a grasp of the way in which Maimonides deals with these same issues, and for this purpose we are best served by turning our attention to the problem of prayer in the *Guide*.

In the *Guide* we confront the full ambiguity of Maimonides' treatment of the problem of prayer, since here he cannot ignore or treat lightly the difficult philosophical questions. Given the admittedly esoteric character of the *Guide*, a book which was written in such a way as to veil its true doctrine, it becomes extremely difficult to determine precisely (and with complete confidence) what Maimonides' views are. Yet the lines emerge with sufficient clarity to allow us to make reasonably sound judgments.

If we consider the purely philosophical doctrines of the *Guide*, then conventional prayer should turn out to be a meaningless and improper activity. Praise of God is impossible, since we have neither the language nor the knowledge to speak about Him in any meaningful way. Petition becomes equally impossible since God is a being so utterly unlike anything that is created that there is no way to conceive intelligibly a relation between Him and us, yet petitionary prayer presupposes just such a relation. Among the many statements that Maimonides makes on this subject, the following is typical.

> In view of the fact that the relation between us and Him, may He be exalted, is considered nonexistent—I mean the relation between Him and that which is other than He—it follows necessarily that likeness between Him and us should also be considered nonexistent.[16]

How, given such a view of God, can He either be praised or petitioned? What do we know of Him that would make such praise in any sense possible or that would make such petition in any way sensible? Maimonides goes on to argue that all terms that are used to speak of God are used in a way which is completely equivocal, that is to say that we use the words in ways which are semantically empty. As Maimonides expresses it,

> the term "existent" is predicated of Him, may He be exalted, and of everything that is other than He, in a purely equivocal sense. Similarly the terms "knowledge," "power," "will," and "life," as applied to Him, may He be exalted, and to all those possessing knowledge, power, will, and life, are purely equivocal, so that their meaning when they are predicated of Him is in no way like their meaning in other applications.[17]

What can it possibly mean, then, to address praise and petition to a being who is so remote and so absolutely inaccessible to our intellect and whose nature is so inexpressible in our language?

The problem grows even more severe when we consider that Maimonides denies all motion to God. In his insistence on an absolutely pure conception of the Divine unity he is driven to eliminate any suggestion of corporeality. Since he holds that, "It has been demonstrated that everything that is capable of motion is endowed with a magnitude that, without any doubt, can be divided,"[18] it follows that God cannot be understood as having motion among His predicates. Though Maimonides does argue subsequently that God may be understood as acting purely through His will, despite the denial of motion to God, this does not help us very much, for he argues that will cannot be understood as a separate faculty in God, otherwise we would compromise the Divine unity. In that case, what can we make of petitionary prayers addressed to a Being who is unlike us in every way and whose mode of causation is utterly unintelligible to us? These difficulties reach a climax when we see the intensity with which

Maimonides defends God against any suggestion that He is subject to external causes which can in any way affect Him. So severe are his strictures against any such views that he classes them as worse than idolatry. Speaking of a man "who does not believe that He exists; or believes that there are two Gods, or that He is a body, or that He is subject to affections," he goes on to say that "such a man is indubitably more blameworthy than a worshipper of idols."[19] It would appear that prayer cannot have any meaningful petitionary function if God is utterly beyond being affected by any force outside Himself. Man's prayers would appear in that case to have no proper object to whom they are directed and his supplications would emerge as utterly pointless. Yet, even in the *Guide*, Maimonides also speaks positively about prayer and about Divine providence. In order to come to terms with this apparent internal contradiction we need to examine systematically the ways in which he treats this topic in the *Guide*.

In a key statement Maimonides expresses what some might well consider his true view of prayer. He has just explained the commandments concerning animal sacrifices as a concession to the needs of a people accustomed to think of such sacrifice as the only proper mode of worship. It would have been impossible for them, he argues, to accept a commandment forbidding them to offer such sacrifices to God. Consequently, they were instructed to sacrifice, but under very carefully specified and restricted conditions. In this way they were turned away from idolatry to the worship of the true God, but with sufficient sensitivity to their general level of development so as not to demand of them what would seem utterly impossible. Maimonides explains the need for concessions to that early Israelite generation by a comparison with his own. For anyone to have tried to eliminate animal sacrifice completely at that time

> would have been similar to the appearance of a prophet in these times who, calling upon the people to worship God, would say: "God has given you a Law forbidding you to pray to Him, to fast, to call upon Him for help in misfortune. Your worship should consist solely in meditation without any works at all."[20]

Maimonides is here treating the laws of prayer as a concession to our present state of religious and intellectual development, comparable to the concessions which were required in an earlier age when worship without animal sacrifices was unthinkable. Prayer is our way of religious expression, as sacrifice was theirs. Neither is ideally desirable, nor is either consistent with a proper metaphysical understanding of God, His nature, and His relationship to the world. However, since men today would almost surely construe a prohibition against prayer as an attack on all religion, we concede this point to them and permit them to pray in controlled ways in order to be able to lead them finally to right opinion in matters of religion. It should be noted, however, that this is not a concession only to those who are intellectually undeveloped or philosophically naive. Prayer is, after all, obligatory for Jews. It is a Divine commandment. No Jew is exempt from that obligation, whatever the level of his knowledge. Maimonides, and even Moses himself, are bound by the statutory duty to pray. If the permission—to say nothing of the obligation—to pray is a concession to man, it is a concession made in the light of man's ultimate intellectual limitations and his spiritual needs. No one ever fully achieves a true intellectual apprehension of God, nor is anyone ever without the deep inner need to express gratitude for God's beneficence, to praise and glorify Him, and to turn to Him for help. Yet the intellectual problems are very real.

Unlike what we saw in our brief survey of the halakhic works, in the *Guide* Maimonides has hardly any statements concerning prayer which can be viewed as purely conventional, and those few are very quickly qualified. To begin with, he stresses in the fullest way the limitations of all language, so that true praise of God is seen to be impossible. What matters most is not saying the correct words, for in truth there are no correct words, but having a sound intellectual apprehension of God. Even in the case of *keriat shema* he holds that "men ought rather to belong to the category of those who represent the truth to themselves and apprehend it, even if they do not utter it . . . for they are told: 'Commune with your own heart upon your bed, and be still. Selah.' "[21] He makes this statement, despite his own (and the Talmud's) explicit ruling that one is required to speak the words of the *Shema* so that they are audible at least to oneself.

The locus classicus for his attack on the language of prayer, and in particular on prayers of praise, is I,59. Since God can only be spoken of without serious error by way of negative attributes, it follows, he holds, that all positive praise must in the very nature of the case be erroneous. His slogan is the verse of the psalmist, "Silence is praise to Thee" (Psalm 65:2). In Maimonides' interpretation it is taken to mean,

> silence with regard to You is praise. For of whatever we say intending to magnify and exalt, on the one hand we find that it can have some application to Him, may He be exalted, and on the other we perceive in it some deficiency. Accordingly, silence and limiting oneself to the apprehensions of the intellects are more appropriate.[22]

This is why, he believes, the Rabbis themselves put such severe limitations on praise of God. He cites with strong approval the well-known talmudic passage in which Rabbi Haninah attacks a Jew who praises God with a series of extravagant adjectives. All that is permitted is the exact language of praise which Moses instituted, and even that limited form is permissible to us only because it was formally enjoined by the men of the Great Synagogue. The best model we can have is that of the heavenly spheres. These are intellects far superior to our own, who constantly pay homage to God, but their praise is wordless silence. "There is no speech, there are no words, neither is their voice heard." Their true praise of God is in their sound intellectual apprehension of Him, and this should be our true praise as well.[23] It would appear, then, that the commandment to praise God in prayer is a grudging accommodation to the limits both of our intellect and our language. Given that we are moved, despite these limitations, to sing out our homage to the Most High, the Torah permitted us as a concession a very restricted mode of expression of praise to Him. The ideal, however, is to come to the point where we render Him the true praise of sound intellectual apprehension, rather than the false praise that is tied to human language.[24]

If even praise is so severely limited, how shall we understand the supplications and petitions which are included in the standard liturgy? What shall we make of the many recommendations and even injunctions in the *halakhah* to turn to God and plead with Him for our needs? What of the biblical passages in which God is petitioned and responds? We must first consider how Maimonides deals with the notion of God's response to prayer, a problem to which we alluded earlier. Given his severe strictures against the doctrine that God is subject to any affections, together with his view of God as utterly unlike man and utterly without relations to anything outside Himself, it is obvious that petitionary prayer can hardly be interpreted by Maimonides in accordance with the common religious view. In fact, he takes a position which is, to say the least, daring, a position which, according to some, may well be open to charges of destroying the foundations of religious faith. His theory is that the Torah at times adopts certain teachings, which are known to be unsound metaphysics, because they are useful means that lead men to certain desirable ends which cannot be achieved otherwise. As he expresses it,

> The Law also makes a call to adopt certain beliefs, belief in which is necessary for the sake of political welfare. Such, for instance, is our belief that He, may He be exalted, is violently angry with those who disobey Him and that it is therefore necessary to fear Him and to dread Him and to take care not to disobey. . . . In some cases a commandment communicates a correct belief, which is the one and only thing aimed at—as, for instance, the belief in the unity and eternity of the deity and in His not being a body. In other cases, the belief is necessary for the abolition of reciprocal wrongdoing or for the acquisition of a noble moral quality—as, for instance, the belief that He, may He be exalted, has a

> violent anger against those who do injustice, according to what is said: "And my wrath shall wax hot, and I will kill, and so on." And as the belief that He, may He be exalted, responds instantaneously to the prayer of someone that is wronged or deceived: "And it shall come to pass, when he crieth unto Me, that I will hear; for I am gracious."[25]

The suggestion is clear enough here that the conventional picture of a God who hears the cry of the oppressed and hastens to their succor is not to be taken literally. It is a doctrine which the Torah, if read literally, teaches, together with the practice of petitionary prayer that it implies, in order to reinforce a belief which is essential for the welfare of the individual and society.

It is the mature view of Maimonides that we have, in fact, no literal understanding at all about the way in which God governs the world. At the one extreme, his views come very close to a theory of fixed natural causation, in which all things are held to depend on God as First Cause, but in which the order of the natural world is adhered to rigorously. When he opts for the theory that the world is created in time out of nothing, he does so for the explicit reason that only in this way can one protect the Jewish faith against the onslaught of fixed natural causation. For, as he sees it, the belief in the eternity of the world "destroys the Law in its principle, necessarily gives the lie to every miracle, and reduces to inanity all the hopes and threats that the Law has held out."[26] Yet, based on the theory of creatio ex nihilo, he never claims to be able to offer any coherent explanation of God's governance of the world, except that all that happens is due to His will. This may be sufficient as a statement of faith. It will not do as a philosophic explanation. When he confronts these as pure philosophical matters, Maimonides can only say that they are matters about which we can claim no proper understanding.

> . . . the character of His governance of the world, the "how" of His providence with respect to what is other than He, the notion of His will . . . it should be considered that these are obscure matters. In fact, they are truly the mysteries of the Torah and the secrets constantly mentioned in the books of the prophets and in the dicta of the Sages.[27]

We have no capacity to understand how the very God whom we seek to grasp in metaphysical purity also functions as a power directly concerned with the world and the affairs of men. It is, nevertheless, of the highest practical importance to inculcate in men the belief that He does direct their affairs. What we must do, he urges, is to treat all events in such a way that we talk about them as flowing from a Being of supreme power whom we conceive on the model of a man. Therefore, we explain events as deriving from God's anger, or compassion, in the same way as we would if such events had been caused by men. Great catastrophes that occur to individuals or communities, had men caused them, "would proceed from one of us in reference to another only because of a violent anger or a great hatred or a desire for vengeance. With reference to these actions He is called 'jealous and avenging and keeping anger and wrathful.' "[28] This is only a way of speaking for the instruction of the masses, not a sound literal representation of God's way in the world. Though Maimonides is almost always careful to add, when he discusses this question, that the men who are affected by God's action merit the treatment that they have received, there is no way in which he can make this intelligible in the light of his general principles.[29] It is easy to trace out consistently in the *Guide* the doctrine that political and social necessity made it mandatory for the Torah to impose such beliefs on the people as a whole, although we cannot claim any systematic knowledge of them.

Given these literalized conventional beliefs, prayer surely makes sense. If God is viewed as subject to passion, even in a manner of speaking, then it is appropriate to try to influence Him by our petitions and supplications. Granted that these prayers must not be merely in words, but must be accompanied by man's repentance and his efforts to become virtuous, this conventional religious notion of prayer is still poor metaphysics. While this manner of speaking about God's actions is also adopted by the Sages, Maimonides holds that they never intended that it should be understood literally by sophisticated men, although they did recognize that one must speak this way for the masses.[30] The Torah itself also teaches a doctrine of prayer aimed at protecting ordinary men from falling into the errors of idolatry as well as for the purpose of maintaining sound social order. As Maimonides understands the matter, to take just one case, the idolatrous cults all held that only through appropriate worship of their particular gods could one bring about rain, fertile fields, and all that is needed for human sustenance. In order to save us from the danger of idolatry the Torah teaches explicitly that if we worship idols, precisely the opposite consequences will follow. No rain will fall, the fields will be barren, and man will suffer grave calamities.

> You will find that this intention is reiterated in the whole of the Torah: I mean that it is a necessary consequence of the worship of the stars that rains will cease to fall, that the land will be devastated, that circumstances will become bad, and that the bodies will suffer from diseases, and that lives will be short: whereas, a necessary consequence of the worship of God will be rainfall, the fertility of the land, good circumstances, health of body, and length of life. This is the contrary of what

was preached by the idolators to the people in order that they worship idols. For the foundation of the Law consists in putting an end to this opinion and effacing its traces, as we have explained.[31]

Now, even in this case, where the reference is to one of the three paragraphs of the *Shema,* that is, Deuteronomy 11: 13–21, Maimonides still does not want to accept it as literally correct from any philosophic point of view. It is rather a mode of worship which is enjoined as a way of combatting the dangers of false gods. Just as we were allowed to continue to offer sacrifices so that we could be weaned away from *avodah zarah,* so are we enjoined to pray in certain ways in order to be brought to the belief in the one true God. No sophisticated man will believe literally that rainfall is a "necessary consequence" of a particular kind of worship, but it is good that unsophisticated men should think so. Furthermore, even the sophisticated must recognize their total dependence on God. As members of a common religious community, the intellectually advanced join with their simpler brothers in common rites and patterns of worship in order to build a community of faith which reinforces movement away from idolatrous practices and toward a sound apprehension of God.

This is not the place to discuss thoroughly Maimonides' theory of Divine Providence. However, we must make some brief reference to it, since it is in the context of that theory that he offers his most sophisticated account of the way in which the truly meritorious are protected by God. He is anxious to give a philosophically acceptable account of God's connection with man, but it turns out to be an account which could hardly justify any conventional notions of prayer. God, on this view, is related to man exclusively by way of the intellect. The higher the level of a man's intellectual development the closer his connection with God. This is due to the fact that the human intellect is activated by way of the Divine overflow that is mediated through the active intellect and activates the rational faculty of man. "Accordingly everyone with whom something of this overflow is united, will be reached by providence to the extent to which he is reached by the intellect."[32]

> When any human individual has obtained, because of the disposition of his matter and his training, a greater portion of this overflow than others, providence will of necessity watch more carefully over him than over others. . . . Accordingly Divine Providence does not watch in an equal manner over all the individuals of the human species, but providence is graded as their human perfection is graded.[33]

This theory of providence has the effect of making all petitionary prayer superfluous and useless. Prayer cannot be legitimately understood as having a direct causal connection with the way in which God governs us and determines our destiny. For, as Maimonides insists, given a certain level of intellectual development, which is to say a certain level of intellectual apprehension of God and concern with the knowledge of God, a given degree of providential care follows "of necessity." In that case, it would appear that prayer has no more direct function than that of directing man toward an intellectually sound apprehension of God and a morally sound social order.

In his discussion of the true form of Divine worship at the end of the *Guide*, Maimonides introduces a brief excursus on providence. There, too, he stresses that being with God is the highest achievement of the intellect, and argues that this is the only way in which man is protected from the evils which might befall him. The Divine overflow elevates man in such a way that,

> The providence of God is constantly watching over those who have obtained this overflow, which is permitted to everyone who makes efforts with a view to obtaining it. If a man's thought is free from distraction, if he apprehends Him, may He be exalted, in the right way and rejoices in what he apprehends, that individual can never be afflicted with evil of any kind. For he is with God and God is with him. When, however, he abandons Him, may He be exalted, and is thus separated from God and God separated from him, he becomes in consequence of this a target for every evil that may happen to befall him. For the thing that necessarily brings about providence and deliverance from the sea of chance consists in that intellectual overflow.[34]

Not prayer, not petition or supplication, but the intellectual apprehension of God is the way in which man is protected from evil and is granted the highest rewards. Without making any attempt to explicate further the theory of providence which has been summarized here, we can still see clearly what a devastating effect it could easily have on literalist notions of petitionary prayer. With all his desire to protect the intellectually innocent from the dangers of discovering truths that they are not able to grasp or cope with, Maimonides still makes his intentions concerning prayer sufficiently clear so that no attentive reader can fail to understand the force and the threat of his doctrine.

The treatment of prayer reaches its climax in the final chapters of the *Guide*, where true worship specifically emerges as a kind of *amor dei intellectualis*. In his famous parable of those who seek to enter the chamber of the king, Maimonides concludes that only those who achieve sound intellectual apprehension of God can be said to worship Him truly. Those who merely observe the commandments without any kind of intellectual reflection on theological questions have no access to God at all. They are, in his language, "ignoramuses who observe the commandments." This group includes the "multitude of the adherents of the Law," who, because of their lack of philosophical interest and development, are remote from God and unprotected by His providence. Traditional *talmidei hakhamim,* who do engage in serious intellectual activity, but do not devote themselves to philosophical-theological studies are only slightly better off. They are at least moving in the right direction, but they are still very far from God. Only those who are fully devoted to philosophic speculation at the highest level and have achieved demonstrative knowledge concerning God are truly with Him. The intellectual activity in which they engage is the mode of worship of these highest of men, and that mode of worship is alone sound; it alone is the ideal toward which all should aspire. What Maimonides explicitly seeks to achieve as the climax of his great book is

> to confirm men in the intention to set their thought to work on God alone after they have achieved knowledge of Him. . . . This is the worship peculiar to those who have apprehended the true realities; the more they think of Him and of being with Him, the more their worship increases.[35]

It is this worship, that is, the intellectual apprehension and contemplation of God, that constitutes the true love of God. This is what is intended in the commandment to love Him with all our capacity. For "love is proportionate to apprehension."[36]

Maimonides sees this as the ultimately true and perfect mode of worship, compared with which every other form is defective. This, he tells us, is the worship that is meant when we speak of *avodah shebelev,* worship of the heart. Yet, he knows full well, and indicates so in his Code, that the normal meaning of this term is *tefillah,* and that this refers to the set liturgical forms. Now, when he appropriates this very term for intellectual worship, which consists of knowledge and contemplation, he is deliberately telling us that the rabbinic tradition will be understood in new ways by those who are at the highest level of intellectual and philosophic sophistication. This is why he can go on to affirm that such true worship is best achieved in solitude, in direct contrast with the ideal for *tefillah,* which is best achieved *bezibbur.*

We have now gone beyond the law and its norms because, presumably, we have achieved those highest ends which the law is intended to foster. Ordinary prayer and fulfillment of *mizvot* serve as a propaedeutic, a discipline which guides and prepares us for the life of true worship. "Know that all the practices of the worship, such as reading the Torah, prayer, and the performance of the other commandments, have only the end of training you to occupy yourself with His commandments, may He be exalted, rather than with matters pertaining to this world."[37] Out of this discipline grows the state of mind and soul in which one is fully preoccupied with God, seeking that demonstrative knowledge and philosophic contemplation that is the highest fulfillment of the human intellect.

Ideally, then, we must move from ordinary prayer and ordinary fulfillment of commandments, to the only life in which man is finally redeemed, the life in which he elevates himself to God and is connected with Him permanently by way of the intellect. The redemptive power of the intellectual apprehension of God is elevated, even in his *Mishneh Torah,* to the level of being the ultimate goal of man's striving. Messianic fulfillment is characterized by Maimonides as the time when, as the prophet puts it, "the earth shall be full of the knowledge of the Lord, as the waters cover the sea." It is not without significance that he chooses these words with which to finish his *Mishneh Torah.*

From our discussion it is clear that we can discern two different theories of prayer in the teachings of Maimonides. What is far less clear is how we should understand the relationship between these different teachings. One standard line of Maimonides scholarship stresses the presence of contradictory teachings and resolves the contradictions by arguing that it is the philosophical view he truly affirms while he sets forth the popular views for political purposes. Whatever merit this approach may have, it is in no sense a resolution of contradictions. It is rather the affirmation of one of the contradictories at the expense of the other. Now it is an elementary rule of logic that contradictories cannot both be true, nor can they both be false. It follows that if we are, in fact, dealing with true contradictories, then we have no choice but to understand Maimonides as affirming one and denying the other. It is a remarkable fact that though much as been written about contradictions in Maimonides' *Guide,* hardly any attention has been given to the task of a rigorous analysis of those alleged contradictions. Are they contradictories, contraries, subcontraries, or perhaps even some other form of opposition? Must we not pay close attention to each case in order to determine exactly what its logical status is? Otherwise we have no ground whatsoever for asserting that Maimonides must necessarily have rejected one and affirmed the other of a pair of seemingly opposed propositions. This task lies beyond the limits of the present study. It is so large that we cannot pursue it here even with respect to the opposed positions which Maimonides sets forth on the subject of prayer. We should, however, recognize that scholarly responsibility requires far more care of us than the simple offhand announcement that we have found a contradiction and that one of the two propositions is necessarily false while the other is true.

Yet, despite our failure to carry out this phase of the investigation in the current inquiry, we must make some attempt to deal with the problem which confronts us as we reflect on the differing views of Maimonides on prayer. While I do not claim to offer any definitive resolution of the problem, I believe that there is good reason for rejecting the kind of solution which has recently become popular. Despite what some contemporary scholars might say, it is by no means obvious that Maimonides intends the conventional theory of prayer only for the masses while the philosophical theory is only for the intellectually sophisticated. Such a solution is neat and easy, but it simply does not take account of all the facts. The Maimonides whose personal life and practice is well known to us was a man of great personal piety. If he was a man of the highest intellectual sophistication and subtlety, he was also a man of very deep religious feelings and impulses. Not only was he meticulous in his concern for the law and in his own religious observance, but he often went far beyond what the law required. If as a decisor he was required to codify the law and to render decisions in accordance with the rules and methods of the Jewish legal system, this does not explain those acts of personal piety which go beyond ordinary legalism.

Let us consider just one case, one that is directly relevant to prayer and worship. On the sea voyage which led him from Fez to Palestine his ship was beset by violent and threatening storms. When the storm ended and the ship was able to sail without further danger, Maimonides declared the day on which the storm began and the day on which it ended (six days later) as permanent fast days for himself and all his descendants. He himself tells us that

> it was my vow that I would spend the tenth day of *Iyyar* [the day of the storm's end] in solitude, that I would see no man but would devote myself to private prayer and study. Just as on that day I found in the stormy sea no one but the Holy One, blessed be He, so would I on the annual day of commemoration see no one unless circumstance forced me to do so.[38]

This is not the thinking or the practice of a man who holds that prayer is intended only for the protection of the masses while the truly educated should serve God exclusively through the activity of the intellect.

Our effort to understand Maimonides' doctrine of prayer must take account of the implications of those aspects of his personal life which are relevant. In this case, we have a striking instance of his assuming a stance of personal piety which seems on the face of it to be far more appropriate for a man of the people than for a philosopher. Should the objection be raised that this is an event that occurred in the early part of his life when he may not yet have reached his full intellectual sophistication, we may reply that the many expressions and acts of prayerful piety which are recorded in all his writings bear witness to the fact that to the very end of his life he engaged in prayer in ways that go far beyond the fixed statutory requirements.

I should like to suggest that the key to understanding the way in which Maimonides keeps both the popular and the philosophic ideas of worship in a single system lies in his notion of "necessary beliefs." It is my contention that if we interpret this notion correctly, we shall be able to see that Maimonides has no choice but to maintain simultaneously conventional and philosophical ideas of prayer. These ideas and practices are not (as many suppose) intended to be mutually exclusive. They are intended to exist side by side within a single system of thought, maintaining a delicate and difficult balance. They are conceptions which live together in severe dialectical tension, and at times the tension may indeed be so strong as to threaten lhe balance. Nevertheless, Maimonides is saying that our very condition as men leaves us no option but to live in this precarious situation in which we affirm and pursue in practice both a philosophically sophisticated conception of divine worship and a popular conventional pattern of prayer.

Speaking of the commandments that are codified and explicated in the second book of the *Mishneh Torah,* specifically those that concern prayer and that which is connected with it, Maimonides says the following:

> The end of these actions pertaining to divine service is the constant commemoration of God, the love of Him and the fear of Him, the obligatory observance of the commandments in general, and the bringing-about of such belief concerning Him, may He be exalted, as is necessary for every one professing the Law.[39]

This idea of necessary belief is introduced earlier also with respect to the view that God hears and answers prayers.[40] It is widely held that Maimonides means by "necessary beliefs" doctrines which are contrary to the truth, but which have great social utility. One recent writer speaks of the necessary beliefs as *hashlayah,* that is, deliberate deception, and goes on to say of them that they are "directly contrary to the true knowledge of God."[41] This seems to me to miss the point completely, and to set up a false interpretation of Maimonides. In the passage from the *Guide* that was just quoted, Maimonides explicitly states that these beliefs are "necessary for everyone professing the Law." The key term here is "everyone" and we must give it its due weight. "Everyone professing the Law" includes the philosophers who are faithful members of the Jewish religious community, even Maimonides himself.

There is not here, in my opinion, a simple opposition between what the philosophers believe and what the masses should be taught to believe, but rather between two kinds of belief, both of which are necessary. The philosophic beliefs are necessary for any reflective man, because they are demonstrated and thus command our assent. These philosophic beliefs, however, are incomplete, as is the case, for example, with respect to the problem of creation. Our own limitations are such that we can never have total and complete philosophic knowledge. We can never avoid the profession of some beliefs which are undemonstrated and, perhaps, indemonstrable. This is the case not only because our intellect is limited. If this were the only problem, then we might just suspend belief and profess agnosticism with respect to such matters. This would, in fact, be the soundest and most defensible intellectual stance. We are, however, not only philosophers. We are men. We live in societies that must be ordered. We have a higher nature which must be served. We have hopes, aspirations, fears, and anxieties, all of which demand attention. Our hearts long for fellowship with God, and our minds are determined to find evidence of His presence in our world. Prayer is one of the most basic and irrepressible expressions of the human spirit. Perhaps the pure intellect that has advanced to the true intellectual apprehension of God no longer needs ordinary prayer. For such an intellect its knowledge is, in the fullest sense, both its worship and its fulfillment, but men, even philosophic men, are not perfect disembodied intellects. The ideal praise of God may well be, as Maimonides suggests, the wordless praise of the spheres, but how can this ideal ever be realized in the actual lives of men? Our apprehension is, at best, imperfect, and our dependence on language is very deep. We cannot conceptualize without language, although we are fully aware that our conceptions are defective and our language inaccurate with respect to God. The spheres have no such problems, but then they are spheres and not men. If the human heart overflows with gratitude and awe before God, men have no way to express these sentiments except in the language of prayer. Their very condition as human makes it necessary for them not only to pray, but to believe sincerely in the significance and meaningfullness of prayer. These are necessary beliefs, not in the unpleasant and morally shoddy sense that they are encouraged for the masses by superior intellects who know them to be false, but in the significant and admirable sense that no religious man can do without them, however sophisticated he may be. If God cannot be praised, if He cannot be thanked, if He cannot be petitioned honestly, then for the religious man He is not God.

Maimonides is thoroughly aware of the dilemma in which religious man finds himself. While aspiring to that intellectual perfection which is pure *amor dei intellectualis,* he never fully achieves that ideal in this life. Not even Moses can claim to have achieved the goal fully or to have freed himself completely from his human limitations. Moses does not only teach others to pray, He prays himself, praises God, thanks Him, and petitions Him. Maimonides understands full well the complexity of the problem confronting man as he seeks to develop his relationship with God within the framework of his human condition. On the one hand, Maimonides wants to make certain that we know what the ultimate ideal is and that we not only aspire toward it, but use all our powers to move ourselves ever closer to it. At the same time, he wants to be certain that no man will so misunderstand his situation that he rejects the Torah and its commandments. These are not only necessary instruments for moving us toward the ideal; they are also the intrinsically precious ways by which we achieve religious fulfillment within those finite limitations of our nature that make the ideal ever beyond our grasp.

Notes

1. *Guide of the Perplexed* I, 60.
2. Deuteronomy 3;26, 27.
3. Exodus 32:10.
4. *Exodus Rabbah* XLII, 10.
5. Exodus 32:14.
6. *Yevamot,* 64a.
7. *Commentary on the Mishnah,* ed. J. Kapah, introduction, p. 36.
8. *Ibid., Berakhot* IV, 2; cf. *ibid.*, IX, 4.
9. For some typical instances in the *Commentary on the Mishnah* in which Maimonides expresses such conventional views concerning the nature and effectiveness of prayer, see his comments in *M. Berakhot* IV, 2; IV, 4; V (passim); IX, 3; IX, 4; *M. Sotah* VII, 5.
10. *M.T., Tefillah* IX, 7.
11. His statement in *M.T., Berakhot* X, 26, that the more one praises God the better, should not be construed as going counter to his general position. This statement comes near the end of his discussion of the laws of *berakhot* and should be seen in its context. By virtue of the fact that the precise text of the *berakhot* was set by the Sages these liturgical forms have a privileged status similar to that accorded to the form of praise that Moses instituted. The point is made in *M.T., Berakhot* I, 3: "Our Sages instituted many *berakhot* as forms of praise, thanks, and supplication so that we might constantly be mindful of our Creator. . . ."
12. *M.T., Teshuvah* II, 6.
13. *M.T., Matnot Aniyyim* X, 16. For similar assurances that God hears and answers man's prayers see, *M.T., Teshuvah* VII, 7; *Tefillah* VIII, 1; XV, 7; *Taanit* I, 1, 2, 3, 4; *Matnot Aniyyim* X, 3; *Mekhirah* XIV, 18.
14. *M.T., Yesode ha-Torah* X, 4.
15. *Ibid.*, I, 11, 12.
16. *Guide of the Perplexed* I, 56.
17. *Ibid.*
18. *Guide* I, 26.
19. *Guide* I, 36.
20. *Guide* III, 32.
21. *Guide* I, 50.

22. *Guide* I, 59.
23. *Guide* II, 5.
24. We should, however, always keep in mind that the ideal is unattainable for man in this life. The intellectual perfection of the spheres is their praise of God, or is a necessary condition for that wordless praise. Man's imperfect intellect, however, can never free itself completely of the limitations of language.
25. *Guide* III, 28.
26. *Guide* II, 25.
27. *Guide* I, 35.
28. *Guide* I, 54.
29. See, for example, *Guide* III, 17, where Maimonides is dealing with Divine Providence. When he sets forth the first version of his own view he states that the events which affect men are "not due to chance, but to Divine will in accordance with the deserts of those people as determined in His judgments." He hastens to add, however, that these are judgments "the rule of which cannot be attained by our intellects."
30. See *Guide* I, 46.
31. *Guide* III, 30.
32. *Guide* III, 17.
33. *Guide* III, 18.
34. *Guide* III, 51. One is inclined to think that the point here is not that God intervenes in the natural order so as to protect the deserving from misfortune, but rather that when one has achieved this very high intellectual level of fellowship with God no earthly misfortune is of any consequence. The troubles of a child are, from a mature perspective, childish troubles of little true importance. Men of true knowledge have a similar view of what ordinary men consider to be great misfortunes, and are thus protected from them.
35. *Guide* III, 51.
36. *Ibid.*
37. *Ibid.*
38. Cited in J. L. Maimon, *Rabbi Moshe ben Maimon* (Jerusalem: 1960), p. 55.
39. *Guide* III, 44.
40. *Guide* III, 28.
41. Yaakov Becker, *Mishnato ha-Pilusufit shel ha-Rambam* (Tel Aviv: 1955), pp. 74–75.

10
The Meaning of Prayer in the Spanish *Kabbalah*

Ephraim Gottlieb*

In this chapter, I will discuss the meaning of prayer among the kabbalists from the first full development of the *Kabbalah* in Provence in the twelfth century until the disappearance of this school (known as Spanish *Kabbalah*) in the East at the beginning of the sixteenth century. There are two reasons for treating this period as one unit: First, this framework constitutes an independent ideological entity in Jewish mysticism, one which differs from its predecessors in the

---

*Professor Ephraim Gottlieb passed away before the publication of this essay. Josef Hecker prepared the text for publication. The portions he edited or reworked are indicated by pointed brackets < > ; other sections were actually added by him for the sake of completeness: these are signified by square brackets ([ ]). In addition, he drew up all of the footnotes and references. This lecture first appeared in print in the posthumous volume *Mehkarim b-Sifrut ha-Kabbalah* by E. Gottlieb (Tel Aviv: 1976), pp. 38–56.

understanding of God and the world, and as a result differs as to the relationship also between man and God; it also differs greatly from the Lurianic trend which emerged in Palestine in the last third of the sixteenth century. Second, there is the aspect of the community. In several communities there were recognized circles of kabbalists who practiced their own customs during the time of prayer, yet there is no historical evidence that they had their own synagogues.[1]

These two points are critical to our discussion. For the kabbalists the established communal prayer was normative. Within its framework and using its vocabulary, its laws and its fixed character, the kabbalist found his "ladder of Beth-El."[2] On the highest rungs of that ladder man discovers the purpose of prayer. This is the clinging to God, according to one kind of emphasis, or the repair of the Divine world, from which comes the repair of everything, according to another emphasis. In this discussion, I will consider these two emphases in greater detail.

1

At this stage of the *Kabbalah,* not only does the kabbalist not feel any need to establish an external framework for himself, in which he can practice his customs, but there is no tendency to break up the existing, traditional framework of prayer. As Gershom Scholem has pointed out in several discussions,[3] the paradoxical side of the doctrine of *kavvanot* lies in the fact that the kabbalists transformed prayer, in its old forms, into mystical prayer by the infusing of a mystical-theosophic element into the old words and verses of prayer, in other words, into a text belonging originally to a way of thinking far removed from that of the kabbalists. < Thus, the kabbalist does not separate himself from the community, nor does he change the *nosah*. Although several specifically kabbalistic prayers were composed in the early period, there is no evidence that they were composed for public recitation, and even if they were recited in certain circles, this does not change the fact that the kabbalists were strict in their adherence to the received texts and forms of prayer.

For the kabbalist, prayer, like the *mizvot,* mirrors the Divine world. He desires to enter into this Divine world by means of due intellectual contemplation. Prayer is the best opportunity for such mental activity, that is for contemplating the Divine world. Such contemplation does not leave the contemplative subject unmoved, for a connection is formed between the contemplative powers and the Divine forces known as *Sefirot*. >

The aim is to connect the soul to the object of this mental activity, to *cleave* by means of thought and thus to achieve a mystical elevation. Yet this mental activity is bound up with certain theosophical notions. The Godhead itself cannot be apprehended. In the words of R. Isaac the Blind:[4]

Thought is incapable of reaching that which is above *Hokhmah* (wisdom); it does not even reach *Hokhmah* itself, except through contemplation, as is said—"understand in *hokhmah*," and *haven* (understand) means source,[5] and if it is a command it is only for the enlightened. Nor does it say, 'understand *Hokhmah*' or 'know *hokhmah*,' but 'understand *in hokhmah*.' For *hokhmah* comes by means of *binah* (understanding, contemplation),[6] for *binah* is the understanding *in* wisdom and not understanding *of* wisdom."[7]

In the continuation of his discussion, he explains this somewhat further. There are hidden realities, which we cannot penetrate with our understanding, but contemplation is directed to those things which emanate from them. "The Single Lord," mentioned in the *Sefer Yetsirah,* is, in his interpretation, "an aspect of the *En sof* that has no end at any side," and thus you cannot direct or concentrate your thoughts on it. However, since these things are all interconnected, and each attribute comes from the one which is above it "they were given to Israel for contemplation by the nearest way toward the *En sof.*"[8] At this point, there is a sentence that describes the nature of prayer: "There is no way to pray, except via the finite things by which a man ascends in his thoughts to the *En sof.*"

The words of traditional prayer are, in the final analysis, a medium to which man's thought is attached in order that he may contemplate the Divine attributes. Prayer is thus an act of contemplation. This is the new meaning of *kavvanah* in prayer.

< It is thus clear that kabbalistic prayer is not fuelled by personal motives. It is a quiet, inner activity, involving a concentration of thought. Moreover, the numerous commentaries which appear, one after another, prove that the kabbalists did not view *kavvanah* as a matter for individual choice. The mysteries of prayer are passed down from teacher to disciple, first in hints proper to those modest ones thought worthy of entering the Divine secrets, and afterward, once the fences were down, there would be a flood of words and a whole series of works would appear explaining the secrets of prayer. These compositions are, in large measure, also guides to correct kabbalistic *kavvanah*. >

It may be noted that the criticism directed against the kabbalists and their practices for hundreds of years was directed primarily against their *kavvanot* for prayer. A first echo of this controversy may be heard in the book, *Milhemet Mitzvah,* of R. Meir ben Rabbi Shimon of Narbonne, which was composed approximately in 1245.[9] This same criticism is heard in more restrained form elsewhere, such as in the responsa of Rabbi Yitzhak ben Sheshet Perfet and in the writings of Rabbi Abraham ben Rabbi Eliezer Halevi.

From this same circle we find a passage dealing with prayer which, upon close examination, indicates that it is impossible to overlook the physical aspect of prayer activity and study. "One who prays must see himself as if He (God) were speaking to him, teaching him and guiding him. He accepts His words with reverence, awe, trembling and fear, and he should bethink himself that all of those things which He teaches man are infinite." However, one must add the reservation that a man cannot reach a thought beyond the level of its source, and the analogy mentioned is that of a spring whose waters cannot rise above the level of their source. Relevant to our discussion is the following:

> "Therefore the early *hasidim* would elevate their thoughts to the source and would remember the *mizvot* and the "words" and through this remembering and this close thinking, the words would be blessed and added to . . . like a man who opens a dam (pool), and the water spreads more and more, for the clinging thought is the ever-flowing source, the pool and the fountain."[10]

In the sequel, we find the idea that the clinging of thought is the clinging spoken of in relation to prophecy.

The goal of prayer as the clinging of the soul to the Divine attributes places the individual in the center, something which is certainly a departure from the normative public-communal character of Jewish prayer. [Further on, however, we will discuss additional distinctions, from which it will become clear that the active principle, a factor beyond the redemption of the individual soul, also exists among these kabbalists and combines with mystical contemplation.] In his analysis of the meaning of *devekut* in the circles we are discussing, Scholem cites the limits which the kabbalist imposes upon himself in his path of mystical contemplation, thus "maintaining even in the most intimate communion[11] something of the mutual relations of two separate personalities."[12] Scholem sees in the kabbalistic understanding of *devekut,* as opposed to the *unio mystica* of other religions, the specific Jewish note, for Judaism preserves the distinction between the soul and the Godhead even on this high level reached in contemplation. Clinging is not union. Y. Tishbi attempts to question this unequivocal thesis of Scholem.[13] However, from a new text which was unavailable to either of these scholars, it now becomes clear that in the new flood of mystical thought and activity, individuals found a way to breach the barriers which the majority had set for themselves.

2

[It would seem that, of all the personalities known to us from this period, Rabbi Isaac of Acre was such an individual. He is the most extreme example of the individualistic, spiritualistic mystical tendency, known to us till now.[14] His path

The Meaning of Prayer in the Spanish *Kabbalah*

can clarify for us the emphases and the maximal development of this tendency which, as mentioned, was one of two primary tendencies amongst the kabbalists of this period.]

From some of the words of Rabbi Isaac of Acre which shall be quoted shortly, it is clear that he had a strong desire to attain the mystic ideal of negation of the outside world, and concentration on the secret of the Godhead to the point of immersion, that is, loss of self in the Divine stream of the *En Sof*. From this follow the contemplative practices which a man should engage in throughout the day and in prayer. According to one of the statements in *Meirat 'Eynayim* it follows that prayer is one of the stages of devotion to the upper realms, leading to the Holy Spirit. There are three stages on the path of ascension to the gift of the Holy Spirit or prophecy, and these are: cleaving, equanimity, and seclusion. Cleaving is the first step, and he gives instructions for its attainment:

> I say to the select few as well as to the many that one who desires to know the secret of connecting his soul above shall have his thought cleave to Almighty God, that, through that constant, uninterrupted thought, he will acquire the World to Come, and God will always be with him, in this world and the next. Let him place before the inner eyes of his mind the letters of the Ineffable Name, as if they were written before him in a book, in Asshurite script, and each letter shall be very large in his eyes, without limit: that is, when he places the letters of the Ineffable Name before his eyes, then the eyes of his mind shall be on them, and the thoughts of his heart, on the *En Sof*: that is, all together, the looking and the thinking, both together. This is the true clinging spoken of in the verse, "and to Him shall you cling." (Deuteronomy 10:20)[15]

These instructions are only the first step, and they are intended both for individuals and for the masses. A man needs to carry out two activities, one the visual one of "placing before the eyes of his mind the letters of the Holy Name as if written in a book." At the same time, he focuses his thought upon the *En Sof* (Infinite). This is the meaning of the verse, "I have always placed God before me" (Psalm 16:18). "When it says, 'before me,' the suggestion is . . . that his eyes and heart shall always be there, as if it were written before him." "His eyes and heart" or, in another expression, "the looking and the thinking, both together."[16]

< This instruction refers to a relatively low stage, and it is to be practiced throughout the day, but not during the time of prayer. At the time of prayer, man goes further into the world of the *Sefirot*. During the day, he stands on the level

of *Tiferet* while during prayer he is in the *Sefirot* of *Hesed* and *Gevurah* and even enters into the realm of *Binah*. As Rabbi Isaac writes in *Otsar Ha-Hayim:*

> Since you know that *Tiferet* means this world, know the intention of our Sages when they say, "A person shall always traverse the distance of two doors and afterward pray (*Berakhot* 8a)." And what, then, should a person do who prays where there are neither doors nor houses? Know then, that to the extent that a man clings to the Sole Lord, that he must always place, day and night, the *Sefirah* of *Tiferet* before his eyes . . . but just as man's thoughts are in *Tiferet* all day, when the time comes for prayer, every God-fearing man must completely purge his heart of all matters of this world—and *Tiferet,* as it is written, is the secret of this world. So that his heart and the eyes of his intellect are now attached to the supreme levels and the total unity.[17]

From the context it would appear that clinging [*devekut*] here refers to concentration of thought of a subjective kind. We are not talking about an objective event, that is, a substantial connection of man with the object to which his looking and thinking are turned. However, it is possible that the carrying out of this contemplation in the proper manner also constitutes a mystical event, for elsewhere in his writings we find instructions for the contemplative way, as follows:

> While I was reading the verse, "*Shema* Yisrael" in the morning prayers, and I was concentrating on the final letter of *Ehad* (one), I saw directly and clearly in my eyes the *kavvanah* of this verse, more clearly than in all of the words of the kabbalists which I have ever read or heard, as follows: While a person says, "*Shema* Yisrael" he shall send out his thoughts about the horizon of the globe to bind together all of the souls of Israel above in *Moshe* for the word Yisrael includes all of them together. And when he says "Elohenu". . . he shall stretch his thought from there to the pillar and to the very head."[18]

That which is described here as an instruction is described elsewhere as an unusual mystical experience of his.[19] It is not impossible that he was excited and overwhelmed from the simple success of an act of contemplation carried out in the correct manner, but it seems more likely that what is described here is not only a reaching out to meet the supreme power, but an actual encounter, for according to the stages of apprehension described further on, there is also a drawing down of the radiance from above, and this radiance is felt to descend through all the worlds to the soul of his understanding.

As has been stated, there are three stages on the path of the ascent to the highest spiritual ideal of the mystic whom we speak of here. This ideal is prophecy, and it has already been pointed out that *devekut* (cleaving) is the first step. The second is the stage of equanimity: this is found in Rabbi Bahye ibn Pakuda in a more obscure fashion, while Rabbi Isaac of Acre, quoting Rabbi Avner (?) states:

> As for the secret of equanimity, R. Avner told me that a lover of wisdom came to one of the recluses, and asked that they accept him as a recluse. The hermit said to him, "My son, you are blessed of heaven for your intention is good. However, tell me if you have acquired equanimity or not?" He said to him, "Rabbi, explain what you mean." He said, "My son, if there were two men, one of whom honours you and one of whom insults you, are they equal in your eyes or not?" He said, "by the life of your soul, I feel pleasure and enjoyment from the one who honours me, and pain from the one who insults me, but I do not desire to take revenge, nor do I bear a grudge." He said, "My son, go in peace, for as long as you have not reached that stage where you do not feel the same and are pained by insult done to you, you are not ready to have your thought connected above that you should come and practice solitude."[20]

From the continuation of this passage, it transpires that the "clinging and connecting of thought" to God, that is, the positive step of *devekut*, qualifies a man to relate with complete indifference to that which surrounds him—both to honors and insults: for these are the "wizards and charms" mentioned in Scripture.[21]

There is with him no single meaning to the concept of *devekut*, but it is clear that the description of *devekut* from the above passages is not the end of the path toward which the mystic strives. His aim is to reach complete immersion in the Godhead, to achieve the loss of selfhood while still alive. The soul which clings to the Divine secret is swallowed in it: "I went to hear the blessings at a circumcision, and I saw the mystery of 'fire eating fire' and 'all is vanity,' and fire is the secret of 'form'[22] and the Divine mystery is compared to fire, for 'the Lord your God is a consuming fire' (Deuteronomy 4:24). And the form is the soul which gives form to a lump of matter, which is the body."[23] The point of this vision is that the soul is made one with that which it apprehends. The idea, and even the formulation, are not new, but the metaphor which is offered to explain the unification of the soul with that which it apprehends is. "It and the mind are made one, like one who pours a pitcher of water into a spring, so that everything is made one." However, the most extreme passage, in content and form, of all the kabbalistic literature of all the generations which has come down to us,[24] is the following, according to which the soul is swallowed up in the deity itself, actually, in the *En Sof*:

> While still writing this, I saw the mystery of, "In the fourth year all its fruit shall be holy for praise unto the Lord" (Leviticus 19:24). That is, that the Holy One, blessed be He, commanded us to strengthen the soul of our mind over our appetites for three years, not to eat its fruits for three years which means the three worlds, so that one's intellectual soul might achieve a clinging in the fourth year: this refers to the mystery of that Divinity that is above the three worlds.[25] And in the fifth year—this refers to the *En Sof* that surrounds everything—this his soul shall cling to the *En Sof* and shall become entire and universal after being specific and separate when locked up within him. . . . And the initiated will understand—Happy is the tongue that speaks to a hearing ear."[26]

Through these words of Rabbi Isaac of Acre we learn that two reservations of the early kabbalists were here abandoned: (1) they spoke of the clinging of the thought and not of immersion or being swallowed up in Divinity; (2) thought, to them, only ascends to a certain point in the revealed Godhead. Prayer is generally not directed to the *En Sof*. Man becomes connected to something which is a sort of transition between the Infinite and the Finite ("an unbounded boundary") while here in the above passage there is a removal of all boundaries.[27] >

3

The contrast between the tendency that places the wholeness of the soul in the center, and that second tendency—which we shall here call the active or theurgic tendency and which focuses on helping the Almighty—is expressed in a very sharp way in regard to prophecy. According to the first approach, the public mission of the prophet (the mission imposed upon him by God to direct the community) in fact disturbs the wholeness of his prophecy. Every contact with the material world or with the community is a stumbling block to the intimate connection between himself and God. Therefore, the prophet longs to be freed from the yoke that has been imposed upon him. This is what Moses desired when he said, "take away my life" (Numbers 11:15); he desired to die," that is, to flee from all and every connection with the world, and not to have to bear the weight of responsibility of leadership of the people. For this responsibility caused him confusion of mind thus constituting a barrier to the clarity of his prophecy. Maimonides contends that Moses and the patriarchs reached a level on which they were able to live material lives and, at the same time, to be in continuous communion with God, as their earthly task was itself a religious function "to bring out a people which would know God and serve him."[28] Rabbi Isaac of Acre, by contrast, holds that there is a certain disturbance involved in the very mission of the prophet to the people. The seventy elders were chosen to aid Moses by reducing those barriers created by the task of teaching the people and "the confusions of the tangible" involved in the work of leadership. The hearing of the words of the people and even teaching them the word of God, whether in the form of ad hoc teachings or "a teaching for generations" is seen as an immersion in the world of "tangible" things, and in order to return to the prophetic state, he "isolates himself from them and strips from his soul the tangible things with which he had been encumbered.[29] "However, in the case of the master of all the prophets, our teacher Moses, the holy Spirit was present constantly[30] (in that ecstatic state the prophet sees his soul "standing over against him and speaking with him as a man speaks with his neighbor . . . and they say that the Holy One, blessed be He, speaks with them"[31]) it never departed from him for even one hour, except when he sank his being into the tangible world so as to hear the words of the children of Israel to guide them or to give them instructions, either ad hoc or for the generations."[32] Since these tangibles are themselves barriers between him and the Divine influence or, in his language, "Because of Moses' concern over these dividing barriers he said before God, 'please take my life and let me not see my evil' – let me not see the evil which will affect my soul." He repeatedly emphasizes that these obstacles are not "because of his wife and children, for he had already separated himself from them . . . but on account of the confusions due to the palpable concerns of leadership of the masses and the honor derived from the masses and things mundane."[33]

From here, we come to the spiritual interpretation of God's promise to Abraham of the land, as being the land of the living (i.e., the World to Come). This allegorization of the term, "the Land of Israel" also appears when he discusses the possibility of prophecy. That is, this materialistic limitation of prophecy, said to be found exclusively in the Land of Israel, is removed allegorically. The Land of Israel is not "a land of earth and soil." "Land" refers to the body. "The secret of the terms, 'Outside of the Land' and 'the Land of Israel' in this context is . . . that the former relates to the souls which dwell in the clump of earth, that is their temple of flesh and blood, and the second refers to the soul which dwells in the Land, which is the seed of Jacob, that surely dwells in the Land of Israel . . . and even if such a one dwells outside of the Land, the *Shekhinah,* which is the Land of Israel, surely dwells with him."[34] The material residue still evident here completely disappears in the dispute with the author of the *Kuzari* with regard to the possibility of prophecy for proselytes in this era.[35]

<The ideal is individual spirituality, and to the extent that there are activities directed toward the whole Jewish People—and this is found only minimally—the tendency is towards the redemption of the soul of the individual as that which is included within the collectivity of Israel. The intent in reciting *Shema Yisrael* is to unite all of the souls of the children of Israel above in Moses, our teacher (*Otzar Ha-haim,* p. 39b). The exile of the *Shekhinah*— which is one of the outstanding motifs of the theosophy of the *Zohar* is interpreted by him as the exile of the "*Shekhinah,* which dwells among the souls of the children of Israel who are in exile under the yoke of the nations of the world." While, on the other hand, the days of the Messiah are described by him as a change which will occur in the status of the souls. He knows the view of the Castilian mystics with regard to the forces of negation. With respect to the days of the Messiah, he is interested in the change which will occur in the individual side by side with the cosmic change. The opposing or negative forces will "return to the depths of the earth which is the place of their emanation." And then the soul will receive only the influence of the upper intellect "in which our soul will be dressed" (and not the influence of the opposition). The purpose of prayer is to draw power from the *En Sof* down to the last *Sefirah,* and, in the penitential prayers (*Tahanun*) "to draw into our souls the influence which we have drawn into the world" (*Otzar Ha-haim,* p. 44b). This stream of influence is the Redeemer "and that is the mystery of the verse 'and a redeemer will come to Zion,' " (Isaiah 59:20). The word Redeemer refers to the aforementioned stream of influence. "To Zion" refers to the souls of the righteous who are outstanding in Torah . . . "and to those who return from sin"—the multitude who are sunk in the tangible or material world, who walk in the darkness of the shadow of the animal soul but who have repented and purified their souls (*Otzar Ha-haim,* p. 44b). The aim of prayer is that the souls of the multitude will also receive the light of the Divine, for by means of purification, their souls are prepared that they may be "ready to receive the flow of purity and holiness" (Otzar Ha-haim, p. 44b). >

4

[While in the description of the path of Rabbi Yitzhak of Acre these matters are sharply defined and distinguished, in most of the kabbalists the two directions are found together. Moreover, had we stressed more the book, *Meirat 'Eynayim,* of Rabbi Yitzhak we could have brought examples from there of the second path, that is, the activist-theurgic direction. But we were primarily interested in posing the extremes against one another in order to clarify the general picture. However, before we turn to the second tendency and its outstanding spokesman, it would be worth saying a word about the trends discernible among the kabbalists of Gerona.

Among these kabbalists, even though the mystical basis is very strong, it is combined with several activist motifs.] In their *kavvanot* for prayer we find that at the time of prayer all things are raised to their source, in fact, even to the point of their extinction! Attention is directed toward that highest point within the Divine realm, which one can only denominate: *Ayin:* that is, "Nothing." This *Ayin* is more real than all of the beings which are in the world. On the other hand, from the viewpoint of the distinct existence of things they reach their extinction when they return to their source. Rabbi Azriel says: "One who prays must push aside every obstacle and interference and return things to their nothingness."[36] The strongest tendency in him is the longing to unite "the upper will and the lower will."[37] And yet, not only is this only a temporary negation of the lower will, but afterward the individual will become strengthened and possess magical powers: "The perfection of the lower will is not in its coming close for its own needs, but in its coming close and in being invested with desire and will to reveal the hidden equation in its secret hiding place and in this approaching, the Upper Will comes near it (i.e., the lower will) and adds strength to it and power to complete everything, even its own purposes which have nothing to do with the upper will."[36] This means that after a man has reached the highest mystical level of which he is capable he still has control over mundane things as well. The paradox here is striking. Man has approached the place of "the equation of secrecy," that is, the place in which there are no conflicts and all contradictions are annulled (the indifferent completeness). This is essentially the highest pantheistic stage of the negation of individuality, yet his private soul does not remain annulled, but afterward rules and dominates the world of experience, the world of differentiation, for the lower will can only rule in a world of distinctions, and he can at will choose and reject it. Scholem has already pointed out that the nature of *kavvanah* in the thoughts of Rabbi Azriel in this passage stresses both sides—the purely mystical and the magical side—two sides that are combined and interwoven with one another.

The two sides—the passive (returning things to their source) and the active (maintaining the independent existence of things), even though they are never cut off from their Divine source, are also found in the conclusion of the paragraph we cited above[38] and its subject is that of the *kavvanah* of prayer according to Rabbi Ezra: "Therefore the early *hasidim* used to elevate their thoughts to their source and would mention the *mizvot* and the 'words,' and through this very dense mentioning and remembering, the things were blessed and multiplied." The dense or clinging thought does not bring about a negation of the separate existence, but strengthens the separateness of things.

The things which were said in the circle of Gerona with regard to prayer reappear with regard to sacrifices. Here, the motif of *tikkun* (repair) — that is, activities and influences directed to the Divine World itself — are stressed more than in the mysteries of prayer, and yet the main thing is the process whereby the soul ascends from the world to its source — the mystical process. "And when the priest offers the sacrifice he causes his soul to cleave to the altar, and the soul rises higher and higher . . . and when his soul is attached on high, the Holy One, blessed be He, counts it as if they themselves had been offered and cling to their Creator." In the continuation we find an explanation how it is possible for the soul to ascend upward. This ascent is made possible through a pantheistic and theosophic understanding of the source of the soul. The ascent by way of the descent of the soul: "For the souls of man come to the upper altar, which comes from above to the throne, which is the throne of the Holy One, blessed be He, and from the fire it descends via the spinal column to the sign of the covenant, and from there they are included on the altar, and from there they come out and take shape in the form of the lowly body. . . . Therefore, when the soul clings up above at the beginning of its ascent (that is when it leaves the land of the living), it returns to its source, from ascent to ascent, like water which ascends to the level from which it originally issued."[39] The same process occurs in the priestly blessing.

The sacrifice is nothing other than a coming near to the point of substantial unity, between the soul and its source, which is one of the upper levels of divine revelation: "Know that the idea of the sacrifices is to elevate the lowly will in order to bring it near and unify it with the Upper Will . . . so that the lower will and the Upper Will may be one." The external act — the slaughter of animals which is seemingly a violent contradiction to the possibility of the connection of his will with the Upper Will — is explained by the kabbalist as follows: At the time of offering a sacrifice, the man is connected with his sacrifice, which is the lowest level of the will, but he elevates it and annuls it through a connection with the Upper Will. "Therefore, the lower being must offer Him his will, and through the sacrifice, which is the lowest of the low of the creatures, and which are 'his strength,' and by honoring God with his wealth, and by connecting his will with the soul of his sacrifice . . . then the lower will becomes close to the Upper Will, and it gains acceptance and completion, from the same matter with which he offered his sacrifice." However, as in prayer, this negation is not in order to attain *nirvana* — it is not the withering away of the world or a permanent abolition of his independent existence. This act of sacrifice ultimately strengthens the (material) universe. After the sacrifice, as after prayer, the world is strengthened in its distinct existence "and upper and lower worlds are blessed, and the souls of those who sacrifice, and this is the meaning of the verse: when a soul sacrifices" (Leviticus

2:1) and the flow is multiplied upon all living creatures and even upon the vegetable kingdom which requires transcendent powers to make it grow and blossom."[40]

5

[In the same way as we took the approach of Rabbi Yitzhak of Acre as representative of the spiritualist trend, we will take the model of Rabbi Meir ibn Gabbai as representative of that approach which saw the purpose of prayer as a repairing of Divine needs. As has been mentioned, this tendency is fundamentally activist. Man is called and created for the supreme purpose of setting the worlds to rights.

The possibility that man, both in his deeds in general and in prayer in particular, should bring about such repair, requires some clarification.

For our present purpose, we ought to explain two concepts: (1) the *mizvah* as a *segulah* (charm); (2) service to supply the needs of Heaven.

< Following several sayings of Rabbi Yehudah Halevi, a new understanding was developed of the notion of the "reward of *mizvot*."[41] According to this notion, there is a special power in the *mizvot* themselves, which connects and unites man with his Creator and forms his character, and this special attribute itself is the "reward of the *mizvah*." In a nonkabbalistic work of Rabbi Joseph Gikatilla, which is found in manuscript,[42] he returns to the idea that the *mizvah* is not in itself a reward to those who fulfill it, but that there is such a consequence hidden in it. He even reaches the radical conclusion that there is really no positive punishment for the violation of commandments, for the punishment is simply the withholding of the positive protection which exists in the *mizvah*.[43] In several sayings, Joseph Gikatilla repeatedly emphasizes that "there is no reward for the *mizvot* in this world." The reward is in the next world, but there is a hidden virtue contained in the *mizvah* and whoever fulfills it has the good contained within it poured upon him—not as a reward but as a natural consequence. "You have learned that the incense has hidden benefits all different from one another, even though the greatest reward is reserved for the world to come." He explicitly compares the *mizvot* to a medicine: "And one need not use the simile of fire, for there are various kinds of drugs and cures in the world, each one of which has various differing effects. How much more so the commandments of the Torah, . . . how many different consequences and virtues ought there to be in each one of them. . . ." And, in conclusion, all of the consequences of the performance of the *mizvah* "are not the reward of that same *mizvah*, but acts and virtues which stem from its own power." >

In his kabbalistic work, *Shaare Zedek,* this same idea is reiterated in somewhat more elaborate form. The magical character of the reward and punishment for *mizvot* is found there too, but there one also finds the notion that this effect is rooted in the *source* of the *mizvah* or the transgression, and that the *mizvah* influences not only those who perform it, but also affects the power which is above it, that is, its source, in the same way as a transgression brings harm to the powers above: "Do not think that these are like the punishments which are meted out to those who neglect or violate them, for this is not so, but whoever neglects one of the *mizvot* is deprived of the good which would have come of it, in the same way as one who fails to sow his field cannot reap. . . ."[44] He brings numerous other examples, all of which come to demonstrate the idea of the negation of the positive good which would have come out of the *mizvah*, for those who neglect them.

Rabbi Joseph Gikatilla did not write any systematic works, but from several of his sayings one may reach the conclusion that he sees the order of all the worlds as a stable hierarchy and while this order is maintained, there is no evil in the world. All of existence is good, as long as it stands in its proper place. Evil begins when the cosmic arrangements are upset, when the forces from below break through to those up above and put themselves in a place not suited to them. Those who are known as *zaddikim* — the saintly — put everything in its place: "Know that they are called *zaddikim*, because they place all of the inner things in their inner place, and the outer things outside, and nothing leaves its set bounds, and in this sense they are called *zaddikim*."[45]

When everything is in its place, there is an infinite continuous flow of abundance from above to below: the act of the *mizvah* straightens the lines and the connection with the world above is renewed. This is in contrast to sin "for there are sins which touch the inner palace, like sexual immorality and violation of the Sabbath . . . and there are those which touch outside of the palace, such as eating forbidden food . . . that one who violates it is as if he had disturbed the lines and broken the pipes and brought an idol into the sanctuary."[46] If sin which strikes above cuts off the connection — something which is described rather as a technical fault, the essence of prayer is that it arouses the upper powers and opens them to receive the continually flowing abundance. And this is not the result of faults in the orderly system of hierarchies. "And through the prayer which man performs below, he arouses the upper chariots and opens the channels from the 'Crown,' and they flow down to 'Majesty' (*Malkhut*) . . . and when it ('Majesty') is blessed, the power of the blessing flows upon the supplicant."[47]

< We thus find that with Gikatilla there is already a combination of the ideas: the *mizvot* as *segulah*, and the influence which the *mizvot* have upon the forces above in repairing (or damaging) the order of the universes. However, the vigorous assertion which considers our worship as needful to God and which sees a blemish in the religious stature of man whose prayer and worship

come as a response to his own need, is repeated in the *Tikkune Zohar* and *Raya Mehemna*. The new concept the kabbalists held of the *Shekhinah,* a concept very difficult to square with pure monotheism, is one of the central motifs of the *Zohar* itself. The status of the *Shekhinah* in exile and its need for repair stand out as a prominent theme, and the author of the *Zohar* speaks about this with great emotion.

In the *Tikkune Zohar* there is a tense striving for the redemption of Divinity. This tension is combined with social criticism and a different understanding of the Torah. The repeated demand of the author of the *Tikkunim* is that we not be slaves, and whoever serves God in order to receive a reward is considered a slave, and his soul belongs to a region below the "world of emanation." All the prayers and deeds of the Jew must be directed to raising the *Shekhinah* from the dust. In his view, prayer in its simple meaning is not the ideal prayer.[48]

The tendency toward active repair reaches its height in the doctrine of Rabbi Meir ibn Gabbai. For him, the mystical way is explicitly subordinated to the way of repair. A few words may be said about the theological basis of ibn Gabbai's teaching. In his view, of the two aspects of Divinity, the *En Sof* and the *Sefirot,* the *En Sof* is hinted at in neither the Talmud nor the Bible. All of the turnings of man to God and the contact of God with man have to do with the various manifestations of God—that is with the *Sefirot*. The intention of one who serves God is not directed to the *En Sof* (Infinite) but to the *Sefirot,* which are the framework of the order of the world or its constitution. Divinity, in its character of *En Sof,* is beyond the world and the law that determines the order of the world, namely, the Torah and its secrets. When the Sages ask, "What does God care whether one slaughters an animal from the neck or from the throat?" their question refers, according to ibn Gabbai, to the infinite aspect of God, the *En Sof,* to "the sole Lord, the Root of Roots, to whom nothing matters at all. And this is what these verses imply."[49] That is, all those verses which state that the righteousness of a man adds nothing to God, and that his evil does not detract, refer to this aspect of God, and not to the Divinity which is revealed. Rabbi Hayim of Volozhin formulated this in a slightly different manner: "That according to the aspect of His own Essence, which is unattached to the worlds, there is no place at all for Torah and *mizvot,* and of this it is said (Job 25:6) "If you sin, what shall you do to him' . . . for to the essence of the Master of all, blessed be He,[50] all of the deeds of man, whether good or bad, touch them not at all."[51]

The ineffable four-letter Name of God points only to the immanent aspect of Divinity which is connected to the worlds and sustains them. "Its meaning is: He Is, Was and Will Be, and He brings everything into being. That is, that He, may He be blessed, connects himself through His will to the worlds, to make them exist and to sustain them at every moment."[52] The religious acts of a man are thus directed not toward the essence of the Godhead but toward the revealed aspect of God. The Torah and *mizvot* are not commandments when viewed from the side of Him who commands but are expressions of His being.

Rabbi Hayim of Volozhin, who was involved in active dispute with the mystical tendency of Hasidism to bring man to a state of *devekut* (clinging) to God, claims that through the performance of the *mizvot* and studying Torah man becomes joined to God, and he thus interprets the saying, "The *mizvot* were not given except to purify man," as follows: "That is, that there is great need of them to refine and purify and to remove the dross from all of the powers and all the created worlds . . . that is, to connect and link all of the powers and worlds, ordered and set right according to the Divine will and intention . . . that only for this purpose did all of the *mizvot* and Holy service come about."[53] However, the source of this idea of Rabbi Hayim Volozhin is in Rabbi Meir ibn Gabbai, who says: "and this is the connection and clinging to the unique Name through the *mizvot*, for they are the thread which links those who do them with the Unique Name."[54] As noted, in Rabbi Hayim we find the thought that the commandments were given to purify us, to unite the worlds and to bring them to their full state of repair and harmony. As a result of this, "the House of Israel, the chosen people are united with the Unique Name as his portion and inheritance," according to Rabbi Hayim. Everything is subjected to this tendency of setting to rights—applied both to the individual and the collective.

However, according to these views also prayer involves an act of *devekut* for, according to one interpretation, "the language of *tefillah* (prayer) is a union of the form of the beseecher with the One besought, so as to receive an abundant flow of blessings from Him, in the secret of the sacrifices." But the highest goal is not *devekut*. If there are those Sages who see in the *mizvot* a charm which brings about the immortality of the soul and *devekut*, even in this world, then Ibn Gabbai holds that all these are means simply to the repair of the "Glory" of God. The meaning of this repair is the putting to rights of the revealed side of the Divine world, that which is manifested in the world "because immortality and the meriting of the life of the world to come is not the final purpose derived from the Torah and the *mizvot*, but this end has another end, more essential, higher, and more elevated, to which the survival of the soul and the life of the life to come are merely contingent."[55]

Man is created, in the example above, so that he may be capable of unifying, that is, to bring about harmony and completion in the Divine world. *Devekut* is merely an aspect of unification. "And it was said, 'to Him shall you cleave,' to hint that the thought should be pure, free of anything furtive, clinging above with a continuous clinging, vigorous to unite the branches with their root, without any separation."[56] This idea stands out even more in the words of Ibn

Gabbai, if we compare his words to his source, namely, the teachings of Rabbi Ezra. Rabbi Ezra also interprets *Avodah* as *kavosh* (overpower), except that for him the aim is to "crush" from it all other thoughts, while in Ibn Gabbai there is a slight change and, in his view, the thought is clinging in order to repair the world above. >

Ibn Gabbai does not content himself with the thought that man's service is for the needs of God. A man who worships correctly is not allowed to include himself in his requests, "for the complete servant, who is faithful, is he who loves God with a continuous love. Moreover, he must intend with his service to unite the great Name to its Glory: he must have no intention in this unification for any of his own needs, at all, whether those of the body or of the soul. . . . For all of the requests and needs come from the mundane side, as is known to the wise of heart, and anyone who intends them and asks for them during prayer, which is the hour of communion, brings profane things into the Temple court, and defiles the Holy Temple."[57] [We may conclude that in man's prayer which has intent for his own needs there is a measure of idol worship, and one who asks also for himself "combines himself to the Almighty."

It seems clear what is meant by prayer and what its character is in the theurgic sense of putting the world to rights. The formulations of Ibn Gabbai, who composed his works after the Expulsion from Spain, are perhaps more extreme than those of other kabbalists who took this line. Perhaps the intense desire for Redemption left its imprint here and led to extreme, one-sided expressions, or perhaps it was due to something in his personality; in any event, his writings call for further study.

The way that we have taken was meant to stress the principal approaches to this subject, which is central in *Kabbalah,* and to sketch a few lines out of a larger canvas. It is proper to point out that among most of the kabbalists these two directions are intermingled, and they are not as unequivocal as would appear in our discussion. There is a vast literature in our possession in which nuances of this subject, found expression both in the period which has been the subject of our discussion, as also in the *Kabbalah* of Safed, and its various offshoots. Much is therefore left for further study.]

Notes

1. On the other hand, the kabbalists in some communities did have special places to gather for prayer, as in the later hasidic "klaus."

2. A symbol rich in associations related to prayer, found in *Tikkune Zohar* and *Raya Mehemna*.

3. See *Reshit Hakabbala"* (Jerusalem: 1947–1948), pp. 93–98, 103–104, 114–118, 141f, and more; *Monatsschrifr für Geschichte und Wissenschaft des Judentums* vol. 78 (1934), s. pp. 492–518.

4. In his commentary on *The Book of Creation.* See G. Scholem, *The Kabbala in Provence* (Jerusalem: 1963), appendix, p. 3.

5. That is, the foundation of contemplation is in the sphere called "Wisdom."

6. Here "comes from" refers to the possibility of grasping; the possibility of grasping the characteristics of "Wisdom" comes gradually from the lower level of "Understanding."

7. Ibid., p. 6. In other words, it is impossible to contemplate and to grasp the essence of "Wisdom."

8. One achieves contemplation of higher attributes through previously understood ones.

9. See G. Scholem, *A New Document in the History of the Early Kabbala, Sefer Bialik* (Tel Aviv: 1933–1934), pp. 148–150.

10. Y. Tishbi, ed., *Commentary on the Aggada by R. Azriel* (Jerusalem: 1944–1945), pp. 39–40.

11. That is, in the intimate bond between the contemplating soul and the Divine power.

12. "Reshit Hakabbala" (Jerusalem: 1947–1948), p. 115.

13. "Mishnat Hazohar," vol. 2 (Jerusalem: 1961), pp. 252f, 292–293.

14. More information about him may be found in E. Gottlieb, "Ha-aroth, Deveikut u-Nevua be-Sefer Otzar Ha-Haim Le-Rabbi Yitzhak de-me-Ácco" in the *Proceedings of the Fourth World Congress for Jewish Studies,* vol II, (Jerusalem 1968–1969), pp. 327–334.

15. Ms. Munich 17, Portion "Ekev," p. 140a.

16. Ibid.

17. *Otzar Ha-haim* (Moscow), Ginsburg ms., 775 p. 129 a–b. Cf. *Me-irat Einaim,* p. 140b.

18. *Otzar Ha-haim,* p. 40 a–b.

19. Ibid., 100a.

20. *Me-irat Einaim,* ibid., p. 140b.

21. Ibid.: "Notice that when God was with Saul, and Saul's thought was bound to God, Saul removed witchcraft from the land while being totally unaware of those who mocked him when Israel crowned him king. When the situation was reversed he sought out a witch."

22. The numerical value of the Hebrew letters of the word *esh* (fire) equals that of *tsurah* (form).

23. *Otzar Ha-haim,* p. 111a.

24. A parallel statement may be found only in Y. P. Schneerson, *H. Gravitser,* pts. 1 and 2 (Tel Aviv: 1954–1955).

25. That is, in the world of the *Sefirot,* which is the self-revealing Divinity.

26. *Otzar Ha-haim,* p. 112b.

27. It would be incorrect to interpret this as a reference to the state after death, for in the notes of the Oxford manuscript (Bodley: 1911) of this work it states "while still imprisoned in it." Cf. also what he writes after speaking of the *devekut* of Abraham and of Moses: "Now, my son attempt to see the upper light, for I have surely brought you in to the sea which encompasses the world . . . and you shall see your world while you are alive, thus fulfilling while your soul is in its sanctuary all our words; for if you do so your soul will produce a divine light and will cling to it both while in its sanctuary and after leaving it. . . ." (Ibid., p. 161b).

28. *Guide for the Perplexed*, pt. 3, chap. 51.

29. *Otzar Ha-haim*, p. 163a.

30. This is in contrast with other prophets. "The soul stands and speaks . . . ," that is, we have here an ecstatic state that takes no account of the crowd of people facing the prophet.

31. *Otzar Ha-haim*, p. 163a.

32. Ibid.

33. Ibid., p. 161a.

34. Ibid., p. 94 a.

35. Ibid., p. 78a.

36. Cf. G. Scholem, *New Fragments of the Writings of R. Azriel from Gerona* (Hebrew), Memorial Volume for A. Gulack and S. Klein (Jerusalem: 1942), p. 215.

37. *Sha-ar Ha-kavannah*, R. Azriel, ed. G. Scholem, *Der Begriff der Kawwana in der alten Kabbala*, MGWJ, vol. 78 (1934), s. p. 511 sq., and *Reshit Ha-Kabbala* (Jerusalem: 1948), p. 143f.

38. Cf. note 10 above.

39. *Perush ha-agadot*, R. Azriel, p. 40.

40. On the concept of sacrifices in the Gerona circle, and on writings on this matter by members of the circle see G. Scholem, *Reshit Ha-kabbala*, p. 141–2; Y. Tishbi, *Mishnat Hazohar* 2: 197–198.

41. Cf., for example, *The Book of the Kuzari*, art. 2, 50; art. 3, 8 (". . . the *hasid* also links his thought to the Divine through various symbols, namely, the *mizvot* . . . which is an irrefutable proof the Divine can have connection with created beings, supervision over them, and knowledge of their actions"); ibid., 19. (Although it would be proper to consider this issue, and to study the writings of the fourteenth and fifteenth century Spanish Sages on this matter, we shall not do so now for lack of space.)

42. *Sefer Klalei Ha-mitzvot*, ms.

43. R. Shem Tov b. Shem Tov accused Maimonides of just this idea.

44. *Shaarei Tzedek* (Cracow: 1880–1881), p. 12b.

45. Ibid.

46. Ibid.

47. Ibid., p. 4b.

48. On the concepts of prayer and *mizvot* in the *Zohar*, in *Tikkune Zohar*, and *Raya Mahemna*, see, for example Y. Tishbi, *Mishnat Hazohar* vol. 2 (Jerusalem: 1961), pp. 261–268, 431–442. Items of immediate interest on *Tikkunei Zohar* may also be found in his unpublished Hebrew work on prayer.

49. *Avodat Ha-kodesh,* pt. 2, chap. 3 (Lemberg 1857–1858), p. 33b.
50. The earlier teachers were insistent on not writing "Blessed be He" in relation to the *En Sof.*
51. *Nefesh Ha-haim* (Vilna: 1874), p. 21a.
52. Ibid., p. 20b.
53. Ibid., p. 21b.
54. *Avodat Ha-kodesh,* ibid., p. 27a.
55. Ibid., chap. 5, p. 36a.
56. Ibid., chap. 6, p. 36b.
57. Ibid.

11
The Idea of Prayer in Franz Rosenzweig's "Star of Redemption"

Moshe Schwartz

Introduction

Our discussions about prayer have centered on two topics: the nature, character, and purpose of prayer; and the crisis of prayer in our time. These two topics are, of course, interrelated, so that one cannot discuss the crisis of prayer without discussing its nature. There is no doubt that Rabbi Steinsaltz is correct in maintaining (see below, "Education for Prayer"), that it is impossible to separate prayer from the theological affirmations which condition it. Jewish prayer is a function of Jewish faith. But is a sense of the presence of God and the expectation of miracle a sufficient foundation for the relation between prayer and Judaism? This may be doubted! Do not the theological premises go far beyond these general premises common to all the historical religions? Rosenzweig's formulations in the matter of prayer point to the unique theological premises of Jewish prayer and may thus help us further.

Moreover, nostalgia has been suggested here as an emotional and spiritual dimension (cf. Dov Sadan, above). Outside of the framework of the nostalgic feelings of the man who prays today is left only a critical standpoint. Yet the doubt arises whether prayer can be limited to the secondary level of naivete, after the fashion of the sentimental poetic style of Schiller. In this context, as well, Rosenzweig has something to teach us.

As for the problem of the crisis of prayer and its renewal, it should be pointed out that among all the reasons Professor Heinemann listed for the lack of fluidity in contemporary prayer, he did not mention any actual theological considerations. And yet, could it not be that the theological problems formulated in so sharp a manner by many theologians today and which bring into question the very possibility of prayer as an individual act of petition—could these not have led to a new emphasis on communal prayer? If this is so, communal prayer should perhaps be given greater weight in the discussion of the relevance of prayer today. In this context, as well, Rosenzweig's theology of prayer is extremely pertinent.

But before going on to Rosenzweig, a word should be said about the basic difference between the treatment of prayer by medieval philosophers and its treatment by contemporaries. In the Middle Ages, the halakhic stature of prayer served as a point of departure for discussion. The various attempts to explain the nature of prayer and its meaning never departed from the search for reasons and justifications. It was a "restorative" activity (to use Professor Schweid's expression), not only in the thematic sense, but in terms of method. True it is that within the framework of the discussion of prayer, questions were asked of considerable metaphysical and ethical importance, such as the well-known dilemma of Josef Albo as to the reconciliation of the idea of prayer with Divine Providence,[1] or that of the unity of awareness and religious practice, discussed by the *Haver* in Halevi's Kuzari.[2] But in all these discussions, prayer is not dealt with as such, apart from its explicit halakhic framework, and far less is there any attempt at a phenomenological description of the types of prayer. No attention is paid to the interrelationships among them and to the level of their importance. In brief, in medieval philosophy a structure of theology is constructed around prayer, but a theology of prayer itself is lacking.

Leo Strauss's characterization of medieval Jewish thought as a speculative activity, guided by Divine law,[3] holds fully with respect to prayer as well. As against this, modern thought freed itself from such dependence and has become an autonomous spiritual activity. The authority of revelation has ceased to be binding. This change has also affected the treatment of prayer by modern thinkers. The autonomous approach to prayer accounts for the description of it as a spiritual phenomenon which has broader philosophical bearings.

Typical of the spiritual situation of modern Jewish thought in this respect is Hermann Cohen's opening of his discussion of prayer with the postulate that prayer is not one of the 613 commandments "but flows and passes through the entire system, in such a manner that it enlightens the entire content of the service of God."[4] Prayer is understood not only as "the special form of monotheism"; it also has a transformative power, which raises man to the level of higher understanding. "He who knows how to pray is not enslaved to superstition and egotism, which only imitate the degenerate form of worship. The man capable of real prayer, finds his worldly fears and earthly burdens set aside and is raised towards the Infinite."[5] Prayer here is not a restorative act, as with Halevi, nor is it analogous to *teshuvah* (repentance) as in Albo's thought, but it is a transformative act, which enables man to ascend from his lower existential level to one as yet unexperienced by him where he may attain a communion with God. Together with this, the dialectic factor stands out in Cohen, as in his earlier metaphysical works: prayer, insofar as it is an expression of man's longing for God, can only be the emotional, "psychological" aspect of a God-Man relationship which is fundamentally rational and logical.[6]

Essentially, Hermann Cohen remained loyal to the notion of a rational structure of reality, and for this reason he was unable to recognize the particular ontological character of prayer as defined in the thought of Rosenzweig.

Rosenzweig's general framework of thought regarding prayer is parallel to that of Cohen. In the *Star of Redemption* prayer is understood as "the content of the worship of God." It is not one of the *mizvot* of the Torah, but is taken out of the context of *halakhah* and treated as a phenomenon sui generis. Nevertheless, despite this resemblance between Rosenzweig and Cohen, they differ in regard to the nature and purpose of prayer. If, in Cohen, we spoke of the transformative character of prayer, in Rosenzweig we would be justified in speaking of its anticipatory power. The essence of prayer, according to Rosenzweig, is not in the elevating of man from a lower to a higher existential condition, but in its being an act which makes possible the realization, in advance, of that state of affairs which constitutes the ultimate purpose of man's existence. Prayer as an anticipatory force in this sense in the life of man is a fundamental idea in Rosenzweig's thinking.

New Thought and Prayer as an Anticipatory Act

Rosenzweig's thought, in contrast to that of Hermann Cohen, is essentially grammatical. Each individual chapter of prayer, and prayer as a whole, is a language articulated at a particular moment of time. The organic connection between time and language is evidenced by the three forms of language—

narrative, dialogue, and chorus—and by the three tenses: past, present, and future.

Friedrich Schelling emphasized the unique connection between time and language and in a late teaching he declared: "The past exists in knowledge, the present in awareness, the future in prayer. That which is known you tell, that which you recognize you describe, that which you anticipate you prophesy."[7] Rosenzweig presents this as the basis of his doctrine. His general idea is that the philosophical understanding of reality requires the description of reality in its variety. And completeness is given to a description only by the connection between various forms of knowledge and their status and standpoint in time.

There is no better way of defining reality as a fixed object inherited from the past and set before us, than the logical-conceptual way. We know the past, not because we have no other means of relating to reality, but because the vehicle of this knowledge, the conceptual category, does not allow us any other form of understanding of reality. The second vehicle of knowledge—speech or dialogue—recognizes reality not as a set, fixed given, but as a presence, a constant event, a dynamic and constantly renewed process of Being. In this form of awareness there is an "age equivalence" between the known and the knower: "As act, creation was founded, and as result it climaxed, in the past. [But] to this tense there here corresponds in dominant fashion the present. Revelation is of the present, indeed it is being-present itself."[8] Its unique expression is the commandment (rather than the experience), and in this it remains within the category of I-Thou dialogue.

Prayer, which is an explicitly liturgical act, presents to our awareness the supreme world where redemption is achieved. As against the last mentioned form of knowledge, that is, the revelatory, "the structures of liturgy do not possess this same simultaneity . . . rather they anticipate. They take something future and turn it into a Today." "Prayer is the force which lifts over the 'threshold.' From out the mutely created mystery of the self-growth of life and the speech-endowed miracle of love, it leads to the silent enlightenment of the completely fulfilling end."[9]

In prayer, there is thus a certain direction toward a reality which has not yet eventuated. The main purpose is the anticipation of the future and its transformation into "today." Prayer has a remarkable representational power, insofar as it is "the whispered anticipation of a world dawning in the silence of the future."

In Rosenzweig's way of understanding prayer, the prophetic is combined with the mystical approach. Heiler, in his book on prayer, characterizes the difference between mystical prayer and prophecy by saying that in mystical prayer the essential thing is individual illumination; there is an intoxicating, ecstatic inwardness, while in prophetic prayer, what stands out is the explicitly social factor. It is concerned specifically not with individual salvation, but with the perfecting of the kingdom of heaven on earth.[10] In Rosenzweig's approach, one can find a blend of the prophetic and the mystical motifs. On the one hand we are told that for prayer "everything comes down to this in the final analysis: is the future of the Kingdom accelerated by it or delayed?"[11] Every prayer, even the petition of the individual, cries out, in the final analysis, for the coming of the Kingdom, because the spiritual root of prayer is the turning of man towards that which has not yet found its realization in life. "One who supplicates for what is past, engages in false prayer," says the Talmud. The face of the true man of prayer is turned toward the future. A man who cannot free himself from his ego, who is entirely confined within the four ells of his own selfhood, lacks the ability to pray truly. The loss of the power to pray is a sign of separation from both the Divine and human "world order." In this, Rosenzweig is loyal to the prophetic view of prayer.

On the other hand, Rosenzweig stresses that since "the suppliant is fixed to the fixed point of his personality . . . this farthest goal which is common to all appears behind the foreground of a wholly personal perspective." The man who desires Divine enlightenment, while his prayer is that of the individual lonely soul, cannot leave the singleness of his perspective. He can see the Divine world order only from his own personal point of view. And yet "His prayer [is not free] from the compulsion to establish his own world-order."[12]

This opposition between the extreme subjectivity of the lonely soul, mystical in nature, and the clearly visualized "infinite objectivity," the opposition between freedom of choice and necessity, is the theological problem of prayer. Rosenzweig propounds an explicit formulation of the problem in the *Star* as follows: "If prayer in essence is no more than prayer for enlightenment, if enlightenment is, consequently, the most that can accrue to the suppliant through the power of prayer, how then is prayer able to intervene in the course of events? Enlightenment, after all, appears to accrue only to the suppliant; his are the eyes that are enlightened. Of what concern is that to the world?"[13]

Rosenzweig's formulation of the problem of prayer clearly testifies to a radical revaluation of the known dichotomy in the philosophical literature of prayer. The main source of spiritual confusion in this area stems from the intellectual difficulty rooted in the two implicit assumptions regarding the reason and purpose of prayer: one is that the main task of prayer is to influence the will or decree of God; the second is that prayer comes to influence the status of the one praying. It would seem that one would need to make an unequivocal decision in favor of one of these two options. Thus, for example, Albo, the author of the *Ikkarim,* thinks that prayer, like *teshuvah,* possesses the power to change decrees which have already been decreed on a man: "When any evil is decreed against a man, this is decreed when he is on a given level of evil and when his level or state changes, then the decree changes also, for good or evil."[14] Rabbi Kook, on the other hand, emphasizes the opposite viewpoint, in placing the emphasis on prayer as a value in itself: "Prayer does not desire to change anything within the Divinity, which is eternal and unchangeable, but to enable the soul to rise, with all its inconstancy . . . to the heights of God. . . . Prayer must be free of any thought of changing the will or influencing the laws of Him, blessed be He . . . for this is a false idea of God, and also undermines our human perfection. . . . Prayer is a wondrous law that the Holy One, blessed be He, instituted in order to perfect His creatures and particularly for the sake of their ethical completion."[15]

Between these two stances, which are diametrically opposed to one another—one stressing prayer as having value in itself, "free of any thought of changing the Divine will," and the other stressing that prayer is an event capable of changing the Divine will—Rosenzweig propounds a third way, from which the sharpness of this dichotomy is removed. Prayer is of value in itself, insofar as it is based upon the direct, immediate needs of man. But, according to its ideal end, prayer is an event of cosmic significance, as it is directed to the elevation of man's requests from the existential-historic dimension to the trans-historic realm of the redeemed world. How radical Rosenzweig's approach is to the transformative power of prayer may be learned from the explanation he appends to Rabbi Yehudah Halevi's poem, *Eloha, Mishkenotekha Yedidot:*

> O God, your dwelling-places are dear
> And your nearness seen, and not in a vision,
> Bring me in my dream to the sanctuary of God,
> And I will sing its precious service,
> And the burnt-offering, and its meal and libation.
> And around, heavy pillars of smoke
> And I will be pleased to hear the Levites sing
> On their secrets of the Temple-worship.
> I awake, and I am with You still,
> And I give praise, and to You praise is fitting.

Rosenzweig interprets the poem as the request of the poet for the renewal of sacrifices, and notes that this request is most difficult, because the difference between set prayer, and voluntary and spontaneous prayer, is that the latter has its source in natural, human need, and expresses immediate needs, while the former comes to educate man and to accustom him to the idea that his basic existence is not limited by the routine of everyday. The reference is primarily to those prayers recited for the establishment of God's kingdom on earth, which are not aimed at all at our relief from the pressure of ordinary life. Every man is connected to natural life in such a manner that he has sufficient reason to pour out petitions before his Creator to change his lot, but he will tend to push away any real radical change. Against this, in the Days of the Messiah, when the Kingdom of the Almighty comes, a radical change is to be expected, which will put an end to all the many-sided historical processes, to their confusion and indecisiveness. It is up to us, writes Rosenzweig, to learn to ask in our prayers for a radical change, even though such prayer entails enormous psychological and spiritual difficulties. The poet is aware of this dual aspect in the stance of the one praying when he says: "I awake, and I am with You still, And I give praise, and to You praise is fitting." The anticipation, in which Rosenzweig sees the essence of prayer, is thus based on the tension between the sense of the close relationship between man and God on the one hand, and the inevitable awakening and estrangement on the other. Prayer in itself is a giving thanks and praise for the continual presence of God.

The various kinds of prayer and their forms of expression arise, necessarily, out of the inevitable tension between the reality of man as he is and that of the redeemed world.

Kinds of Prayer and Their Different Levels

The experience of tension, according to Rosenzweig, creates a distinction among different levels of prayer. In his attempt to classify he distinguishes between the prayer of the believer and the prayer of (a) the sinner, (b) the fanatic, or the self-deceived, or (c) the nonbeliever. This division seemingly corresponds to the accepted division between public prayer and private prayer; the last three are included in the category of personal prayer while the former, which is alone considered true prayer, corresponds to communal prayer.

What is the meaning of this division and how does Rosenzweig arrive at it? Rosenzweig's profoundly subtle approach to prayer can be discovered only through an examination of its various nuances.

Rabbi Yehudah Halevi, in attempting to provide a basis for the preference of communal prayer over private prayer, brings, as the first reason, "that the community does not pray for anything which would bring harm to individuals, while it is possible that an individual might pray for something which would bring harm to other individuals, just as those others might pray for something that would harm him."[16] Rosenzweig also, in speaking of the prayer of the sinner, counts the evil involved in egotistic prayer. But, in his opinion, the sin does not lie in the fact that the request is sinful, for "there is no plea which on the basis of content it is sinful to utter. By creating the supplicant as individual, God has already fulfilled his prayer before it is uttered, even as criminal a prayer, say, as that for the death of another: it is after all true already without any prayer that the other must die."[17]

True, Rosenzweig agrees with Halevi that "one of the conditions of prayer being accepted is that it be a prayer to bring benefit to the world, and not to cause harm in any manner."[18] But, in keeping with his view of the existential nature of man, he is not able to hold that the requirement regarding "that which brings benefit to the world" is a sufficient reason for disparaging the importance of individual prayer. The sin in individual prayer is to be seen primarily as error and confusion. "Rather than treating this content as already fulfilled and therefore thanking God for his own-being . . . instead, [he] requests it and thus treats it as something as yet unfulfilled."[19] The order of the world is confused in such a prayer. Instead of praying for that which man ought to pray for—namely, the coming of the Kingdom—the prayer of the sinner becomes a factor which delays this. It misses the essence of prayer, in imposing upon the liturgical language of prayer a way of speaking which is fundamentally foreign to it. This is like a poet who expresses in poetic language ideas more properly framed in conceptual language.

The exact opposite of the prayer of the sinner is that of the fanatic or the self-deceived. "He seeks to capture the kingdom forcibly at the point which the searchlight of his prayer shows as the next one, but which never is closer than next-but-one."[20] This, too, does not belong to the category of "a time of favour," for he has not the power to realize the central goal which is: "to take something future, and turn it into a Today."[21]

From these criticisms directed against the fanatic or self-deceived, it is clear that to Rosenzweig prayer cannot accomplish its objective so long as it is not based on a special time-dimension. This is the focus of Rosenzweig's doctrine of prayer. For him, there is a central role for the various modifications of the notion of time: "Time," "eternity," "moment," "hour," "future," and "present." Prayer establishes a new world-order in freeing man from his daily existence, which can be described by the term "moment." The nature of momentary time is constant change, and in this process of rapid change there is no permanence or fixity—what the Germans call *Stunde* (hour) from the verb, *stehen* (to stand).

We find, then, that the value of prayer is to be understood in terms of the connection between the present and the future. The uniqueness of every prayer, whether that of the fanatic, the unbeliever, or the believer, is in the seriousness of its turning towards the future. Rosenzweig's words, that "the searchlight of prayer illuminates for each only that which it illuminates for all"[22] apply to all types of prayer, including those of the sinner. Without this forward-looking gesture, this hope for illumination, prayer does not exist in its true form. The difference between the various types of prayer is only in their depth and power. As mentioned, the prayers of the sinner and of the self-deceived confound the correct order of the world, whether through excessive emphasis on the status of the I (the prayer of the sinner) or on the status of the world (fanatical or self-deceived prayer); in either case the correct relationship between present and future is broken, and as a result the wholeness of the "hour" as "an hour of favour" is impaired.

Rosenzweig's view of prayer is clarified further with the aid of the third type of prayer, the prayer of the scoffer and, specifically, that of Goethe. Rosenzweig sees in Goethe one of the great spiritual figures in history, and a new phenomenon for the Christian world. The development of religious awareness in Goethe's writings reaches a high level in which one can see the true fulfillment of the Christian vision. Goethe is "the first Christian according to Christ, that is, the first complete Man."[23]

What is the basis for such an extraordinary estimation? Rosenzweig explains this in a short sentence: "This is a great moment in human history: for the first time man thus lifts his hands in prayer to his own fate."[24] Christianity in its two historical embodiments, the Church of Peter and the faith of Paul, set up a division between man and the world. The Church, being a universal religion, a "world kingdom," spread its protection over the world and, in so doing, denied to man the possibility of remaining alone with his soul. It made its faithful used to the way of prayer of the fanatic: "Whatever he may do, man is now fused into the whole world, the fate of his act indissolubly tied up with the fate of all the world."[25] In the Pauline faith (specifically that of the Lutheran Church), on the other hand, a rift is created between man and the other side of his destiny. This faith came to free the soul "from all fences and walls, and it lived in the unconditional."[26] Luther's Reformation, which placed faith alone as its highest principle, encouraged the illusion that through the power of personal faith "man will be capable of truly achieving everything." However, it forgot the body, so that "the world had escaped it."

Goethe succeeded in correcting the faults which appeared in the historical forms of Christianity. He prays that Supreme Fortune should establish the work of his hands, that he may himself complete it."[27] Goethe's form of prayer contains a radical innovation in contrast to the accepted prayers of Christianity, for here the individual prays for the fulfillment of his destiny, in the hope that "whatever comes should merge in his life, that he be privileged to offer up all in the sanctuary of his own fate, own as well as alien, alien as well as own, all."[28]

Whoever prays in this fashion desires not only to guard his possessions, but seeks to magnify his own poor existence to the condition of eternity. One can therefore discover in the Goethean prayer the correct *structure* of every true prayer, that is, anticipation of the perfected Being, not in an arbitrary fashion but through the confirming of the link connecting Man and the World.

The Prayer of the Believer

Everything up to this point has been a background to the understanding of the true character of prayer. Goethe's prayer, despite its importance for a true understanding of our subject, is only a transition to "the prayer of Moses, our teacher," which is the model of all true prayer. What is the difference between Goethe's "Establish, Supreme joy, the works of my hands that I may complete them" and "A Prayer of Moses, the man of God . . . May the pleasantness of the Lord our God be upon us and may the work of our hands be established upon us, and may he establish the work of our hands"? We can clarify the difference by means of the distinction in the *Midrash* (*Devarim Rabbah* 80:2), between prayer which is answered when it is pronounced, and prayer which is answered even before it is pronounced. "There is prayer which is answered when it is pronounced. From whom does one learn this? From David, of whom it is said, 'And my prayer to you, O God, may it be in an acceptable time' (Psalm 69:14), and there is a prayer which, before it is uttered, is answered by the Holy One, blessed be He, as is said, 'Before they call, I answer them' " (Isaiah 65:24).

It is possible to say that the distinction between the prayer of the unbeliever and that of the believer is that the one is answered in "due time" and the other is answered before it is uttered. The prayer of the heretic is for an "acceptable time" – it is always uttered "in its time." The man of little faith does not wish to hasten the end, to bring eternity close and make it "today." This is prayer which is answered in its time, for its accomplishment is immediate. The individual prays for the full achievement of his own fortune, of that which is allotted to him, and thus, despite his prayer for completeness, he remains in his isolation.

Not so the prayer of the believer. It is not recited, as the prayer of the heretic, on behalf of the fortunes of the individual, that is, it speaks of prospering the work, "not of my hands or thine or his, but of *our* hands, so that He, (not I) complete it."[29] The prayer of the believer is the true religious act of devotion, because it stands on one and only one request: "The perfection of the world in the Kingdom of the Almighty." Not that other prayers of a more immediate nature are completely pushed aside, but that these only come as an annex to the main request wherein the needs of the individual and those of the general body of worshippers are inseparably joined together: "Only the end of days is common to all. The searchlight of prayer illuminates for each only that which it illuminates for all, only the farthest: the kingdom."[30]

As said above, in commenting on a poem of Yehudah Halevi, true prayer demands a real change in man's life. This demand can only be fulfilled in communal prayer, for "The prayer of the congregation [which] is addressed not to the personal fate but directly to the Eternal . . . looks beyond everything individual to the Universal and to it alone. With a mighty grip it snatches the eternal into the moment, and endows the individual piece of life, which at this moment has become wholly alive in the nonbelieving prayer, with the spark of eternal life, brought down from on high."[31] From here, it follows that the proper prayer of the believer is the request that "this hour be an hour of Grace and Mercy before You." In this verse, all of the demands of true prayer are condensed, the essence of prayer being anticipation. The "hour" has eternal value, and we hope in our prayers for the redemptive advent of the eternal into time."[32]

This hope is false if it includes only a request for "an hour of grace," for prayer is not true prayer if "it does not awaken the human in man." Prayer is an act which always rises out of a specific human situation, and it must be said "from the foreground of a wholly human perspective."[33] Prayer remains fanatical if it does not express the stature of the "lonely soul" and if it is not an expression of "a time of Grace," in the sense of "the fate of the (individual) action as connected with the fate of the entire world"—as is said of Goethe's prayer. At the same time the completion of prayer and its wholeness require that the "hour" of prayer be "an hour of Mercy"—that is, that it anticipate that situation of spiritual completeness, putting an end to the harsh rule of history and the rift in human relations which it entails.

Proper prayer is founded upon the unavoidable tension between the entreaty for a radical change, the desire for the millennium, and the strong desire to see immediate reality, of which one is neither able nor willing to be deprived. A remarkable expression of this double perspective, which is the sufficient reason for man's turning to God, is found in a poem of Uri Zvi Greenberg:

> I am astonished if there is one who rejoices
> and does not weep to remember the End.
> I am astonished if there is one who groans
> and does not rejoice in the spreading of life.
> For each moment is beyond price.
> Every hour of evening and morning
> in the cycle of the last things
> upon the earth.
> [From *Anacreon at the Pole of Despondency*]

He who does not recognize the necessary combination of petition and praise, individual and communal prayer, does not know the true nature of prayer. In Judaism, this awareness attains its full expression in the coupling of individual prayer and collective prayer; in the clear preference for communal prayer over that of the individual; and last of all—in the nature of "the constant awareness of God through all the days of the year," that is, in the liturgy of the

Jewish festivals, which came into being as a way of anticipating an ideal order of reality and of "bringing the redemptive power of eternity into the realm of time."

Concluding Note

The idea of prayer in the thought of Franz Rosenzweig suggests various thoughts about the reason for the crisis of prayer in our own day.

What emerges from this analysis is that the gates of every true prayer are open in two directions—petition and praise, that is, the natural impulse within man for the fulfillment of his own needs, and the pure longing for the fulfillment of that nonimmediate need which is not within the grasp of any man. This latter alone serves to bring about spiritual growth, and establish a new reality, in which the spirit of man can find its full completion.

The circumstances in which we live here and now with the rise of the State of Israel and the renewal of our political independence do not in any way detract from the basic assumptions of the theology of prayer. But we must be conscious of the psychological and spiritual difficulties which we face when we seek the meaning of the religious changes which have come about together with the first signs of the fulfillment of our age-old dream. Is not the great turning point which has occurred in the life of the Jew in the last generation also a dangerous temptation to remake our prayers on the model of the prayers of the sinner or of the self-deceived? Are we as capable, as those who lived in previous generations of "weeping when we remember the end"— in the words of the poet? Does the joy which fills the hearts of the sons returning to the borders of their promised land not perhaps serve to obscure the "dream of the Sanctuary of God," and the "precious songs of the service"—that is, the idea of worship and sacrifice as an unattained need, as the "remembrance of the latter days"? Do not those moments in history, which come into existence through the power of our actions, and which are not seen as "patriarchal nightmares" but as elevated visions of fulfillment—do not they show that we have slackened in the attempt to live "each hour of evening and morning in the cycle of the End"? Such questions arise naturally out of a consideration of Rosenzweig's theology of prayer.

Notes

1. "That which has brought people to have doubts about prayer . . . is that they say there is an unavoidable dilemma. Either it has been divinely ordained that a certain good should come to a certain person or it has not been so ordained; if it has been ordained then prayer is superfluous, and if it has not been ordained then how could prayer effect a

change in the Divine will to ordain a certain good after it had not been ordained, since God does not change from willing to not willing or vice versa." Y. Albo, *Sefer Ha-Ikkarim* 4, chap. 18.

2. "Afterward the *hasid* arranges the fundamental principles that complete Jewish faith . . . ," R. Judah Halevi, *The Kuzari*, art. 3, 17.

3. Cf. Leo Strauss, *Philosophie und Gesetz* (Berlin: 1935), s. pp. 68–86.

4. Hermann Cohen, "Dat Ha-tevuna Mi-mekorot Ha-yahadut" (Jerusalem: 1971–1972), p. 396.

5. Ibid., p. 422.

6. Ibid., p. 398.

7. In the original; "Das Vergangene wird gewusst, das Gegetwartige erkannt, das Zukunftige wird geahndet. Das Gewusste wird erzahlt, das Erkannte wird dargestellt, das Geahndete wird geweissagt." F. W. Schelling, "Die Weltalter, Schellings Werke," *Munchner Jubileumsdruck*, Bd. IV. s. p. 575.

8. F. Rosenzweig, *The Star of Redemption*, trans. William W. Hallo (London: 1971), p. 186.

9. Ibid, pp. 295–294. Cf, *Der Atem des Geistes,* Eugen Rosestock-Huessey: "Natural grammar differs from liturgy of the word in that it does not see as central the language's vitality, its transformative character, the forms, the words, and even the language itself are perceived as objects," ibid., p. 83.

10. F. Heiler, *Das Gebet*, p. 255.

11. *The Star of Redemption*, p. 272.

12. Ibid, pp. 270–268.

13. Ibid., p. 268.

14. Y. Albo, *Sefer Ha-ikkarim* 4, 18.

15. R. A. Ha-cohen Kook, *Olat Reiyah*, pt. 1, p. 14.

16. R. Judah Halevi, *The Kuzari*, art. 3, 19.

17. *The Star of Redemption*, p. 273.

18. *The Kuzari*, ibid.

19. *The Star of Redemption*, p. 274.

20. Ibid., p. 275.

21. Ibid., p. 295.

22. Ibid., p. 293.

23. F. Rosenzweig, *Naharaim* (Hebrew), [Jerusalem: 1960] p. 206.

24. F. Rosenzweig, *The Star of Redemption*, p. 277.

25. Ibid., pp. 280–279.

26. Cf., ibid., p. 281.

27. Cf., ibid., p. 275.

28. Ibid., p. 276.

29. Ibid., p. 294.

30. Ibid., p. 293.

31. Ibid., p. 294.

32. Ibid., p. 293.

33. Ibid., p. 293.

Part III

12
Education for Prayer

Adin Steinsaltz

The question as to whether and how it is possible to educate for prayer seems to me to lead directly to another, far more fundamental question: namely, What is the nature of prayer?

I would like to explain at the outset why I think that this is the fundamental question. An individual who prays for himself only can pray parrot-fashion, or like a professor; and he does not need to give any account either of the reason for praying or of the content of his prayer. And even if he does think about these things, he is under no obligation to account for himself to anyone else, which is not the case when he has to act as an educator. A true teacher cannot avoid a long list of complicated and painful questions regarding the nature, value, subject matter, and function of prayer, for the simple reason that that is what is required of him. This is the case not only for the professional educator, but for anyone who finds himself, in one way or another, called upon to inculcate in others the desire and the ability to pray.

In the same manner as this question poses itself to the teacher or educator, it is asked no less (and sometimes in a far sharper and more personal fashion) of every Jewish father who wishes that his children should pray (and there are still such fathers around). A father, even if he has no wish to become involved in theology, will be confronted with a pile of questions, which he will be required to clarify, at least to his own satisfaction, as to what he is doing and what he has in mind when he prays, and what his intention is in educating others to pray. Why, in fact, is he teaching them this?

That is to say: anyone who goes beyond the task of imparting purely formal and external information about prayer, encounters the question of the nature and function of prayer long before he deals with other questions in this area. To be sure, the question is not always asked in a direct and unequivocal manner. But this question is always there and appears in one form or another. If I would attempt to describe what is being done now, in practice, in the area of education, I would say that it is confined to two objects. One object of education in this area is to see to it that one's charges behave like "good children"—that is, that they pray three times a day. There are teachers and parents for whom the primary meaning of education for prayer—and, in practice, the only thing they do in this area—is to make their children or students accustomed to pray regularly, in an almost mechanical fashion. In most of the religious institutions in Israel, whether those of the *Hinukh Atsmai* (Independent) system or of the State Religious school network, education for prayer is concentrated on the acquisition of the habit of organized prayer, every morning. (Through this, various oddities come about. For example, an acquaintance of mine, who had been raised in a religious home, told me that it was only by accident that he discovered one day the existence of the *Minhah* (Afternoon) prayer, as he had not heard about this in school, nor at home, because he never saw people reciting this prayer. But this is really part of another problem, that of the real religious character of the so-called *datti* home.)

The school thus sees itself as responsible for inculcating the habit of regular, mechanical prayer. To a considerable extent, it succeeds in this. The student acquires the technical ability, the knowledge of how it is done, as well as the moral stamina required to enable him to rise every morning and pray, without skipping a day. This is no mean accomplishment, and I do not intend to belittle it. I remember that once a quite mature young man, who had grown up on a kibbutz and had studied at Bar-Ilan University for a number of years, came to our synagogue to learn how to pray. One of the things which astonished him was how the small children in the synagogue knew what to do. He asked again and again how they knew when to stand, when to sit, what page to open, and so on. All of this is part of education, and it has achieved a certain success. It is one of the objects of education for prayer.

The other aspect of education for prayer concerns itself, and I would almost say concludes, with what is called in several places "the *kavvanah* (intention) of prayer." And here the main object has been to understand what is written in the prayer book. Of course, I do not oppose the idea that people should know and understand what is written in the *Siddur;* on the contrary, I personally tried, at one time, to exert pressure that the *Siddur* be introduced into the religious schools as a compulsory subject of study, so that those children who use it should know what they are saying. One of the Inspectors of the religious schools told me that this was unnecessary, because "they all know," but I contend that this is simply not so. This subject, however, important though it is, is not what I have in mind in this essay.

Education for prayer in this sense may be accomplished by any good school, any good teacher, and sometimes by a good father or even a good rabbi, who can explain to the children what prayers to say, how they are related to one another, why each blessing is formulated in its particular way, what is its subject and context, and so forth. One teacher will explain things in terms of numerology (*gematria*) and mysteries; another, by means of history—each according to the style which he prefers. However, with all the importance and value which this has—this is not true and deep education for prayer. Such explanations are useful as an aid, but this is not education for prayer as such, education which comes to grips with the nature and foundation of prayer. I would like to give a personal illustration of this.

After some years during which we had not seen one another, I met an old friend who is now the dean of one of the *yeshivot* in Israel, and asked him what he does during his prayers, whether he concentrates on prayer itself. "Yes," he answered, he has *kavvanah* (devotion). I asked him, "What *kavvanah* do you have?" He explained that his intent during prayer was to understand the connection between one sentence and the next, between one word and another, between the various sections, and so on. He thinks about and concentrates on these matters—and this he terms *kavvanah* in prayer. I told him, rather shortly, that these are things which I do on *Shabbat* after eating dinner, and that sometimes I study these problems and look into books which deal with and explain prayer in this manner. But to regard the analysis of the text (which is what his *kavvanah* amounted to, though he did not use this expression) as a proper form of devotion for, say, the service of the High Holy Days—this I cannot agree with or accept as *kavvanah* in the true sense.

In order to explain something about this subject of *kavvanah,* I will quote a well-known anecdote: They tell of a simple Jew, almost an ignoramus, who stood on Rosh Hashanah and recited with great fervor the liturgical poems, "These and these shout with a shouting, these and these roar with a roaring. . . ." They asked him why this great fervor over *befetsah mefatshim,* and what did he understand by these prayers? The Jew answered, "What do I care what is written there? I know that all of the prayers have one meaning: Master of the Universe, help us to make a living."

To my mind, in terms of what is truly connected to the nature of prayer, the Jew in this story was far closer to the depths of prayer than the one who knows the exact date of composition of the prayers, and knows all about two- and three-letter roots in ancient and modern *piyyutim,* and so on.

When I come to teach what I regard as the true apprehension of prayer, it seems to me that the questions raised are not first and foremost technical. The basic thing is not the understanding of the prayer-text, what words I use and how I understand them. Long before this, prayer raises two fundamental questions, one greater and more fundamental, the other perhaps a partial question within a larger one. When a man prays, he says in every prayer and in every *nosah:* "Blessed art Thou, O Lord." When a man says, "Blessed art Thou, O Lord," he finds himself standing before God—in direct confrontation with Him. That is to say, the moment a person says these words and does not wish to be a liar or a deceiver or the like, he makes an affirmation and places himself before God—and this fact far outweighs any textual or technical consideration, such as whether this form of prayer is attractive or not, and so forth. In every prayer, before all else, we face this great issue. It amounts to this: When a man prays, he addresses the Holy One, blessed be He.

I was confronted with this question, not as a teacher, but as a parent. Once, while I was in the middle of my prayers, my little daughter tried to talk to me, and when I failed to respond, she was very angry with me: "Why don't you speak to me?" Later on, I answered her by saying: "I was busy, I was speaking with God." She then replied, with great understanding, that she hadn't noticed that God was answering me. This second question was very deep and it goes beyond the limits of our discussion here. In any event, a four- or five-year-old girl was prepared to accept the notion that I speak with God, when I pray, but she wanted this to be a two-way conversation and not just a speech on my part.

The point is that every prayer boils down in the final analysis to a very basic point: that is, to the words "blessed art Thou," and especially the "Thou." That is: If I feel the presence of the "Thou" before me. If I have someone with whom to speak, then I can pray; if I have no one with whom to speak, then what is the point of all these words, and all the things I say, new, old, good, bad, ugly? What good is all this if I have no feeling of presence, in the simplest sense?

What I am saying here is so simple that it should not need to be said, except that it still does need to be said, and stressed: prayer is an expression of faith. It is impossible to pray, except out of faith in the encounter with God, in the standing of the I before the Thou. I don't want to enter into the niceties of this subject; it is not a question of Buberian philosophy; it is a simple point, so simple that any child can understand it. And yet, it is a problem which confronts adults, the more they wish to delve into the problem of prayer, the intention of prayer, and especially the question of education for prayer. It is a theological problem, perhaps the most important problem of all, and it arises in regard to every single prayer and blessing we say. Whoever deals with people trying to find their way to religious faith, knows that these are critical, existential questions.

When I pray, I speak with someone. I must necessarily believe in His existence, and not only in His existence. Moreover, I do not thereby accept just an abstract metaphysical existence, in the fashion of those who opt for orthopraxis (which is so intellectually a little too easy). It is not enough that I place God in some corner, from which He won't touch me or come to me, and that I take care that I have no contact with Him except in that peculiar region known as "the observance of the *mizvot*"—something no one quite understands. For, when a man prays, he explicitly places himself before somebody. And he must assume that this "somebody" hears what he says to Him.

Thus, education for prayer raises the whole question of the reality of the awareness of God in the heart and mind of the person praying, and his ability to pass on this awareness to others. This is the first, more inclusive question regarding prayer. There is also a less general, more personal question. In almost every prayer, besides the doxologies and affirmations (as in a portion of the Eighteen Benedictions), there are also petitionary prayers. I pray, in short, means: I request. And this includes all of the middle twelve of the Eighteen Benedictions.

One ought to remember that every request contains within it the expectations of a kind of miracle, and the assumption that such a miracle can, in fact, occur. When a man requests, "Master of the Universe, heal the sick of your people Israel," he requests something specific. That is, he asks that something happen, a certain change in the world, be it large or small. But, in essence, it is a request that something occur, and that something occur which would not have occurred had he not prayed. True, I am putting this in the simplest manner, in the form which is understood and felt even by the smallest children, but it is also the case for adults who would put it in more sophisticated, precise, and elegant form. There is no other way to understand all of the blessings and prayers, except as a request for a trans-natural occurrence; within nature or above nature, but always involving a certain departure from ordinary laws. That is to say: before one enters into discussion of the details of the external components of prayer, whether large or small, one must remember that prayer is not like any other act that we perform, or any other mode of discourse. Consequently, education for prayer is not simply education on a defined and limited track and aimed at a defined and specific *mizvah*. Education for prayer is of necessity far broader: it is concerned with the necessary and essential ground of education as a whole. We may term this ground the striving for faith.

If we wish to educate for prayer, we need to pass on the basic assumptions which exist in every prayer in the world. Whoever accepts these basic principles can and ought to pass them on in the process of education, and if he is unable to do this, then there is no point in him getting involved in the details which follow. Whoever gives up on these basic points, has given up on any meaningful contact with prayer.

In his day, Rabbi Yitshak Meir of Gur said similar things, but using his own formulations, as for instance, the following: When the Evil One succeeds in stealing a a man's soul, he leaves him with all his foolish niceties of observance intact—even to being particular about saying *hodu* before *barukh sheamar* in the morning service—because then none of these things really matter. The foolish things can remain. From then on, a person can say the prayers with or without the passage dealing with the Temple-sacrifices, because they have become irrelevant. He relates to prayer as in the saying, "He swears with his lips, but denies it in his heart." It is as if he had said in his heart before he started praying, that whatever he is about to say is a heap of lies and falsehood, from beginning to end; for it would seem that he speaks and there is no one to hear, no one to answer, so that his whole prayer is a matter of empty words addressed to an emptiness. To be sure, I have put the matter crudely, but without doubt there are many people (belonging to what are called "religious circles") for whom this is their inner sense of prayer. Prayer, for them, is a certain duty, a 'chore' which every man is required to perform, like all the other not-understood and meaningless performances. He is obliged to put on a *tallit;* and he is obliged to utter such and such words. From this standpoint, the education toward mechanical recitation of prayers solves the problem. The interpretations given of "what is my duty that I shall do it" show very well how to deal with this situation as well. In the same way as they teach one how to wrap oneself up in a *tallit,* they can teach us when to accent the penultimate syllable and when the last, and in this way they solve the problem.

However, if prayer has any sort of content, and a man genuinely wishes to relate to this content, then each and every prayer becomes primarily an inward declaration of certain points of faith.

The problematic nature of education for prayer is the visible part of a more general crisis, viz. the crisis of faith. The existing debates regarding the *nosah,* and so forth, are generally speaking ways of hiding oneself from this more general theological crisis. The real issue is not that this or another prayer is not up to date. Prayer, in general, expresses a certain posture and a certain path and it is not so particularized that it cannot be reconciled with changed circumstances and details. But prayer, without doubt, postulates certain broad theological attitudes and I see no place for prayer without prior theological affirmations. I know that there is, these days, a general withdrawal from all theology and from metaphysical definitions. There is an attempt to reach a compromise and not to take risks or raise inner doubts and difficulties,

Education for Prayer

to resolve the lack of faith by relating to a text, which one tries to void of all inner content.

In order to demonstrate – against a slightly different background – just how far this goes, I may mention an article which appeared recently in the monthly journal *Masa,* describing a piece of biblical research which was done in all seriousness. This was an attempt to demonstrate that all the *malakhim* (angels: messengers) mentioned in the Bible were in fact human beings, the basic assumption being: How is it possible that a book as sublime as the Bible could deal with the supernatural? This was an extremely serious article, which attempted to resolve speculative theological problems (which also exist for many who pray). Of course, the solution was only partial, because God did not enter into the picture. As a matter of fact, left-wing Zionist movement *Hashomer Hatsair* once published a *Tanakh* (Bible) which corrected this error also: This edition eliminated every mention of the name of God, and thus resolved the problem. This Bible (which was published and then withdrawn from circulation), was an attempt to solve a theological problem, by eliminating it completely. This is an approach one can use towards the *Siddur* as well, and it could be done by a staff of serious religious scholars. It would be possible to create a popular *Siddur* which would speak to the heart and create no problems. To begin with, one would remove all those passages dealing with animal sacrifices (as some people have done), the passages dealing with a bodily resurrection of the dead and a personal Messiah (as has been done in various places), and in the end one would also remove the name of the Almighty, from the *Siddur,* and then we should have a truly magnificent prayer book. So that this not seem to you like a mere fantasy, I suggest that you examine almost any Passover *Haggadah* from the *kibbutzim* of forty years ago. It is possible to see there that such a thing is not only possible, but was in fact done, and evidently in all seriousness. It is possible to perform a Passover Seder and to pronounce blessings in which there is not only no mention of the Passover Sacrifice, but no mention of the Name of Heaven; in the same way as was done (and perhaps still is done) in the "ceremony of bringing of the firstfruits" on the Feast of Weeks, where the theological content has been removed from the ceremony, so as to make it speak equally to all. In brief: enlightened, aesthetic, and clear.

All these examples are mentioned simply to explain that the concern with external details is not only superficial but also misleading. The question of old and out-of-date forms of prayer is in the final analysis, an extremely peripheral issue. The basic cause of the discomfort people feel with the *Siddur* is – as I have explained earlier – the very deep problem people have with regard to faith and theology, and every attempt to hide behind problems of text or of varying *minhag* shows a lack of seriousness. This basic point, that prayer is an expression of a living faith, is known to everyone, and is almost tautological.

With all this, these problems are not openly expressed or stated. Perhaps a group of scholars and thinkers can allow itself to hide from such a central problem in the course of a series of abstract discussions, but an educator—on any level—cannot allow himself to do this. The educator, even if he is not aware of it, must sense that education for prayer is one of the important—and essential—elements of education towards faith. And education for faith, through the means of prayer, means education toward a certain *kind* of faith as defined by the content of the prayers themselves.

One of the specific components of this faith is the personal relation between the one who hears and the one who speaks. I must believe (and be prepared to pass on this belief to others), that when I stand with my face toward the wall, I am *not* speaking to the wall, but I *am* speaking to God, and He hears my prayer and answers it in some fashion. This is part of the education for faith and there must be an injection of this understanding into ordinary life.

If a man wishes to relate to God, he cannot jail Him in the synagogue, without any connection with the surrounding world. If I wish to explain to a small child or to a grown man what prayer is, I must of necessity say that there is one "who hears prayer," and by this relate not only to the specific blessing in the *Amidah* ("Blessed is He who hears our prayer"), but to the actual concept itself. And if there is one who hears me, then the blessing "He who hears prayer," is part of the nature of life—not only when I pray, but at other times as well.

If a man cannot live with this awareness, then this would suggest that he has a theological problem—one relating to his general worldview. One who takes the view that he cannot tell a child, a student, a man who comes to pour out his heart, that God in fact exists and really is, has a personal problem that he has to settle with himself first. Instead of educating another person in prayer, he had better first stand and pray that he be granted the ability to pray. Doubtless, there exist such prayers, both ancient and very modern, both in circles far from and close to Judaism. There are prayers in which people pray for faith, for the ability to pray. It is possible that such a prayer creates its own problems, but it is at least real, and it is needed as a preliminary to any discussion on this subject.

In every attempt at meeting, whether with adults or with children, there is no other solution to the problem of education for prayer (and even to the question of education for *mizvot,* with all the difference between the two) than to come to a confrontation—a self-confrontation, if you like, and this must be faced up to both before the educational act and during it.

To summarize: to the extent that it is possible to educate to pray, this may only be done within a more general framework of education toward faith. Even ostensibly religious schools, which include in their curriculum every subject under the sun, do not deal properly with this topic, either openly or, in a general and indirect fashion. It is astonishing that the professedly religious school does not deal directly with the question of faith. Why must the religious child, like every other child, pass his own crises of faith in such awful loneliness, with no one to ask—neither teacher nor rabbi, no one with the background to enable him even to frame the question?

It is possible that because of the inability to decide whether to follow *Nosah Sefarad* or *Nosah Ashkenaz,* whether to decide the basics in this *nosah* or another, people have decided not to teach anything and not to try to attain to anything basic. The same is customary in the subject known as "Jewish Thought," which is mainly taught by placing before the student scores of passages from various sources, and saying, "This is how Jews thought," without attempting to bring the students to any basic consideration of what *they* think or should think, as Jews, and without setting any line or standard as to actual thought or faith. Again—prayer can only be taught as part of an education toward faith in general. Education means taking a stand; it means that the educator is prepared to defend his religious position. If he believes in it, well and good; if he does not believe, then he must face the question, whether he ought to pretend that he is more God-fearing than he really is. This is a large question, which comes up wherever a teacher (even the *melamed* in the most old-fashioned *heder*) attempts to talk about prayer. Every teacher must attempt then to settle this problem with his own conscience, and the solution is not easy.

In any event, when a worldview founded on faith exists, there is a possibility of building on it a relationship to prayer. Only when such faith exists is there a reason to pray; that is—to pronounce certain words seriously. And if not—then one is reciting parrot-fashion, and it is to be regretted that so much energy is spent in mechanically teaching things which have no meaning to those who say them. He who prays (i.e., "speaks with God") necessarily requests various things. If he is serious, then his requests are sincere. But one who recites the blessings from *Tsemah David* (for the restoration of the Davidic dynasty) to *Retzeh* (for the restoration of sacrifices), and very much hopes that these things will *not* happen—has no educational problems at all, since he contradicts the very essence of education. On the other hand, the serious worshipper may have problems to confront, but they are problems of faith. Prayer is a structure raised upon the foundations of faith; it is by no means a subject in itself. It is impossible to separate it from the problem of faith generally, without which it has no existence.

To be sure, it is possible to discuss Jewish prayer with detachment as one would discuss Tibetan prayer, when a man is concerned with comparative religion. But when one deals with prayer as a subject in life, and as a subject of education, one must relate to the subject in a personal fashion. And a personal approach requires faith. I know that to speak about faith to a group of people involved in Jewish Thought is somewhat embarrassing—it is a subject which is almost taboo, one which people are ashamed to talk about in public. With all this, I think that there are more believers than those who make themselves out to be such in public. That is, even in the religious community there are more believers than one thinks.

My late uncle once quoted the great Rabbi of Kotsk, who said—in reference to the story of Judah and Tamar (Genesis 38:20)—that every man must have a close friend, so close that he can reveal his heart to him and even tell him that he has had dealings with a prostitute. And my uncle added that this was said in those days. Today, one can talk about such things in the street with anybody. But today, ironically, one needs a close, soul-friend, to whom one can speak of one's belief in God, and tell him that, despite the fact of being religious and carrying out the *mizvot,* "I nevertheless believe in God." I think that part of the job of religious education is in the personal ability to throw off our philosophical, intellectual, and academic baggage, which has become an encumbrance rather than a staff to support us, and to say what many people think in their hearts—that God truly exists (in spite of the declarations that He exists) and that it is actually possible to turn to Him. Only in this way is it possible to speak of prayer and to educate for prayer.

13
Teaching *Siddur* to Enhance Devotion in Prayer

Uriel Simon

The *Hazon Ish* made the following observation in one of his letters: "Even though *tefillah* became a *mizvah* to be performed by a physical act after the Men of the Great Assembly had ordained a fixed and unchangeable prayer text, nevertheless *tefillah* remains essentially a devotional *mizvah,* a duty of the heart. If one fails to fulfill the devotional obligation, he has accomplished nothing even in action, since *tefillah* is none other than worship performed with the heart, as our Sages noted in expounding the verse, '*To serve Him with all your heart'* (Deuteronomy 11:1) 'What is the service performed with the heart? It is prayer' (*Ta'anit* 2,b).[1]

This extrahalakhic norm, that there is no *tefillah* without the devotion of the heart, has not apparently furnished the guideline for the labor performance-oriented approach followed today in the state religious educational system. It would seem that on the "operative" plane, the success has been quite impressive, the evidence being the ability of so many graduates of the system to officiate as congregational readers and read the Torah. While not always easy to bring together a *minyan* among a company of reservists, there is usually no difficulty in finding the necessary functionaries among the ten. Nevertheless I feel that it is high time to acknowledge that the expectation among educators and teachers—that mere performance would lead to internalization, and recitation in the course of time to devotion, has not generally been fulfilled. In congregations outside of the *yeshivot* and their sphere of influence—that is to say, in urban neighborhoods, in the Religious Kibbutz movement, at youth services—the prayers seem to be marked by an almost mechanical mumbling, the speed with which they are recited precluding any kind of fervor or concentration on content, and often by a noisy murmur issuing from the mouths of people "who trample the courts of the Lord" (Isaiah 1:12). Many of the worshippers have their eyes blank and their faces numb and in their regular weekday and Sabbath services they remain uninspired except in a few moments of grace.

Rarely do those assembled combine to form a real congregation of worshippers. When they do, it is because of their performing some act in unison or through congregational singing, rather than from an inner identification with the plural form of the prayers: "You have loved *us*," "Restore *us*," and "Heal *us*." Listening to the recitation (in the Morning Service) of the petition for mercy for "our brothers given over to trouble and captivity," one becomes clearly aware that the worshippers do not have in mind their real brothers groaning in ghettos or languishing in hostile imprisonment. Even where much has been done to improve the synagogue in its physical appearance, in its organization and administration, by the introduction of lessons and youth activities and the like, almost nothing has been done to improve the quality of prayer itself.

The first of the factors possibly contributing to this grave situation is the inherent difficulty of the task. "Indeed how difficult it is for man to be cured of this malady and to achieve perfection in the performance of the *mizvah* of *tefillah*," the *Hazon Ish* continues, "For even though prayer regarded as an appointed routine is to be rejected outright, nevertheless making a real supplication to the Allpresent, may He be blessed, requires nothing but a supreme degree of human perfection."

Yet, humbly acknowledging the difficulty does not exempt us from attempting to clarify the particular circumstances that render it so difficult for us to pray properly. The *Hazon Ish* attributes our failing to the paucity of our faith in Divine providence, and, when people like ourselves are spoken of, it seems that this idea can be broadened and our deficiency ascribed to the general lack of intensity in our religious lives. This weakness is manifested, *inter alia,* in the lack of cohesiveness in communal life, in the lack of authoritative religious leadership, and in the lukewarm attitude of the individual to the community and the community to the individual, among adults and children alike. These factors seem not so prevalent in *yeshivah* prayer and where there is *yeshivah* influence. For this *yeshivot* are to be envied. An atmosphere permeated with intense fear of Heaven endows prayer with the intense fervor of the worship of God. And as far as I can judge, such effort is attended by abundant reward: the meticulous fulfillment of the halakhic prescriptions regarding *tefillah* confers upon it both gravity and glory.

A second factor, by which, too, *yeshivah* students are not affected, is the distinct gap between the content of not a few of the *tefillot* and the world outlook and convictions of many of the worshippers. Prayers for the resurrection of the dead, the revival of the monarchy, and the restoration of the sacrificial service arouse varying degrees of failure to identify, spiritual discomfort or mental confusion. Not only have Jerusalem and the Jewish people ceased being a "reproach for all that are around us," but in general a member of our generation finds it quite difficult to bow his head as a sign of weakness, or in supplication and lamentation. It seems to me that this tension, arising from the content of several of the prayers and the obligation to recite them, generates an alienation on a broad scale from the words printed in the *Siddur*. Unwittingly, the worshipper tends to maintain a certain distance from the words of the *Siddur,* to refrain from reflections that may lead him he knows not where, and to satisfy himself with fulfilling what has been imposed upon him, that is, simply to pronounce the words with his lips.

The third factor stems from the fact that the language of the prayers has ceased to be *leshon hakodesh* (literally, "the holy tongue"), but has instead become the vernacular. I cannot determine the extent to which worshippers in the Diaspora understood the language of the prayers; but I am sure that, even where the words are not understood, prayer can be deeply meaningful Divine worship. But when those who speak Hebrew and study its literature attempt to follow this pattern of behavior, of necessity some type of short circuit is produced. For a generation that understands what it is saying, much of the magic and sublimity of the Hebrew word is lost, and so it becomes awkward for the worshipper to recite *kinot* and *selihot* couched in stilted language and teeming with hidden allusions. No less does it become difficult for him to tolerate the frequent repetitions of prayers that he understands; how can he concentrate when the reader repeats the identical *Amidah* he has just recited? How can he help losing respect for the *Kaddish* when he hears it repeated four times over, with only slight intervals, at the conclusion of the Morning Service? Furthermore, not only the words as such have to be understood, but the content as well. It is no wonder that a person who has not decided for himself who the *minim* and *malshinim* (lit. "heretics" and "slanderers") may be, for whose destruction he prays, does not, by the same token, have in mind, when praying for mercy on behalf of the *Gerei Hazedik* (literally, "righteous proselytes") those of our own day who have attached themselves to the Jewish people. And so our lack of understanding and of devotion leads to an impoverishment of spirit which is accepted as a kind of necessity.

Accordingly *iyyun tefillah* — in its original sense of praying attentively — is a skill that can only be acquired by dint of intensive effort. The thesis that I submit, in this connection, is that much can be accomplished in improving prayer by teaching it in depth. According to the *Hazon Ish* it is the effort to understand the *Torah Shebe'al Peh* that produces an increase in one's spiritual powers, and *ipso facto* a revitalization of prayer. Those educated in Torah who have not deviated in their mental outlook from the *Bet Midrash* are familiar with this approach. As for people like us and our pupils, the proposal is that we concentrate our efforts directly on the *Siddur* itself, and regard its content as study material suited to youth and adults alike. This seems so logical to me that I fail to understand why it has not been tried long ago.

An examination of the primary and high school curricula of the State Religious Educational System reveals that *Siddur* is not taught beyond the fifth year of primary school! During the entire four years of high school no genuine attempt is made to come to terms with the *Siddur,* the exception being that, within the framework of the course in *Mahshevet Yisrael* (literally, "Jewish thought" or Jewish philosophy and theology), it is optional, by no means compulsory, to allocate a maximum of ten hours to the subject bearing the name, *Tefillah*. It is proposed that in this absurdly limited period of time the basic conceptions of *tefillah* of nine Jewish thinkers — from Rabbi Saadiah Gaon and Rabbi Judah Halevi through Rabbi Samson Raphael Hirsch and Rav Kook — be imparted.

As an argument against teaching the prayers themselves, it may perhaps be urged that *tefillah* is so delicate and precious an experience, that it is better to leave it to the individual worshipper and not to introduce it into the profane world of the classroom, of homework and examination subjects. Such arguments are raised today against the teaching of Hebrew literature in school. Yet it seems that this contention was raised in the first place only in order to draw attention to the amount of damage that classroom instruction can cause. I, too, would prefer that instruction in *Siddur* on the high school level be confined in practice, in the first stages, to voluntary study groups, such as study circles in synagogues and the cultural programs of youth movements.[2]

The main issue, however, is not the framework but the approach, and this must be adjusted to the spiritual and intellectual needs of each student group. If my evaluation of the situation and my analysis of its main causes are correct, the conclusion inevitably follows that the first goal of systematic instruction in

Siddur is to bring the student to recognize that the *Siddur* is comprised of literary selections, rich in meaning, which require understanding, study and personal involvement. The teacher should impart to his students a minimum of information on the dates when the prayers were composed and the evolution of the various prayer-texts. The emphasis, however, must be on study of the meaning and personal significance of the prayer.[3] The same applies to the *halakhot* of prayer. Only the indispensable minimum should be mentioned, and this only as part of the attempt to penetrate to the depths of the reason for the *halakhah* and its significance for the worshipper. Rabbi Kook achieved great success in joining the *halakhic* and devotional aspects together in his commentary on the *Siddur, Olat Reiyah.*

The danger exists that the teacher, will follow the beaten track of long ago, because he has no text book to follow. Although a large quantity of historical, exegetical, and devotional material has been collected in the late Rabbi B. S. Jacobson's *Netiv Binah,*[4] this is presented almost as raw material, and indecisive eclecticism may serve as a negative example for the teacher. From the spiritual and ideational point of view, there is no source of inspiration comparable to the *Olat Reiyah,* provided that the teacher is capable of translating Rabbi Kook's words into his own terms. Accordingly, in the final analysis, the teacher cannot avoid presenting to his pupils the fruits of his own, personal encounters with *tefillah,* and submitting these as possible interpretations.

An additional difficulty is to be found in the long strings of synonyms and the repetitions of the same ideas in different words, which abound in the liturgy. These make it unnecessary to dispense with any precise, literary analysis of the type we customarily employ in teaching *Tanakh* and literature in general. Indeed it is not at all necessary to elucidate and analyze the particular section of the liturgy that is under discussion from beginning to end. The goal must be to enrich and to intensify the language of the *Siddur,* just as chemists enrich natural uranium and farmers fertilize their fields. Since such teaching will of necessity and justifiably be very personal, it would do no harm, in my opinion, to leave the choice of the study material to the personal predilection of the teacher and his understanding of the needs of the class.

As a possible starting point, the teacher could ask his pupils to review a certain section of the Morning Service at home, and to designate the prayer they find "easiest" to recite and the one they find "most difficult" to identify with. If a significant number choose the same passage as "the easiest" to recite, this will afford the teacher the clue as to which elements arouse and stimulate his students in prayer, and he can begin the enriching process with this passage. Their designation of certain *tefillot* as "difficult" will enable him to isolate those elements where our mentality and the prayers conflict and challenge our powers of reconciliation. The statistical compilation of the pupils choices can also furnish a topic for discussion, and its analysis an effective introduction to the course.

In the second stage, various pupils will be called upon to indicate the *tefillah* they had chosen and give a detailed "defense" of their choice. Obviously, the teacher is not precluded from suggesting a *tefillah* that in his opinion lends itself most readily to recitation. For myself, I think my choice would be: *Ahavah rabbah ahavtanu* ("With abundant love hast Thou loved us"). In explaining my choice, I would point out, inter alia, that God's love for His people precedes the command to love Him! *Veahavta* ("And you shall love the Lord your God"). As expressed in that prayer, the sublimest expression of God's love for His people is His having taught our fathers "the statutes of life," and the essential feature is our request that He continue to manifest this loving-kindness in the giving of the Torah to us: "So shalt Thou favor us and teach us." It becomes possible, within this context, to take up other *tefillot* in which gratitude is offered for the election of Israel, and to deal with the various aspects of this central idea. Other *tefillot* could be utilized to generate discussion on the significance of *kedushah*, on the nature of our expectation of redemption, of our attitude toward nature as creation, the relationship of the individual and community in the striving for repentance, and the like.

These enriching interpretations must be combined with the reinterpretations that are to bridge the gaps. By using the pupils' choices of the *tefillot* that leave them cold or even arouse their antipathy, it is possible, first of all, to make them aware of these points of difficulty. And if the pupils are not themselves ready for this type of approach, it behooves the teacher, in my opinion, to reveal to the class some of his own difficulties, obviously while adapting himself to their level of comprehension and degree of maturity. Openhearted discussion and intellectual honesty in dealing with the problem involved in so central a verse as "Thou openest Thy hand and satisfieth the desire of every living thing" (Psalm 145:16) will yield rich educational reward.

The mere raising of questions is not sufficient. Answers and solutions must be propounded. When the scientific view of nature and the language of prayer conflict (e.g., "Who opens the windows of the firmament?") the ancient conceptions are to be interpreted as metaphors. Some teachers might even adopt this approach with respect to the mention in the prayers of the restoration of the sacrificial service.

The prayer, "And for the slanderers let there be no hope" might be understood best in historical perspective, although it would not be difficult to show how this petition would be uttered with special fervor in lands where Jews are persecuted and their religion suppressed, and the danger ever present that slanderers and informers might be planted among them.

Teaching *Siddur* to Enhance Devotion in Prayer 195

Rabbi Kook has written most effectively on the problem inherent in praying for the destruction of sinners, rather than their sin, and his words may well serve as an antidote to the strong expressions of animosity to be found in this same blessing.[5] Nevertheless, just as the teacher may become a party to the expressed or suppressed reservations of his pupils, so may he categorically reject their views. The obligation to reconcile prayer and worshipper must not be taken to indicate that always and as a matter of course the *tefillot* must be adapted to the taste of the worshipper. On the contrary, the true goal of classroom instruction here is to arouse within the pupil the aspiration to bring himself nearer to *tefillah*, and to learn, from the fixed formulae established by the Sages who instituted the *tefillot*, how to stand in the presence of God and worship Him.

No less vital than the clarification of the devotional and theological aspects of prayer is the elucidation of the existential and experiential aspects. Many important observations are to be found in Joseph Shechter's *Mavo Lasiddur*,[6] on what he calls "the basic emotions" of the prayers: the experience of the morning embodied in the *Yotzer* blessing; the experience of the evening which finds expression in *Hama'ariv Aravim* and *Hashkivenu*. Indeed, it is possible, in this spirit, to teach the preliminary Morning Blessings as the sequence of the gradual, step-by-step awakening of one's religious consciousness at the beginning of a new day. Each of the literary genres that are current in *tefillah* — blessing, thanksgiving, confession, supplication, petitions for needs — is tied to a specific religious posture. Anyone can sense the difference between *berakhah* and *hallel* intuitively, but comprehension can be deepened considerably by articulating the spiritual attitude embodied within each of them.[7] In this connection, the very problem of prayer can be dealt with: Why does God "desire the prayer of the pious"? Why does He "choose song and psalm"? And why is prayer itself included in the gifts for which we pray?[8]

Finally, one should examine the ritual context of the prayers. The individual prayers, whatever their origin may have been, are fitted into the *Siddur* in a new context that endows them with meaningful continuity. Explaining the overall structure of the Morning Service as contrasted with the Evening Service must complement the teaching of the individual *tefillot*, and can serve as a summing up. This context makes it possible to deal with the problems of repetitions and strings of synonyms, and the reward and price of congregational worship. One would also wish to explain the difference between prayer and aesthetic experience, and whatever follows therefrom.[9]

I shall conclude with a measure of self-criticism. The weakness in the proposal I have submitted here is its almost exclusive stress on the intellectual aspect of praying and on the ability of the power of comprehension to improve its quality. Indeed, my proposal is not intended as a substitute for teaching through doing but rather as an addition. Undoubtedly the personal example of parents and educators is many times more important and effective. But with respect to our pupils this is not enough. Similarly, it is obvious that the ultimate gift of prayer will not come from the school but from the congregation at prayer, once it becomes awakened and alert and assumes the strength to impress the seal of our generation on the *Siddur* and on Divine worship generally.[10] These considerations, however, lie beyond the teacher's control, and he cannot wait for them to come about. In the meantime he can increase his pupils' comprehension of the standard prayers and develop their ability to endow them with new significance, in the spirit of "Sing unto the Lord a new song" (Psalm 149:1).

Notes

1. The letter is printed in the anthology *Sefer Yesodot Neemanim,* ed. N. Weintraub (Bne Brak: 1968), privately published pp. 133–134.

2. These remarks refer to religious youth, since this article deals with the improvement of the quality of prayer by those who do pray. Nevertheless, to my mind there is no room for doubt with regard to the suitability of the classroom for teaching *tefillah* to pupils who have had almost no contact with it. My experience in teaching *Siddur* in a general nonreligious high school has taught me that pupils who enter the world of prayer from without are liable to find true interest in it (after they have overcome their initial antagonism). The proposal that instruction in *Siddur* be included in seventh grade, utilizing the motivation stemming from the preparation for *bar mizvah,* seems eminently reasonable. Eliezer Schweid's article, "Teaching Jewish Subjects in Israeli High Schools" [(Hebrew), *Petahim* 21 *Iyyar* 1972]) does not deal with *Siddur* teaching, but charts the course to some extent for honest, upright, and courageous teaching of religious texts in a secular school. See also, Joseph Schechter, *Mavo Lasiddur* (Tel Aviv: 1958).

3. In the discussion that followed this lecture, the late Joseph Heinemann observed that the comparison of prayer texts can also serve as a fruitful starting point for exegetical discussion. As an example, he cited the variants in the conclusion of the *Yotzer Or* prayer. In R. Saadiah Gaon's *Siddur* the sentence, "O cause a new light to shine on Zion. . . ." is missing, and this conforms to his explicit assertion that "the Sages did not institute this *berakhah* for the future light of the Messianic era, but for the light that shines every day . . . hence it were good to silence those who mention it (the messianic light) at this point." Indeed, the Sephardi *Siddur* concludes with "And ordained luminaries to delight His world which He created," and it stands to reason that this is the original version, which has been displaced from most *Siddurim* because of the messianic conclusion. See Ismar Elbogen, *Der jüdische Gottesdienst in seiner geschichtlichen Entwicklung,* third ed. (Frankfurt am Main: 1931), pp. 19–20; (Hebrew tr. [Tel Aviv: 1972], p. 15); and similarly Joseph Heinemann, "Rav Saadiah Gaon's attitude towards Changes in Prayer Texts" (Hebrew), *Bar Ilan Annual* 1 (1963): 221ff.

4. R. Issachar Ya'akovson, *Netiv Binah* (Tel Aviv: 1968); in English, B. S. Jacobson, *Meditations on the Siddur* (Tel Aviv: 1966), and *The Weekday Siddur* (Tel Aviv: 1973). See also R. Elie Munk, *The World of Prayer,* vol. 1 (New York: 1954), vol. 2 [New York: 1963].

5. R. Abraham Isaac Kook, *Seder Tefillah* with the commentary, *Olat Reiyah,* vol. 1 (Jerusalem: 1939), p. 275.

6. Schechter, *Maro Lasiddur* (Tel Aviv: 1958), pp. 17–18.

7. On the *berakhah,* see Pinchas Peli, "The *Berakhah*—The Gateway to *Tefillah,*" (Hebrew), *Petahim* 16 (*Adar* 1971): 31–38.

8. Cf. Eliezer Berkowits, *Prayer* (New York: 1962).

9. Cf. E. Schweid, "Hameyahalim Litefillah" (Hebrew), *Moznayim* 36: 6 (*Iyyar* 1973): 402–497.

10. After the manner of the prayer of R. Nahman of Bratslav: ". . . Master of the Universe, Master of the Universe, awesome and fearful! Give me new speech now. Give me the speech now with which to propitiate Thee where I am now, only now, that I should have the merit of returning to Thee in truth now. . . ." (R. Nathan of Bratslav, ed., *Sefer Likkute Tefillot* [Warsaw: 1930], pt. 2, 57.

14
The *Siddur* and the Contemporary Community

Jules Harlow

I take some comfort in a line attributed to Thomas Hobbes, who is quoted as having said that whoever says something that never has been said before is very likely saying something that will never be said again. Let me put my thesis into a personal perspective.

I come from Sioux City, Iowa. Actually, I was only born there. The town that we lived in at the time had no hospital, and my mother went to Sioux City and its hospital for the occasion. I still have family living there, whom I visit from time to time. Several years ago, soon after the congregation in Sioux City had acquired a prayer book in which I had been involved as a translator and editor, a distant cousin of mine arrived at the morning *minyan* in time to hear a conversation between two men, whose true identities will be protected. We'll call them Greenberg and Goldberg. My cousin came in when these two gentlemen, their backs to the door, were leafing through the newly acquired

Siddur. Greenberg had taught my mother the *aleph bet* in the local *heder* and both Greenberg and Goldberg knew of our family's wanderings through the mercantile wilds of Iowa and Nebraska, where very often we had been the only Jewish family in a small town.

They were looking at a page on which my name appears when my cousin entered in time to hear Greenberg say, "Nu Goldberg, a wonderful country America! Jules Harlow tells *us* how to *daven!*" That is just part of the problem, Greenberg and Goldberg's problem and my problem. It often paralyzes me, when I think of them looking over my shoulder.

Part of the problem for them lies in the fact that they are not "modern" men. They are not "modern" in part because certain modern questions do not exist for them. Dietrich Bonhoeffer has asked a modern question: "What is the place of prayer in the entire absence of religion?" That's not a problem for Greenberg and Goldberg, except in so far as it is a problem for their children and grandchildren. It does not affect their own *daven*ing. That question borders on cuteness, but it is a valid and disturbing question. And it's a question which also can lead to cynicism and despair. We don't lack problems. Too few Jews enter the synagogue at all, too few Jews are involved in the life of the synagogue. Even among those who are involved, problems remain: problems of faith and the absence of faith, problems of apathy and antagonism.

Abraham Joshua Heschel, of blessed memory, stated that the problem of prayer is the problem of God, that is, the problem of faith. The times in which we live can hardly be characterized as an era of prayer. The same point has been made by Adin Steinsaltz (see above). There are Jews who pray, of course. But their number does not even include all the Jews who come to the synagogue. It is very easy to say that people who are involved in producing new editions of the *Mahzor* and the *Siddur,* or in producing experimental booklets of prayer, are essentially producing books of prayer for Jews who don't pray. It's very easy to say that because it is so true. But, having said it, then what? Should we give up on all Jews who are not *daven*ers? That means most of the Jews in the world, probably. Shall we not even *try* to involve them meaningfully in prayer? They are a significant group, in terms of the Jewish future. Will they exist as dead weight for those who are concerned with the life of prayer in the community? I think that they cannot be ignored. Whatever problems exist, including the absence of religion, Jews, certainly in the United States and Canada, do at certain times bring at least their bodies to the synagogue.

Even though the basic questions, like the question of faith, may not be completely answered, there is an obligation to consider another question, a practical question. What books or booklets of prayer do you put into the hands of the Jews who do come to temple and synagogue sanctuaries? With what do you confront them in a service of prayer, with what do you enable them to be involved in any way?

Basic education is an obvious necessity. Any congregation should have a series of lectures or courses for adults and for the young on the *Siddur,* so that a Jew coming to *shul* can at least bring with him a basic knowledge of what happens at a service.

But it is also necessary, and perhaps more essential at this time, for certain people, to make judicious additions and judicious deletions, to help make it more apparent to a Jew today that the service of prayer (and, by extension, Judaism in general) is meaningful for his particular life. It must be made more apparent that his concerns are reflected and confronted in the service of prayer. And then he perhaps could be led farther along in prayer, from that level.

This is not a problem for all Jews. What is meaningful for some is not meaningful for others. Jews who *daven* because it is a *mizvah,* and part of their life, are surely involved in meaningful activity, and are aware that it has deep meaning for their lives. But we are talking now about other Jews.

I would like to focus upon experimental booklets of prayer. I have a collection of about 175 booklets containing experimental services and readings, from Reform and Conservative congregations in the United States. My collection is not complete, but from what I know of the others, it is a representative collection. To my knowledge, there is no parallel development in Israel, although we should at least mention the *Seder L'yom Ha-atzmaut* (Independence Day Service) published by the *Kibbutz Hadatti,* and the various *Haggadot shel Pesach* (Passover Haggadahs) and booklets of prayer and meditation and reflective material published by various kibbutzim which are not identified as religious.

To a large degree, it is misleading to present any description of the services in these American publications. Most of them were conceived as part of a total experience which is not limited to the printed word. In order to really know what they are, you must have experienced them or, at least, have observed others experiencing them. I think that these are attempts to involve people through an experience, people who are generally uninvolved in the liturgical life of the synagogue. People are asked to hold hands, to touch each other, there is an attempt to break down a frozen attitude to oneself and to others. Describing it makes it sound forced, even silly. People come, hold hands. Is that going to make a difference? However, I have been in communities where this obviously has been part of a moving experience for many of the people there. I am not saying that it is prayer. I am saying that for some people it can perhaps be a step on the road to prayer. Until you have people really trying to involve themselves, trying at least to express an emotion, you will find it more difficult to lead them into an experience of public prayer. And this is just one dimension of the total experience aimed for by those who compile some of these booklets.

The booklets have come out in great quantity and variety in the past few years, the late 'sixties and early 'seventies. They vary greatly in size and in appearance, as well as in content and quality. There are eight-page pamphlets and 180-page booklets, there are poorly mimeographed sheets and there are nicely printed booklets, with artwork in four colors and with photographs. There are some serious, knowledgeable, thoughtful, and tasteful attempts, and there are some trivial, uninformed, flippant, and vulgar trials.

What moves a rabbi to produce such a booklet for his congregation? I'd like to read from the introduction to one of these booklets. "Why don't the issues of this generation have an echo in our prayer book? The burning crisis questions of our time must find a place in our prayer book, or the synagogue becomes an anachronism. We need new liturgical expression to channel into our prayer book the fears and hopes of this present age."

This particular introduction appears in a loose-leaf booklet of prayer. Why a loose-leaf? "Because the dynamics of our time demand that whatever changes we introduce remain fluid, flexible, responsive to the desperate concerns of now and here."

I think that an analysis of these lines will produce some serious criticism. They state a case in the extreme, presenting a case of either/or, implying that if this booklet is not used, the synagogue becomes an anachronism and the service becomes irrelevant!

It also implies, along with many of the other booklets, that what's old is bad and what's new is good, by definition. This is manifestly untrue. But we should not forget that the opposite also is not true, namely, that the old is good, and that the new is bad, by definition. The introduction from which I have quoted does represent many of the others, and it does reflect a felt need for (for want of a better term) new prayer. Rabbis and laymen, throughout the United States, are investing great efforts and a certain amount of funds to produce these booklets or to purchase them, in some cases from commercial publishers. The booklets exist, primarily, due to the feeling that the hardbound prayer book lacks something that can be found in these softbound collections.

The largest number of booklets have been produced for the Friday evening service. Not for the traditional *kabbalat shabbat,* at sundown, but for what has come to be known as the "Late Friday Evening Service." (For those who are inclined to be critical, I would say, "Better late than never.") The next largest number of services in this collection were produced for the *Kol Nidre* eve (Day of Atonement) service, reflecting the time when the largest number of Jews are gathered in congregations. Most of them are essentially unfamiliar with the text of any printed service, in any hardbound prayer book. In addition, there are a few booklets which are not complete services, but which contain supplementary prose and poetry, largely produced for the *Yamim Noraim.* The booklet often contains an entire service, with the new material interspersed among the traditional texts. By "traditional" here, I mean any text which has been canonized by publication and use in a hardbound prayer book. This includes prayer books within the Reform movement. There is a dissatisfaction with the "old" texts there as well as elsewhere.

A concern for contemporary relevance is not something invented only with the appearance of these booklets. If you will consider prayer books published with English translations in the United States in this century, including the Sabbath and Festival *Prayerbook* published for the Orthodox Rabbinical Council of America in 1960, and edited by Rabbi David De Sola Pool, you will see that they contain supplementary prayers, usually set up as responsive readings, on various topical subjects of general as well as Jewish concern. Such readings are generally found collected at the end of the book, or at the end of sections. The booklets are different, however, in that their compilers obviously feel that the new material should be integral to the fabric of a service, that you should not have to look to the back of the book for the relevant readings, that they are part of the service itself.

I would like to run through some of the most popular themes in the new material: *Self-understanding.* Often found as a sort of *kavvanah,* or devotional introduction to a service. *Brotherhood.* This reflects the situation in the United States, not so much at this moment, but certainly in previous years. There were a number of readings on brotherhood, trying to reflect the fact that black and white, rich and poor, are brothers. *Democracy.* All men are created equal. *Ghettoes.* Interestingly, in the United States these days, ghetto does not mean a place where Jews live. And whenever the word appears in these booklets, as in the newspapers, it refers to the "black ghettoes." *Poverty. Love. Holiness. Pollution.* Ecology and pollution are very much on the minds of children and adults. The threat of ecological disaster is more real for them than the threat of extinction by a crusade. Concern over and reaction to pollution articulates something that people feel. *War.* Especially the war in Vietnam. *Peace. Violence.*

For more strictly Jewish themes, Soviet Jewry, Jews in Arab lands, Israel, Jerusalem, the Six Day War, the Holocaust, and Jewish Commitment head the list.

What kind of material is used? What are the sources? Sometimes the new matter is written by the rabbi, sometimes by other Jews in a particular congregation, often by teenagers, especially in services produced for the youth. The quality of this material varies widely. Often, too often, it is quite poor, and very disappointing.

The following Jewish sources are those that appear most often in the collection of 175 services: Rabbi Kook, Martin Buber, Rabbi Nachman of

Bratslav, Abraham Joshua Heschel, Naomi Shemer (especially in the months following the Six Day War, "Jerusalem of Gold," which at times took the place of *Adon Olam* or other closing hymns), Uri Zvi Greenberg, Hillel Zeitlin, Aharon Zeitlin, Eli Wiesel, Saul Tchernichovsky, Chaim Nahman Bialik, Anne Frank, selections from the children's poems written in Theresienstadt, Hannah Senesh, Levi Ben-Amitai, Yosef Tzvi Rimon, and the song *b'shanah ha-ba-ah* (many services ended with that).

There are a great many non-Jews represented in these booklets, perhaps too many. Walt Whitman, Eugene O'Neil, Tagore (mostly in English translations made from Frishman's Hebrew translations), Robert Frost, e. e. cummings, Michael Quoist (a French priest), Martin Luther King, Dag Hammarskjold, Harlow Shapely (a scientist), Cesar Chavez (on the meaning of fasting, Chavez being active as a farm labor leader and protest organizer in western United States), Oscar Wilde, Wallace Stevens, Yevtushenko (a number of congregations introduced his poem Babi Yar between *Alenu* and the mourners' *kaddish*). Many rock lyrics are introduced. From the Beatles, "He's a Real Nowhere Man" is a typical selection. Simon and Garfunkel are mostly represented by "The Sounds of Silence." Bob Dylan, "The Times They are A-Changing." Peter Yarrow, "The Great Mandalla." Joan Baez.

As good as many of these selections may be in a song or in a concert hall or at a poetry reading, they are often intrusions into what is presumed to be a service of prayer. Ideally, the best way of involving people in prayer is by involving them in *prayer,* hopefully after teaching them, and even discussing it with them. The other selections, if not used in clearly delimited ways, can be distractions in terms of the goal of a community in prayer. One among many basic weaknesses is the material used for responsive readings. Many people do not like responsive readings. However, it is one of the few things that can be done with a congregation if you want to involve them vocally. Most of the readings included in the booklets are essentially unrealistic, if the goal is to involve people in a real experience. More often than not, they are essays broken up into readings. One absurd, extreme example, is a selection from Buber's *I and Thou* broken up into a responsive reading. Very often there are meditations or reflections upon candle lighting or *kiddush*. Wine is presented in various readings as a symbol of joy, of family, of laughter, of Israel's destiny. Each such statement limits the meaning and connotations of wine and *kiddush*. Readings preceding candlelighting speak of light as the symbol of the Divine, the Divine in man, the Divine law, Israel's mission, gratitude, holiness, hope, warmth, and so on.

Obviously, such material can be an intrusion and it certainly is not as sustaining as the essential act of simply lighting the candles at home, or chanting *kiddush* at home. These acts and the memories of these acts, are sustaining. The readings about the act and its significance are not. They are unsuccessful attempts at instant education. The education is so often sorely needed, but a longer process is required, and not during a service.

There are often readings on the meaning of worship included, as well as readings on the meaning of *Shabbat.* C. S. Lewis, a remarkable writer, wrote a book called *Letters to Malcolm: Chiefly on Prayer,* which includes the following comment on this kind of material "As long as you're counting the steps, looking at your feet, you're not dancing; you're learning to dance."

Many of these services try to teach something to prepare people for an experience. But that should be done *before* the service of prayer. Consider the titles of some of the *Shabbat* services: A Service Devoted to Jewish Mysticism, An Experiment in Religion, Dialogue for the Ambivalent. These are far more appropriate as lectures or discussions than as "services." Many of these booklets are inclined to present collections of prose paragraphs, poetry and lyrics of popular songs, and expository discussions of services as prayer.

These occasional publications do reflect a search for significance, for relevance and creative involvement. One cannot question the motives of the compilers. But one can wonder about the technique. Time, and the Jews, will judge whether these services have any sustaining value. This Jew questions it. A great number of these publications bear such subtitles as: "A Creative Service" or "A Service for our Time." Title pages often contain the word "relevant." The words "creative" and "relevant" are very holy words in our time. A little *too* holy, perhaps.

One implication of such self-applied descriptions of these booklets is that the mimeographed booklet is creative while the prayers of the Sages are not creative. The new, flexible booklet is relevant to our time. The hardbound *Siddur* is not relevant to our time.

It is very easy to criticize these booklets. They are easy targets. Many of them are beneath criticism. But the significant fact about them is that they exist at all. They are faulty, and I think they are a passing phenomenon, but we have erred for too long in the opposite direction, producing very little and hardly encouraging experimentation on the part of rabbis or laymen.

Just as a first-rate poet moves forward from the efforts of many lesser poets, so perhaps we need many experiments with services in order to produce something of sustaining value for our congregants. Certainly, we will not develop by discouraging attempts at this stage. The process must be encouraged, even though it brings along with it mediocrities and worse. Our condition would be much worse, I think, if none of these services existed at all. Active involvement is at least a sign of life.

I now would like to focus briefly on one booklet which also is not free of faults. I edited it myself and I am not satisfied with it. It was an experiment, part of our attempts at developing an approach to supplementary prose and poetry to be included in the hardbound *Mahzor.* The booklet is called *Yearnings,* subtitled "Prayer and Meditation for the Days of Awe." It is not meant to be a service, but a supplement to a service. Not all of it is prayer. Reaction from laymen and rabbis who acquired 100,000 copies of this booklet was helpful, in terms of seeing what kinds of material worked and what did not work for our purposes. It was also, happily, a welcome addition to many services.

The booklet begins with a few words on *kavvanah* as a general introduction to a service, to the experience of prayer. One should not expect to benefit from a service without some sort of preparation. These words were written by Abraham Joshua Heschel:

> In prayer there is a danger of relying on the word, of depending upon a text, of forgetting that the word is a challenge to the soul rather than a substitute for the outburst of the heart. Prayer as a way of speaking is a way that leads nowhere. The text must never be more important than inner devotion, *kavvanah.* The life of prayer depends not so much upon loyalty to custom, as upon inner participation, not so much upon the *length* as upon the *depth* of the service. Those who run precipitately through the liturgy, rushing in and out of the prayer text as if the task were to cover a maximum of space in a minimum of time, will derive little from worship. To be able to pray is to know how to stand still and to dwell upon a word. This is how some worshippers of the past would act. They would repeat the same word many times, because they loved it and cherished it so much that they could not part from it. There is a classical principle in regard to prayer. Better is a little with inner devotion than much without it.

This booklet includes a prayer on behalf of Soviet Jewry, in the stylistic framework of a *yekum purkan.* It contains reflective material (not prayers) reacting to the Six Day War, including excerpts from *Siach Lochamim* (taped conversations with soldiers who took part in the battle for the Temple Mount.) and an excerpt from a speech by General Yitzhak Rabin, since the booklet was first published in 1967. It also contains a supplement to *al chet* (the great confession of sins), some selections from which follow:

"For the sins we have committed by not crying out for peace. For the sins we have committed by making guns easily available, by ignoring the poor, by trying to outdo each other in displaying wealth, by closing our hearts and our neighborhoods to other races, by teaching children prejudice through our attitudes, by tolerating the existence of slums. For the sin we have committed by false advertising, by ruthless competition, by selling inferior goods, by keeping silent in the face of evil, by neglecting our parents, by indulging our children, by

The *Siddur* and the Contemporary Community 207

rejecting our tradition, though in ignorance of it, by rebelling for the sake of rebellion, by wasting our lives on vanity, by running after recognition."

This received much favorable reaction. And some unfavorable. Essentially I am afraid that it is more an indirect sermon than a prayer or confessional.

I now would like to turn to the High Holy Day *Mahzor (A Prayer Book for the Days of Awe)* published by the Rabbinical Assembly (New York, 1972), which I edited. It is very difficult to speak about such a many-faceted project in a limited amount of time. First I would like to point out that the concept of *hiddur mizvah* should be revived in the manufacture of prayer books. People today are exposed to some of the most handsome products of contemporary design. Why should the synagogue come off tenth best or worse by comparison?

This volume is printed in two colors, for esthetic, design, and also utilitarian factors. Passages recited only on the Sabbath usually printed in smaller type or within parentheses, are printed here in the second color. The second color is also used for rubrics, short introductions, and *kavvanot*.

Print sanctifies, which is both good and bad. In many ways, I think, the printing press is the enemy. For we feel that our own words, since they are not in print, are not quite legitimate parts of prayer. Let me give one example.

Most people think that the *Amidah* ends with the words *elokai netzor* ("My God, keep my tongue from telling evil"). Of course, those closing sentences are not part of the *Amidah,* but one distinguished Jew's private prayer which has become beloved by the Jewish People. It is not the only way in which one can end the *Amidah*. But the point is not very effectively made by just stating it. You have to legitimize alternatives. Preceding this prayer of Mar bar Ravina after the *Amidah,* we have inserted the rubric: "At the end of the *Amidah* personal prayers may be added, before or instead of, the following" (p. 39).

We have also added alternatives to *elokai netzor* in the printed text. Thus, on Yom Kippur, the above rubric appears before a selection from a long prayer by Rabbi Elimelech of Lyzhansk:

> Keep me far from petty self-regard and petty pride, from anger, impatience, despair, gossip and bad traits. Let me not be overwhelmed by jealousy of others; let others not be overwhelmed by jealousy of me. Grant me the gift of seeing other people's merits, not their faults.

Printing various prayers after the *Amidah,* preceded by the note about personal prayer, is one way of stating that there are legitimate options, melting the freeze that so many of us are in by encouraging our own contributions to prayer as valuable and legitimate. Some of the best "new" sources we have included are so old that they are new! Thus, for example, I re-introduced Psalm 130. That is a great novelty! It usually appeared in the traditional *Mahzor*. But many prayer books published in the United States with English translation unfortunately have not included it in the High Holy Day service.

We have some laymen who serve as readers. When I send new material to them, in translation, I never note the sources. Later, if they ask, I will give them the sources. I sent out my translations of Psalm 130, arranged for responsive reading. One layman reacted by writing, "This is one of the best modern readings on sin that I've seen."

Another "radical innovation" of mine is the introduction of Psalm 103. I use it to introduce a section of the thirteen divine attributes *(middot)* in the evening service of the Day of Atonement. This psalm appears in the ancient Palestinian *nosah* for that service.

I also wanted to do something about the arrangement of certain sections of the *Mahzor,* highlighting themes without converting the volume into a text book. Let me take the thirteen *middot* (from Exodus 34:6–7) in part as an example of this. Too often they appear as a hodgepodge, here and there, without rubrics or emphasis. Rubrics and emphasis are needed, certainly for most congregants today. The *middot* should stand out typographically, first of all. And the emphasis on compassion should be very clear, through the use of a brief note on the traditional *piyyut* and through the use of newly added poetry. I tried to introduce and emphasize themes through the presentation of both old and new material. One "new" selection is taken from a book printed in Metz in 1788. It is an expansion of the *Tosafot* in the talmudic tractate *Rosh Hashanah*. I inserted it after one of the times when the thirteen *middot* are chanted. It is arranged in columns in the *Mahzor,* the *middot* in one column and the exposition of them in the other column. The text follows:

> THE LORD I am He before you sin
> THE LORD I am He after you sin
> GOD merciful to all, Gentile and Jew
> GRACIOUS to those with merit
> AND COMPASSIONATE to those without merit
> PATIENT with the wicked, who may repent
> ABOUNDING IN KINDNESS with those in need of kindness
> AND FAITHFULNESS rewarding those who do My will
> ASSURING LOVE FOR A THOUSAND GENERATIONS when you
>   do good deeds
> FORGIVING INIQUITY when you sin deliberately
> TRANSGRESSION when you rebel maliciously
> AND SIN when you sin unintentionally
> AND GRANTING PARDON when you repent

The service then continues: "Forgive us, our Father, for we have sinned. . . ."

Another new addition to this section of the thirteen *middot* is taken from the Middle Ages. It is a *piyyut* which had been used in some Sephardic communities. I would like to quote part of it. It appears in the *Mahzor* I edited right after *ki hinei kachomer* ("As clay in the hand of the potter," p. 395), which emphasizes our need and our hope and our prayer for God's compassion, that He should recall the Covenant by being compassionate in spite of our natures. *Laberit habbet ve'al tefen layetzer* (Your covenant recall, and not our imperfection").

The "new" *piyyut* then follows:

Whom can I accuse, of whom revenge demand,
When I have borne deep suffering at my own hand?
    Other hearts have held hatred for me,
    But my own heart hates me more than anyone knows.
My body bears the wounds of relentless foes,
But none can match my self-inflicted wounds.
    I have been seduced for my own destruction
    But none have lured me more than my own eyes.
I have been burned by countless fires,
But none compare to the heat of my desires.
    In traps I've been ensnared by old and young,
    But none have trapped me better than my tongue.
Bandits have pursued me, fast and fleet,
But none pursue me better than my feet.
    Pain overwhelms me, but no pain more than my rebellion.
    Anguish increases, but never faster than transgression.
Whom can I blame, how can I function,
When I am the source of my own destruction?
    I seek shelter for my soul, which You alone did fashion,
    For You, our God and King, are enthroned upon compassion.

This last line, of course, leads naturally into another *piyyut* associated with the thirteen *middot*, since this last line is the first line of the other *piyyut*. Some people have attributed this newly included *piyyut* from thirteenth century Spain to Abudraham, but according to Schirmann, the author is unknown.

Another "innovation" is my adaptation of *tefillah zakah*, (composed by Rabbi Abraham Danzig, 1748–1820). It is important to include prayer in the first person singular, to be recited silently. We inserted a great deal of meditative and reflective prose with which a Jew might confront himself during some silent moments on days of introspection and self-examination and search.

Inserting new prose and poetry from the modern period poses problems. One problem is that there is precious little new material appropriate for a service of prayer. I was unable to find any writer in Hebrew, Yiddish, or English to compose new prose or poetry specifically for this edition of the *Mahzor*. I did find material already written and which I adapted, and/or translated, with permission, for inclusion in the *Mahzor,* namely, selections by Miriam Kubovy, Zeev Falk, Hillel Zeitlin, Hillel Bavli, A. M. Klein, Nelly Sachs, Soma Morgenstern, and Anthony Hecht. (I also included passages from, among others, S. Y. Agnon, Martin Buber, Samson Raphael Hirsch, Isaac Luria, Ibn Gabirol, Maimonides, Bahya ibn Pakuda, Rabbi Simcha Bunam, Will Herberg, Leo Baeck, C. N. Bialik, and Avraham Holtz.)

To illustrate some of the considerations and sensitivities involved in the search for new material, I would like to quote part of a letter which I received from a writer whom I had invited to write for the prayer book. She is Cynthia Ozick. She was unable to write a poem which she felt to be suitable for inclusion.

> . . . the whole method of contemporary poetry is alien—one might even say with precise attention to its root-meaning, goyish—for your purposes. Poetry is the aesthetic way, the Greek way, and it is not the way to speak directly into the inner being of man-in-the-congregation. What I mean to tell you is that my efforts have all turned into poetry, into convoluted, over-compressed aesthetic designs . . . It seems that I cannot leap out of my place in the congregation; the learning must flow from the rabbinical sources to me. The rabbis must instruct the congregation, not the other way around. Learning makes simplicity; ignorance makes complexity. This has been my trouble in trying to meet your request. A bit of talent isn't enough, in fact nothing, without learning. And if you say, "No one's asking you for learning, we're perfectly aware how you stand as to *that,* we're asking for a response out of emotion," . . . I have discovered what (for me) seems to be a truthful answer: Emotion without learning is impossible. Or, if it turns out to be possible, it leads one into alien ways. . . .

In addition to everything else that she says here, Cynthia Ozick provides a certain critique of so much of the new material included in the various booklets. "Emotion without learning . . . leads one into alien ways."

Another problem that must be faced while producing a book of prayer for contemporaries is reflected in the fact that prayer refers to the *kudsha berikh hu* (the Holy One, Blessed be He) as a king. At one time, that was a powerful image. In the real world, at one time, a king had the power of God on earth. The power of life and death was in his hands. Who is a king today? The image has lost its power. Today a king has trouble with the guerrillas in Spain, a king is kicked out of Greece, royalty is that rather nice gentleman who accompanies that rather nice lady, the Queen, in England. But this is not the locus of awesome power. What can we suggest? Perhaps the most appropriate image for absolute power on earth in our time would be MC^2. Our MC^2 and MC^2 of our fathers! This alternative, like others, becomes rather silly, frivolous. President, chairman of the board, secretary-general. We cannot stop using the word "king"—*melekh*. But the problem exists, consciously or subconsciously, for many people. Somewhere in the *Mahzor,* in the *Siddur,* you have to confront the problem, and try to help people answer the question (or at least confront it): If God is King, so what? What does that mean for my life, and for my children's life?

We try to help answer or pose the question in a prelude to the verses of kingship for Rosh Hashanah. In this *Mahzor,* each of the *musaf* sections of *malkhuyot, zikhronot, shofarot,* is introduced by two pages, one page for each of the days of Rosh Hashanah, with one selection each in poetry and prose. They are a kind of *kavvanah,* for the sections.

One of the prose selections preceding *malkhuyot* is adapted from Will Herberg.

> To live a human life means to live in terms of something taken as the object of your supreme loyalty and devotion. This object of supreme loyalty and devotion is your god. Faith is your relation to your god. In this sense, every man has his god and his faith, whether he knows it or not, whether he wants it or not.
>
> The real problem, therefore, is not *whether* to have faith, but what *kind* of faith, faith in *what?* The basic choice is startlingly simple. It is: God or an idol. The choice is inescapable and it is all-important. It is a choice between some god and the God. Whether you are loyal to a god or to God defines the kind of person you are and the kind of life you lead.
>
> The decision for or against God is the primary decision of life. If we do not decide for God, quite inevitably we decide for some idol. "Choose this day whom you will serve."
>
> The world is idolatry-ridden, and in rebellion against God. Our vocation as members of the people Israel is to stand witness to our King, and the King of all mankind, amidst this universal rebellion and disobedience, to say no to every idolatrous pretension, to reject every claim to absolute devotion made by any earthly power—whether person, institution or idea—and to call man to knowledge and to service of the living God."

If God is King, *that's* what it means, among other things.

Another way of articulating the search is found in a poem by the late A. M. Klein, that extraordinarily gifted Canadian-Jewish poet. The poetry on the page with the Herberg quotation (p. 257), presented as another *kavvanah* for *malkhuyot,* is a poem by A. M. Klein.

> O incognito God, anonymous Lord,
> with what name shall I call You? Where shall I
> discover the syllable, the mystic word,
> that shall evoke You from eternity?
> Is that sweet sound a heart makes, clocking life,
> Your appellation? Is the noise of thunder, it?
> Is it the hush of peace, the sound of strife?
> I have no title for Your glorious throne,
> and for Your presence not a golden word—
> only that wanting You, by that alone
> I do evoke You, knowing I am heard.*

Finally, I would like to turn to two longer, difficult sections, known as *eleh ezkerah* (a martyrology) and *seder ha-avodah* (an account of the Temple ritual on the Day of Atonement). One problem with these sections is that traditionally each is a *piyyut*. *Piyyut* is inaccessible, for the most part, to congregants today. First of all, the various allusions are lost on most contemporaries. Then, too, in modern English (and in modern Hebrew), emotional impact is made through the use of nouns and verbs, not through the piling up of adjectives and adverbs, or obscure and semiobscure allusions to texts with which most people are not familiar.

In this "Operation Hutzpah: Of Presenting a New Version of *eleh ezkerah*," I retained only the refrain beginning with the words *eleh ezkerah*. The refrain reads, in English, "These I recall and pour my heart out./ How the arrogant have devoured us!" (p. 562). This refrain is used as a link between the various parts of the revised martyrology which includes liturgical reactions to various martyrdoms throughout our history. For the martyrology of the talmudic Sages I included passages from the Talmud describing those martyrdoms rather than the medieval passages, for the narrative in the Talmud uses nouns and verbs (rather than adverbs and adjectives) and also is a simpler text which is more readily appreciated by people today, in Hebrew or in English, than is the

---

* Published in *Poems of A. M. Klein* (Philadelphia: 1944), this poem, originally entitled "Psalm XXIV," is reprinted here by kind permission of the copyright holders, The Jewish Publication Society of America.

medieval poem about their martyrdom. I also included selections from the book of Psalms, from Bialik, Hillel Bavli, A. M. Klein (a long poem about those slaughtered in the *Shoah*), Nelly Sachs, Soma Morgenstern.

Finally, a few words on *seder ha-avodah*—the description of the Temple-worship. All the problems of *piyyut* mentioned before apply here as well. There are also additional problems. If one does not know the *Mishnah* tractate *Yoma*, dealing with the Day of Atonement, then the *piyyutim* for this section are rather remote in content. Rather than present and translate the text beginning with the words *amitz koach* ("Thou art strong and powerful") or any of the other *piyyutim*, I presented an anthology from *Mishnah Yoma*, preceded by a reading which tries to put into context the great significance of the sacrifices for our ancestors. Some modern editions of the *Mahzor*, as well as some essays, have presented an "understanding" of our ancestors, as primitive people, much caught up with blood and animals and all that! I tried rather to put the Temple sacrifices into their proper context as a very meaningful experience for those who went up to Jerusalem in majesty, in awe, and in solemn joy to be led to atonement and purification through the Temple Service of the High Priest.

Interspersed in the abridgement of *Mishnah Yoma* are the appropriate traditional liturgical sections accompanying the act of *koreim* (kneeling and prostrating oneself). Rubrics are used, in a few words each, to outline what is happening in the Temple service of the High Priest and his various confessions and ritual acts.

After the abridgement of *Mishnah Yoma,* and after a description of the *Kohen Gadol* (High Priest) taken from Ben Sira, and the prayer of the *Kohen Gadol,* the question is posed: How do we gain atonement in a world without animal sacrifice at the Temple? This, too, is not a new question. It was asked by Rabbi Yehoshua. We present his question, and the answer by his teacher, Rabbi Yochanan ben Zakkai: through *gemilut hasadim* (charity), which is probably more difficult than bringing a sacrifice. The section then closes with a reading presenting specific examples of charity including those found in the morning reading from the prophet Isaiah.

The section ends with another adapted quotation from Ben Sira (Ecclesiasticus):

Let us now praise the God of Israel
who works wonders throughout the world,
who ennobles us from our birth
and deals with us in mercy,
May He grant us wisdom of the heart.
And may there be peace among us. Amen.

Part IV

15
Prayer in Hasidism

Samuel Dresner

There once was a king who so loved music that he directed his musicians to play before him at a certain hour each morning. Those who came at the appointed time and performed received a reward, and those who arrived early, even before sunrise, received a double reward. But whether they arrived at the appointed time or earlier, they came not for the sake of the reward but only out of love for the king. For many years all went well. The musicians delighted in playing each morning before the king, and the king delighted in hearing their music.

When at last the musicians died, their sons sought to take their places. But alas, they had neither mastered the art of their fathers nor had they kept their instruments in proper condition. Worse still, the sons no longer loved the king as did their fathers and set their eyes only upon the reward, blindly following their fathers' custom of arriving early each morning at the palace to perform. But the harsh sounds that emerged were so offensive to the ear that the king gradually stopped listening to their music. So intent were the sons upon the reward, however, that greed closed their eyes to this reality, and they continued to come each day to play as usual.

Still, there were some among the sons of the old musicians who recognized that they were not worthy to play before the king. And they

were determined to correct the situation. They set about the difficult task of relearning the forgotten art. Before coming to the king, they would now first try to tune their instruments and in so doing would often arrive late. Upon entering the king's court and hearing the racket of the other musicians who were already present, they sought out an obscure corner for themselves where they could play undisturbed in accordance with their ability. It was there that they gathered each morning to perform, remaining long after the other musicians had departed so that they might improve their skill. And long before leaving their homes for the palace each morning, they continued to struggle with their poor instruments. The king was aware of their efforts and its was good in his eyes. For even though they did not play with the same talent as their fathers, still they strove, within their limits, to once more bring joy to the king. Thus was their music received by the king with favor.
Vikkuha Rabba (Pietrokov, 1912), p. 38

This parable was told by a disciple of one of the great masters of hasidic prayer, Rabbi Levi Yitzhak of Berditchev, from whom it may have originated. It contains allusions to some of the issues raised in the development of hasidic worship: criticism of rote prayer, establishment of separate Houses of Worship, and the delayed time for prayer. While in the generations prior to the rise of Hasidism, the study of Torah took precedence over prayer, for the Besht they were of equal importance. What had been endangered by perfunctory performance was transformed by *hitlahavut* and *devekut*.

The material that follows is a collection of hasidic sources on prayer that concentrates on the work of the early generations, for the direction of hasidic prayer was set by the Besht and his circle. The selection is organized according to certain of the aspects on which Hasidism laid stress. These texts should provide the reader with some idea of the wealth of material awaiting analysis by scholars.[1]

The Power of Man

Who Can Praise?

How is it possible for this clod of clay, man, to praise Him Who no angel can praise in accordance with the majesty of His Holiness?

But the question itself contains the answer. For if there were even a single creature in all the worlds who was able to glorify God as He deserves to be glorified, then it would be fitting that only he should do so. However, since there is none who can so praise Him, neither in Heaven above nor on earth below, therefore anyone is permitted to praise Him, even the humblest of the humble — even man.

This is the meaning of the verse, "Who can utter the mighty acts of the Lord, or make all His praise be heard" (Psalms 106:2)? It seems to impugn the possibility of prayer but actually affirms it, if scanned thus: "*Who* can utter the mighty acts of the Lord?" None can. Therefore, "*all of us* should make His praise be heard (Yashmiya kol tehilato)"

Levi Yitzhak of Berditchev
Kedushat Levi (Jerusalem: 1954), pp. 300, 301

Self-Abasement

I heard from my teacher [The Besht] that man's service of God is hampered through his self-abasement. For it is on this account that he may fail to believe that it is man, who, by his prayer and his study of Torah, brings blessings to all the worlds and even sustains the angels. Once believing this, with what joy and awe would man serve God, and with what care would he pronounce every word, every letter and every vowel. He would remember that the Holy One, blessed-be-He, watches over the lips of man to kiss them when he utters words of Torah and prayer with awe and love. Should man set his heart on this, how would he not be seized with fear and trembling at the thought that the great and awesome King watches the lips of mortal man. And this is what the Sages have said (*Gittin* 56a), "The self-abasement of R. Zechariah caused the destruction of the temple, etc." Man must understand that he is the "ladder fixed in the earth whose head reaches the Heavens" and whose every deed, every step, every word and every gesture leaves its impression on the Heavens. Surely, then, he should take care that all he does be for the sake of Heaven.

All this would not be the case were he to think: "Who am I to help or hinder; how could my deeds influence heaven?" But truly, this is not so. For through the good deeds of man, he can in fact cleave to the Blessed One, as it is written, "And you shall walk in His ways" (Deuteronomy 8:6), for as man is merciful on earth, so is mercy roused in Heaven. As I have explained the words to *Avot* (2:1), *Da ma lema'alah mimkha:* "Know that what is above, is from you." What you do here has effect there.

Ya'akov Yosef ha-Kohen *Toldot Ya'akov Yosef* (Koretz: 1780), f. 172c

One Word

The Divine Presence rejoices in the words of one who prays with love and awe, as a mother rejoices when her son speaks wisely, exclaiming, "Who is like Your people, Israel, a unique nation" (Chronicles 27:21)? Therefore, you should try to pray with love and fear—at least one word—for thereby you incite the angels and all the worlds to sing praises to the Lord. When, through the efforts of man, such words ascend to heaven, they are adorned, "splendor" is born, and the angels cry out.

Keter Shem Tov (Brooklyn: 1974), pt. 2, f. 40a, #306

Great Splendor

"Blessed is the king who is thus praised in his house," in such manner that [man's] body becomes God's house. . . . For God created the material world and created man within it in His image in order that His presence should reside within man. . . . But the angels, who comprise one third of the universe, provide much light and beauty, so what need is there for man? [Man's] beauty, however, is similar to the bird that sings before the king. Although the song of the bird is "silly", yet it pleases the king more than that which is more profound. Similarly, when base matter [i.e., man] elevates all the worlds by his [contemplative] thought, then a great awe and trembling seizes them [i.e., the angels] because of their fear of God, and they behold a great and resplendent light. All this becomes manifest through lowly man who dwells in the world, and [through him] a great splendour is born . . . through the body [i.e. matter] great beauty comes into being.

"Let us lift up our heart with our hands unto God in the heavens" (Lamentations 3:41). This means that the person who performs a Divine commandment brings new life to this world, for he brings prosperity to this world [if he intended so] or to the world to come [if his intention was directed thither]. "Hands" refer to the commandments, because they are the cause of the gift of the divine influx, like a hand that is stretched out for giving. And the right manner of performing the commandments is to act only with the intention of pleasing God, as in the [aforementioned] simile of the bird. Then God foresakes the song of all the countless worlds, and all the angels come to hear the utterance of man. But man thinks: who am I, despised and lowly, that I should cause great pleasure to God in all the worlds? Let him not think that owing to his lowliness God cannot derive pleasure from him. On the contrary, God dwells with the downtrodden and the humble. And pleasure is an important matter, as it is written, "Then shall you delight yourself in God" (Isaiah 58:14). This is the purpose of the commandments. And this is the meaning of "lift up our heart", that is, our thoughts, "with our hands", that is, by doing the commandments for the sake of God in heaven. David said, "the earth is full of the goodness of the Lord" (Psalm 33:5), for it is a great goodness that God should fill the earth, and that such a coarse thing should contain such a spiritual reality. When God['s presence] rests on [man's] words, then a great fear seizes him and he does not know where he is and he neither sees nor hears, because all corporeality has been annihilated. This is the meaning of the [above-mentioned] saying, "Blessing is the king who is thus praised in his house", for the body should be the house of God, and man ought to pray with all his strength until he is divested of corporeality and forgets his own self, so that only the life that is in God remains, and all his thoughts are directed to Him. [In this state of orison] man must not be aware of the intensity of his prayer, for every awareness is awareness of his own self. And all this occurs in the flash of a moment, which shows that it derives from the supratemporal.

Dov Ber of Mezeritch
Shemuah Tovah (Warsaw: 1938), f. 2b

What is Prayer?

My Child My Child

A father and son, who were once travelling together by wagon, came to the edge of a forest where great bunches of delicious berries, sweet to the taste, were to be found. When the boy saw the fruit, he asked his father to stop the wagon and wait for him while he gathered some. His father agreed but advised him to be quick about it, for they had no time to linger. The boy, however, delighting in the berries, gathered heap after heap, until the father complained: "My son, we must be on our way, for the moments are fleeting and the road still lies before us." To no avail; the boy's desire was his master. Now the father, seeing that nothing could be done with his son, at last called to the boy:

"Hearken to me, my child, and I shall give you good counsel, so that in your search for the berries you do not stray from the path which leads to me.

"Keep calling: 'My father! My father,' and I shall answer you: 'My son! My son!' So long as you hear my voice, know that I too hear your voice. But, beware, should you fail to hear my voice, then know that you are lost in the thickets of the forest. And run to me with all your strength, until you find me."

Shmuel Shmelke of Nikolsburg
Divrey Shmuel (Jerusalem: 1953), p. 124

Hidden in the Light of God

The Holy One, Blessed-be-He, encompasses all worlds. There is no place where He is not. The Besht said that when one desires to experience God's Presence, he should dwell upon the thought that he himself is as nothing and that there is naught in him but the Divine.

A parable: When one dives into the sea for pearls, he must beware of two things: not to suffocate, and to gather pearls. Otherwise, all his labor is for naught.

One may learn from this parable the way to serve the Creator. For God created the sea (which represents the fifty gates of understanding) in order that

Israel, that is, the souls of Israel, might go down into the waters by means of the boats, which are their bodies, to collect pearls, which are the letters of the Torah and the *mizvot*. Thus it is written, "those who go down to the sea in ships do their business in the great waters, they see the work of the Lord and His wonders in the depths" (Psalm 107:23-24). If a man is about to do a mizvah or study Torah or pray, let him reflect that he is hidden in the light of God, as it is written, "He who dwelleth in the secret place of the Most High" (Psalm 91:1), that is, in the light of the *En Sof*. Thereby will he merit to "abide under the shadow of the Almighty" (ibid.). And he will gather pearls, i.e., words of holiness, which he himself will not speak, but they will be spoken through him by the Divine power.

Thus, for example, when a person prays with proper *kavvanah* the words [of the *Amidah*]—"Blessed art thou [O Lord our God . . . great, mighty and revered . . ."—the spoken words represent divine Names]: "Blessed (*Barukh*) is a divine Name; "[art] thou" (*atah*) is a divine Name; "great, mighty and revered," which signify *sefirot*, are certainly [divine Names]. Then awe will descend upon him. When a person utters the word, "great", he should think on repenting out of love; when he utters the word, "mighty", he should think on repenting out of awe; and when he utters the word, "revered", he should think on how his repentance out of love and awe will bring "glory" to God. One should concentrate on joining the letters to their source through love, and to bring about a *yihud* in all the worlds from the unity in which man is included.

Or Ganuz la-Zaddikim (Warsaw: 1887), *par. pinhas*, p. 49

Minhah

The morning prayer is called *Shaharit*, which means "dawn," because it refers to the dawn of the day, while the evening prayer is called *Ma'ariv* because it refers to the eventide of the day. Rabbi Yomtov Heller explained that the afternoon prayer is called *Minhah* because it refers to the repose (*menuhah*) of the sun.

But I would like to give a different reason.

We are obliged to say the morning prayer because God has returned our souls to us and has brought us the light of the sun and so many other good things. Thus, in the morning service, we say, "true and abiding" has been the Lord. We are also obliged to pray the evening prayer, because we are giving over our souls to the Lord and trust that He will be faithful to return them to us. Thus, in the evening service, we say, "true and faithful" is He. But we are not at all obliged to pray the afternoon prayer. We offer it to God of our own free will. Therefore do we call it *Minhah*, for that is what it is—a "gift".

Levi Yitzhak of Berditchev
Kedushat Levi, p. 40

How to Judge

There is a way a man may judge the thought he thinks. If, when he prays to God, that thought does not obstruct his prayer but, on the contrary, strengthens it, then the thought is pure. But should it in any way disturb or weaken his prayer, he is obliged to cleanse his mind, as one would refine a precious metal by removing the dross—even though, at first, he believed this to be a holy thought.

Levi Yitzhak of Berditchev
Kedushat Levi, p. 193

Prayer Is the Shekhinah

I Am Prayer

I heard from my teacher [the Besht] that the *Shekhinah,* the Divine Presence, is called prayer. For the verse in Psalms (109:4) may be read, "and I [the Lord] am prayer."

Ya'akov Yosef *Zafenat Paneah* (Koretz: 1782), f. 1a.

Lord, Lord

Rabbi Levi Yitzhak of Berditchev taught:
It is written:
"And Moses rose up early in the morning and went up unto Mount Sinai as the Lord commanded him and took in his hands two tables of stone . . . and he cried out, 'the Lord, the Lord, merciful and gracious, long-suffering, abundant in goodness and truth . . .' " (Exodus 34:4, 6).

In the phrase ". . . he cried out, 'the Lord, the Lord . . .'," why is "the Lord" repeated twice? Would once not have been enough? But read it thus: "The Lord cried out—'O Lord'! . . . (*"Vayikra Adonai—'Adonai'* ").

"It is the *neshamah,* man's soul", he explained, "calling to the Holy One, blessed-be-He. For the soul of man is a divine portion from above. Thus when "the Lord passed by", that is, when the feeling of love and awe for Heaven overwhelms one, the divine within—'the Lord'—cries out to the divine above—'O Lord' ".

Siftey Zaddikim (Lemberg: 1863), f. 32b–33a

Prayer Itself Is God

People think that they pray *to* God. But this is not so.
Prayer itself is God.

For it is written, "Your prayer is your God" ("*Hu tehilatkha ve-Hu Elohekha*") (Deuteronomy 10:21).

Pinhas of Koretz
Midrash Pinhas (Jerusalem: 1953), #52

Preparing for Prayer

A Passage of *Zohar*

The Baal Shem Tov directed his disciples to study a passage of the *Zohar* before they prayed.

(*Likutey Torah*, Lemberg: 1884, #7)

Before Sunrise

No matter what the season, one should take special care to begin his prayer before sunrise. That is, the prayers preceding the *Shema* should be recited before daybreak. For so great is the difference between prayer at dawn and prayer recited later in the day that it can hardly be imagined. Before dawn one can still combat the destructive forces of the coming day. Do not take this lightly. The Baal Shem was so exact about this matter that he would even begin to worship without a *minyan* in order to pray at the proper hour.

Zeva'at ha-Baal Shem Tov (Brooklyn: 1975): p. 5, #16

Daybreak

I like to pray at daybreak before the world fills up with foolishness and vanity.

Pinhas of Koretz
Midrash Pinhas, #35

From a Book

When one is on a lower rung, it is better to pray from a book, for seeing the letters of the worlds helps one pray with greater *kavvanah*. But when one cleaves to the upper worlds, then it is best to close one's eyes, that what he sees not distract him from cleaving.

Zeva'at, p. 11, #40

Letter and Word

God Dwells within the Letters

In worship, you should have in mind that the letters of prayer are the garments of God. And say to yourself: "I am making a garment for so great a king; I should make it joyously". In this way you become one with God who dwells within the letters.

Zeva'at, p. 37, #108

Tevah

"Build yourself an ark of gopher wood. Make a light for the ark; make it with lower, second and third decks. Go into the ark, you and all your household" (Genesis 6:15–17).
"Make a light for the ark (*tevah*)"
That is, every word (*tevah*) of prayer we utter should give forth light.
"Make it with lower, second and third decks."
That is, every letter contains worlds, souls and the Presence of God. As the letters are joined to one another and form the words of prayer, all that is within them rises up to God. He who joins his soul to this process brings all the worlds together in boundless joy.
"Go into the ark (*tevah*), you and all your house."
That is, enter into the word (*tevah*) with all your body and all your strength.

Zeva'at, p. 23, #65

Into the Word

"Go into the *tevah* (= 'ark' or 'word'), you and all your house." For the Torah and the Holy One, Blessed-be-He, are all one, and so the Holy One, Blessed-be-He, is present in the Torah. Now when man utters a word (*tevah*) [of Torah or prayer] with all his power, then he too is present in that word. And this power is the soul which pervades his whole body, and which is a part of the Godhead. In this manner that part is completely attached to the root, for the souls of the righteous are, as it were, the limbs of the *Shekhinah*. And this is the meaning of the unification of the Holy One, Blessed-be-He, and His *Shekhinah*.

Or ha-Emet, f. 36b

Entering into the Letters

The holy Rabbi, the sacred light, our master, Rabbi Dov Ber, of blessed memory, who said in the name of the Besht, of blessed memory, that the passage in the *Zohar* which states that man was judged in every "heavenly hall" (*heykhal*), referred to the words and the letters of the prayers, which are called heavenly halls. There man is judged whether he is worthy of entering into the letters of the prayers; if he is unworthy he is driven away, that is, he is visited by alien thoughts and is thus thrust away.

Orah le-Hayim (Jerusalem, 1960), f. 98a.

From Letter to Letter

You should put all your strength into the words, proceeding from letter to letter with such concentration that you lose awareness of your bodily self. It then seems to you that the letters themselves are flowing into one another. This uniting of the letters brings great happiness. For if joy is felt at physical joining, how much greater must be the joy of this union in spirit! Thus do you ascend to the world of *Yezirah* or Creation. From there you rise to the level where you no longer hear what you say, which is the world of *Beriah* or Ideas. After this, you come to the level of total unawareness of self (*ayin*), which is the world of *Azilut* or Emanation.

Keter Shem Tov, pt. 2, f. 56a, #387

Kavvanah

The Merit of the Besht (in the *Baal Shem Tov*)

The soul told the Besht that the reason why heavenly matters were revealed to him was not because he had studied many tractates of the Talmud and Codes of Law, but because of his prayer. For at all times he worshipped with great *kavvanah*.

Zeva'at, p. 12, #41

Ready to Die

Before you begin to pray, decide that you are ready to die in that very prayer.

There are some people who worship with such *kavvanah,* giving up so much of their strength to prayer, that if not for a miracle, they would die after uttering only two or three words. It is only through God's great kindness that their souls do not depart from them when they are joined to Him in prayer, and they live.

Zeva'at, p. 12, #42

The Meaning of the Word

I heard from my teacher [the Besht]:
  In study or worship, if one understands the clear meaning of the law or of the words of prayer, then one joins the lower *Sefirah,* which is the word, to the higher *Sefirah,* which is the mind.

Toledot, f. 167b

Renewed Vigor

A parable:
  There was once a musician, well known for the great beauty of his music, who came to play before the king. One particular melody was so loved by the king that he ordered the musician to play it for him several times each day. And so it was. After a time, however, the musician began to weary of the tune; no longer could he play it with the same passion and excitement as before. The king, to rekindle his musician's love for this favorite tune, ordered that a man be brought in from the market, one who had never heard the tune before. Seeing someone who had never heard him play, the musician's vigor was renewed, and he played the tune in all its beauty. Thus the king ordered a new man brought each day.
  After some time, the king sought other counsel, for to find a new audience each day was not an easy matter. It was decided that the musician should be blinded so that he never see a human form again. Now the blind musician sat before the king, and whenever the king sought to hear his favorite tune, he would simply say: "Here comes someone new, one who has never heard you play before!" And the musician would play his tune with the greatest joy.
  The parable is not explained.

Or ha-Meir (Koretz: 1788), f. 60a

Sabbath and Weekday

One should not say: "I will be concerned to pray with *kavvanah* on the Sabbath, but not necessarily on an ordinary weekday." This would be like serving the king when the king is before his eyes, while doing him no obeisance when he is absent. Such a one is not a faithful subject of the king. On the contrary, the proper attitude would be to recognize that to be away from the king is intolerable, and thus he should not hesitate to break down any and all obstacles to his presence. Moreover, though he may not be able properly to address the king and certainly is not worthy even to come into his presence, the king will grant him his favor, for the king is exceedingly merciful.

Zeva'at, pp. 27, 28, #88

Unable to Pray

If you cannot say your prayers properly, you should not therefore abandon worship that day. Rather should you exert yourself all the more, that you might experience more and more awe of the Lord.

A parable:

Once a king went out to battle and disguised himself. Perceptive persons were capable of recognizing the king on the battlefield by his characteristic movements. Less perceptive people knew where the king was by the fact that his was the most protected place in the ranks.

Similarly, when you are unable to pray with *kavvanah,* know that it is because there are guards protecting the King and you cannot come close for the large retinue which surrounds Him. Therefore, it is necessary to gird yourself with awe and with *kavvanah,* that you may draw near and pray before the Lord. In so doing, you will be able to worship with even more *kavvanah.*

Zeva'at, pp. 22, 27, 28, #88, 72

Melody

There are those who sing their prayers, being particular to select just the right melody for each prayer. They hold that this is proper worship, through which they will reach *hitlahavut* and bring joy to the Lord. But this is not the true way of prayer. Those who pursue it are fools and walk in darkness. They have not even begun to understand the proper manner of worship, which is the following:

Divest yourself of all worldliness, until you have reached the stage where you no longer are aware of this world. Recite the words aloud in a simple, clear voice. Then, of itself, you will suddenly be aflame with an all-consuming awe and love of God.

I have received this holy way of worship from my teacher [Rabbi Levi Yitzhak]. And he received it from his teacher, the Maggid. And he received it from the Baal Shem Tov. And he received it from his teacher, Ahiya ha-Shiloni. For this is the true manner of serving the Holy One, blessed-be-He.

Aaron of Zhitomir
Pitgamim Kadishin (Warsaw: 1886), p. 17

Kavvanah and Kavvanot

He who attempts to pray with *kavvanah,* utilizing all the *kavvanot* familiar to him, can, of course, employ only those which are known by him. On the other hand, if one pronounces a word of prayer with much *hitkashrut,* then every *kavvanah,* known or unknown to him, is included with it. This is because every letter is a complete world, and when a word is uttered with *hitkashrut,* the worlds represented by the letters are awakened and deeds of cosmic significance are effected. Consequently, a man should see to it that he pray with much *hitkashrut* and *hitlahavut* so that each letter can bring about an awakening in the spheres above.

Zeva'at, p. 41, #118

Kavvanah for the Mikveh

To welcome the Sabbath in holiness and purity, one should visit the *mikveh* on the preceding day. In preparation for this one humbles himself, casts off his sins and accepts the yoke of heaven. Then he is ready to serve the Lord in love (which is the *Sefirah* of *Besed*) and awe (which is the *Sefirah* of *Gevurah*), in order that the Holy One, blessed-be-He, might glory in him (the *Sefirah* of *Tiferet*), as it is written, "Israel in whom I glory" (Isaiah 49:3). He gives himself up to the sanctification of the holy Name. Through his faith that God will return the cast off, the "other side" will be vanquished (*Sefirah* of *Nezah*). One must thank God (*Sefirah* of *Hod*), that he has been delivered from the depths of the sea. Then is he counted as righteous, for the righteous one is the foundation of the world (*Sefirah* of *Yesod*). Thus is God magnified, and the glory of His kingdom (*Sefirah* of *Malkhut*) is recognized forever. [And all seven *Sefirot* are encompassed.]

Having prepared oneself in this fashion, he enters the *mikveh*. And the following is his *kavvanah* there:

The Name *ADoNoY* is the mystery of the "word"; the Name *HaVaYaH* is the mystery of the "voice"; the Name *EHYeH* is the mystery of "thought". The ceiling of the *mikveh* represents the Name *EHYeH;* the four walls of the *mikveh* represent the four letters of the Name *HaVaYaH,* blessed-be-He; and the floor of the *mikveh* represents the Name *ADoNoY.* The *gematria* (numerical equivalent) of these three names equals the *gematria* of the Hebrew letters *YBK* (112) and is an acronym for Y*ihud,* "unification," B*erakhah,* "blessing," and K*edushah,* "holiness."

Concentrate upon asking the Holy One, blessed-be-He, that you enter the *mikveh* so that your "thought", your "voice" and your "word" might be pure and holy.

If you concentrate upon this, [all will be well], for "though the righteous stumbles seven times, he will yet rise (Prov. 24:16)"; and though he falls back seven rungs, God will yet heal him and make a new covenant with him which will not be broken. His soul will be enlightened by a spiritual force (= *KoMaH,* the same letters as *MiKVeH*). And let him recite the verse, "the *mikveh* of Israel is the Lord, who delivers him in time of trouble" (Jeremiah 14:8).

Ba'al Shem Tov
Kedushat Levi al Pirkey Avot

(Grosswarden: 1863), the end

Awe, Love, Joy

Awe Is the Gate

Begin to pray out of awe (*yirah*), which is the gate to God's presence. Think to yourself: "To Whom do I wish to cleave? To Him Who by His word created, constituted and sustains all the worlds". Dwell upon His greatness and His exaltedness and subsequently you will ascend to the higher worlds.

Zeva'at, p. 106, #66

From Awe to Love

To worship God in truth one must do so from love and awe. Some confuse melancholy with awe and emotion with love, when they pray. But those who genuinely pray out of love, feel shame, yearn to extol God and to conquer the evil desire. And genuine awe is not the result of man's efforts but of God's grace, descending from above, bringing trembling and tears which flow of themselves. The gateway to love is awe, without which one fools oneself to think he prays out of love. For how can one who has failed to pass through the gate of awe enter the gate of love? His prayer is perfunctory and the "joy" he feels may be only the joy of frivolity. Such a one should turn to the Lord with all his heart and soul.

Likutey Yekarim (Levov: 1792), f. 2a

Joy

How much more pleasing to God is prayer in joy than that which is said in sadness and tears!

Zeva'at, p. 37, #107

All My Bones

Motions

Do not laugh at one who moves his body, even violently, during prayer. He who is drowning in a river makes all kinds of motions to try to save himself. That is no time for others to laugh.

Baal Shem Tov
Likutey Yekarim, 14d

Vigor

You can only achieve prayer with *kavvanah* by exerting great vigor yourself and by petitioning the Lord for help.

Zeva'at, p. 19, #60

Rung

If, while at prayer, one should fall from the rung of his spiritual "ladder" let him recite the words of that prayer with as much *kavvanah* as he can muster. Then let him exert his entire being in order to return to the higher level, even if it means reciting a single prayer several times. At first, let him speak the "body" of the words; afterwards investing the words with "soul". Analogously, a man must first awaken his body to Divine service: only then will the power of the soul shine forth within him. This we find in the *Zohar* (*Shelah* 168a): "If a piece of wood fails to burn, it should be stirred until it catches fire." Afterward it will be possible for him to serve God in the mind alone without any movement of the body. When one has attained the grade of cleaving to the upper spheres, that is, to the Creator of the world, he must take care not to move even a portion of his body, lest he destroy his cleaving.

Zeva'at pp. 18, 19, #58, 59

Old Age

There are times when you cannot pray with *hitlahavut,* though you want to. Rabbi Israel Baal Shem said that it was of this that King David petitioned: "Cast me not off in old age" (Psalm 17:9). For he felt tired, like an old man.

Or Torah (Lemberg: 1863), *par. ekev*

Katnut

I heard an important principle from my teacher [the Besht]:

You should bind yourself to the innermost essence of the Torah that you study, or the *mizvah* that you perform. When, at times, you fall to a low spiritual level (*katnut*), do not abandon the yoke of proper Torah-study and prayer by saying the words hastily and perfunctorily.

Though the "word" is in exile, you can strengthen yourself by raising your voice. Do not be ashamed before others—Sages or those who mock. For it is written, "Whatever comes to hand, do with all your strength." The power of the cry is known, and when you shout, you disperse the *kelipot,* and then will ascend to the rung of "their heart cried out to the Lord" (Lamen. 2:18), truly pouring out your soul before the Creator, until you are faint.

Hekhal ha-Berakhah (Lvov: 1863), pt. 5, f. 210d

The Silent Cry

Learn to pray quietly. Even God's praises should be said softly. Your shouts should be whispers. Nevertheless, say the words of worship or study with all your strength, as it is written: "All my bones shall say: 'Lord, who is like unto Thee?' " (Psalm 35:10)

Zeva'at, p. 10, #33

Converse with the Shekhinah

Prayer is converse with the *Shekhinah.* Just as one moves his body in beginning the act of love, so must one do when he commences to pray. Later, one is able to stand still, without any movement, cleaving to the *Shekhinah* with great *devekut.*

Zeva'at, p. 21, #68

Motionless

There are times when one should serve God with the soul alone; that is, in thought, keeping his body quite motionless. For man can, on occasion, pray with awe and love and great *hitlahavut* without his body at all. To others it may appear that he is praying without cleaving; in reality, his prayers are on the highest rung and his words ascend to God more rapidly and with more *devekut* than prayer accompanied with the outwardly visible movement of his bodily members. What is more, the *kelipah* has no dominion over such prayer, since it is all inward.

Zeva'at, p. 37, #104–105

Devekut

Drunk with Joy

At times, you are drunk with the joy of the Torah that burns as a fierce love in your heart. At times, the love of God burns so powerfully within your heart, that the words of prayer seem to rush forth quickly of themselves. At such times, it is not you yourself who speak; rather it is through you that the words are spoken.

Likutey Yekarim, f. 15a, b

Prolonging Each Word

Cleaving in prayer is manifested by prolonging each word as if one does not wish to separate himself from it.

Zeva'at, p. 21, #70

Too Many Psalms

One should not recite too many psalms before commencing formal prayer, lest he weaken himself and consequently be unable properly to recite the essential liturgy of the day (that is, the introductory psalms, the *Shema,* and the Silent Devotion). He should not exhaust himself with less important things, but rather first utter the essential prayers with as much cleaving as he can. If [when he has completed his worship] God should grant him additional strength, then let him recite a number of extra psalms and read the Song of Songs with a spirit of cleaving. Before *Neilah,* which are the closing prayers on the Day of Atonement, one should review the prayers of the High Holydays without cleaving, as a preparation to cleaving during the closing prayers. . . .

Zeva'at, p. 11, #38

The Last Part

One should consider himself fortunate that God has enabled him to recite half his prayers with true *kavvanah.* Toward the last part of the service, when he weakens and loses the state of cleaving, let him continue to recite the prayers until the end of *Alenu* as best he can, even with diminished *kavvanah.*

Zeva'at, p. 19, #61

"Blessed Art Thou"

As long as you can still say the words, "Blessed art Thou", by your own will, know that you have not yet reached the deeper levels of prayer. Be so stripped of selfhood that you have neither the awareness nor the power to say a single word on your own.

R. Gerhson of Kitov
Avodat Yisrael (Yusafaf: 1842), p. 47a

Miraculously

R. Gershon said of his brother-in-law, the Baal Shem, that he achieved the rung of *hitpashtut,* (divesting) being so divested of all worldliness that he was no longer aware of himself, nor could he speak, his lips miraculously whispering prayers.

Zohar Hay, vol. 2, 27a

Conversing with People

I heard from the Rav of the holy community of Polnoy that the Besht was not able to converse with people, so wholly did he cleave to God. Then his teacher [Ahijah the prophet] taught him which verses of the psalms to recite each day, until he was able to learn how to converse with people without ceasing to cleave to God.

Zohar Hay, vol. 4, (Lemberg: 1885–1891), p. 228

Rung

You cannot begin your prayers in *devekut*. Do not, therefore, exhaust your strength at the beginning, but proceed from rung to rung. Say the words with close attention and grow in strength, until God will help you to draw near and remain in his presence (*devekut*). Commence with composure and by the middle of your worship effect the great cleaving to God.

Zeva'at, 56, #32

Contemplation

Sometimes a man lies in his bed and it appears to others that he is asleep, while in reality he is communing with God in solitude.

One has attained a very exalted rung when one can "see" God with the eye of his mind, as clearly as one can see another person. Also, one should be aware that God is watching him in the same manner as he is watched by other persons. Therefore, let his thoughts always be pure and clear.

At first let him cleave properly to God in the Lower World. Later, he will be able to ascend to the Upper Worlds. It will be necessary to descend a number of times during the day in order to rest from [the exertion of] his contemplation and there will be occasions when one will be unable to serve God save on the level of *katnut,* that is, he will not be able to ascend to the highest world.

Should one, when at prayer, be incapable of ascending to the Upper Worlds, let him serve God in the Lower World with love and awe. By virtue of such cleaving to God, he will merit the ascent to that world above all firmaments, thrones, *ofanim,* and *seraphim,* where he will be able to speak [to God].

When thinking of God, let one be reminded that "the whole earth is full of His glory," and that God's *Shekhinah* is constantly at his side. Although God is pure spirit, He is the Lord of all actions performed in the world and He can accomplish whatever His servant desires. Consequently, one should put one's trust in none save God alone. Let him think that he can perceive the *Shekhinah* at his side as clearly as he can see material things. This is the service of God in *katnut*.

Sometimes a man comes to realize that above him lie many spheres while he is standing on a small portion of an earth, which is an insignificant part of a universe created by God in the act of *tsimtsum* and is nothing when compared to Him. However, despite this realization, he is unable to ascend to the Upper Worlds. This is what is meant by the verse: "From afar the Lord appeared to me" (Jeremiah 31:3). That is, the person is able to see God only from afar.

On the other hand, if he serves the Creator in *gadlut*, namely, he girds his strength, ascends in contemplation, splitting all the upper spheres simultaneously, rises higher than the angels, the *ofanim*, the *seraphim* and the thrones—then he has attained the perfect service of God.

Dov Ber of Mezeritch
Zeva'at, pp. 49, 50, #135-137

For Heaven's Sake

Why Pray?

I have heard from my teacher [the Besht] that the righteous are agents of the *Shekhinah*. From the want that one feels, he can know the want of the *Shekhinah*, and it is to fill this latter need that one should pray. For thereby the *Shekhinah* is joined to the Holy One, blessed-be-He. And this is the purpose of prayer.

To the question asked by Sages of previous generations as to why we pray at all, since God is aware of our needs, my teacher replied according to that which is written above. Prayer is for Heaven's sake. For from man's needs, he knows what God needs, since the one comes from the other. Man's prayer should be that the *Shekhinah's* needs are met. He should pray not for himself but for the *Shekhinah*.

Zafenat Paneah (Koretz: 1782), 39b

Needs

All of man's prayers should be for the sake of *Shekhinah* who herself is called prayer. Each of man's needs is only a reflection of some lack in the Divine Presence. He should pray for her fulfillment, not merely his own. As man brings oneness to the upper worlds and restores that which is lacking above, his own needs too will be fulfilled.

Hekhal ha-Berakhah 4:82a

Needs

I heard from my teacher [the Besht]:

The *Shekhinah* is called "prayer," as the passage "and I am prayer" (Psalm 109:4) is explained in the mystical writings. In prayer, one should be concerned not with oneself but with the divine union of the *Shekhinah* and her Master. My teacher explained further: One whose prayer asks that his own physical needs be met creates a wall of separation, for he introduces material concerns into what should be the realm of the spiritual. His prayer will not be answered.

Zafenat Paneah, f. 1b

In Order not to Receive a Reward

"Do not be like those who serve the master in order to receive a reward. Be rather like those who serve the master not in order to receive a reward" (*Avot* 1:3).

But another version of this text reads: "Be rather like those who serve the master in order *not* to receive a reward!"

I heard from my grandfather, the Baal Shem Tov, that both versions are correct, but the latter speaks of a higher rung of service.

The first version—serving the master "not in order to receive a reward"—surely speaks of a proper kind of prayer, one in which the worshipper directs his thoughts only to the needs of God. It matters little to him whether his own personal petition is granted or denied. All of this servant's deeds are for the sake of heaven.

But there is yet a higher rung, of which the second version speaks. There is a man who lives with a burning desire to speak with the king. The king has issued a decree that anyone who comes forward with a petition shall have his wish granted. This man, however, longs only to stand before the king and speak with him always. In him the king's decree arouses only fear: "whatever I ask, the king will grant, and no longer will I be able to speak with him!" He would rather his petition *not* be granted, so that he might have reason always to return to the presence of the king! This man serves "in order *not* to receive a reward."

This is the meaning of: "a prayer of a poor man who is faint, pouring forth his words before the Lord" (Psalm 102:1). This "poor man" seeks nothing more in prayer than that his words "pour forth before the Lord."

Hekhal ha-Berakha, pt. 5, p. 209a;
Degel Mahaney Efrayim (Koretz: 1811), *par. tetzey,* f.95a

To Speak to the King

Once there was a wonderfully kind king who decreed that on a certain festive day all requests would be granted. Some asked for gold, others for land and titles. But there was one wiser than the rest. His request was only that he be permitted to enter the palace and speak in person with his royal highness, the king, three times a day.

His request found more favor in the eyes of the king than all the others.

Baal Shem Tov
Toledot, f.169a

The Poor Man

The psalmist says: "A prayer from a poor man" (*Tefillah le-ani*, 102:1). But if this is what it means, should it not have been written "*Tefila* mey-*ani*", instead of "*Tefillah* le-*ani*", which seems to mean, "A prayer *to* a poor man?"

I have heard the following explanation from my teacher [the Besht]:

Though the treasure houses of the king are full, they are managed by the king's officials. Having nothing to do with all his treasures, the king himself is like a poor man. He who comes in search of treasure will never see the King of kings. Only one who seeks no riches, who prays as to a poor man, can come before the King Himself.

Toledot, f.169a

One and Many

All Israel

Any prayer that is not said in the name of all Israel is not a prayer.

Pinhas of Koretz
Midrash Pinhas, p. 12, #18

Community of Love

I heard this incident from the Baal Shem Tov, who reported that it occurred to him once when he prayed with his friends. Not able to draw out their prayers as was his practice, they finished before him and waited. But after a time, when he still had not completed the *Amidah,* they left him, each going to take care of his own needs. Later they reassembled in the synagogue.

Subsequently the Besht told them: By leaving me alone, you have brought about *perud* (separation).

Then he recounted this parable:

Once in a tropical country, a certain splendid bird, more colorful than any that had ever been seen, was sighted at the top of the tallest tree. The bird's plumage contained within it all the colors in the world. But the bird was perched so high that no single person could ever hope to reach it.

When news of the bird reached the ears of the king, he ordered that a number of men try to bring the bird to him. They were to stand on one another's shoulders, until the highest man could reach the bird and bring it to the king. The men assembled near the tree, but while they were standing balanced on one another's shoulders, some of those near the bottom decided to wander off. As soon as the first man moved, the entire chain collapsed, injuring several of the men. Still the bird remained uncaptured.

The men had doubly failed the king. For even greater than his desire to see the bird was his wish to see his people closely joined to one another.

From the above parable we understand the custom of saying the verse, "Thou shalt love they neighbor as thyself" (Leviticus 19:18) before reciting the *Amidah* prayer. For the worshippers should be joined in love.

The Besht explained: While you were at prayer all was well, but when you departed, each going his separate way, it seemed that you did not love one another, and because of this you dispersed. Then everything collapsed.

For since it was with the Torah that God created all the worlds, and all this was for the sake of Israel, therefore each Israelite has his source in a single letter of the Torah. And just as the worlds created through the Torah stand one above the other, so with the people Israel. Since they find their source in the letters of the Torah, they must always be joined together in love. For as the Torah is one, so must they be as one. And thereby they have the power to reach the divine outpouring through him who is closest to the supernal mercy. But you dispersed for your own personal needs, which implied that there was no bond of affection among you. And that there was surely not a bond of affection for the one above you. Thus everything collapsed. The proper way is for each to be bound in love to his neighbour and to his leader, that they may be able to reach the higher Mercy.

Or ha-Hokhmah (Leshtzov: 1815), *par. beha'alotekha,* f. 44d

The Mighty Warrior

I heard from my teacher [the Besht]:

In a certain country there was a mighty warrior in whom all the people of the land put their trust. They did not bother to learn the arts of war, for they relied upon this mighty warrior who was among them. War broke out later and the mighty warrior wanted to make ready his weapons, but one of the enemy, a clever man, had stolen these weapons one by one, until the warrior was left with nothing to fight with. The people, who had relied on him, were taken captive with him. (The words of the wise are full of grace!)

Thus we can understand the verse, "Happy is the people who know the joyful shout" (Psalm 89:16). That is to say, when the people do not rely on a mighty warrior, but they themselves know the joyful shout of war, then "they walk, O Lord, in the light of Thy countenance (ibid.)." They do not rely on the great ones alone.

Toledot, f.210d

Cantors

I heard from my teacher [the Besht]:

The people should not rely upon the cantors for the Days of Awe. Each one should pray for himself.

Ben Porat Yosef, f.34b

Alone before God

I have heard in the name of R. Nahman:

"No man shall ascend with you . . . upon that mountain" (Exodus 34:3).

When you stand before God in prayer, you should feel that you stand before Him alone. Then you will be freed from all distractions.

Ben Porat Yosef, f. 69d

Use has been made of material from the following works, for which acknowledgement is hereby given: Green and Holtz, *Your Word Is Fire* (New York: 1977); Dr. H. Stern, "The Testament of the Baal Shem Tov" (diss., Northwestern University, 1976); S. Dresner, *The Zaddik* (New York: 1977); S. Dresner, *Rabbi Levi Yitzhak of Berditchev*, (Bridgeport: 1974); S. Dresner, *Prayer, Humility and Compassion* (Bridgeport: 1974); and R. Schatz, "Contemplative Prayer in Hasidism," *Studies in Mysticism and Religion for G. Scholem* (Jerusalem: 1967). In most cases, where former translations have been consulted, they have been modified for this volume.

Note

1. See L. Jacobs, *Hasidic Prayer* (London: 1972).

16
My New Prayer Book

S. Y. Agnon

It was a new prayer book that my father brought me from the fair. White were its columns, its letters lit up your eyes, its binding was beautiful. This was to be *my* prayer book, my friend and comrade, my holy companion.

All that day I pored over it, leafed its pages, thumbed it. How many prayers this little prayer book contained! Prayers for the Sabbath and prayers for the weekdays, for Rosh Hashanah and Yom Kippur, for Hanukkah and Purim. It was as if the Holy One, blessed be He, had bound together all His sacred days into my one little prayer book.

Everything in that prayer book, it seems, is for me alone. Just the same there are in it a number of things that I don't quite need, such as the prayers for the washing of hands, or the putting on of *zizit,* or the *kiddush* for the Sabbath, for I know them by heart. It may be that the prayer book maker really made this *Siddur* for my younger brother, or made it two or three years ago, before these minor prayers came easily to me. However, I am grateful that he has included the texts for the donning of phylacteries; I have not yet reached, it is true, the age of discretion and *tfillin,* but already have I felt, on my brow and on my left hand, upon the places where the phylacteries are supposed to rest, that special thrill that comes to me when they first touch the skin.

There were a lot of other things in that *Siddur* that I wanted to go over, but the *shamash* was already in the streets, crying: "Holy Jews, the Holy

Sabbath hastens and approaches!" The stores and shops, in fact, were already closed, Jews were hurrying from the bathhouse, the sun was setting, and candles were being lit. So I washed my hands and face, put on my Sabbath clothes, and went with my father to the synagogue, taking with me, of course, my new prayer book.

When I came there, I kissed the *mezuzah,* and then opening my *Siddur,* read *The Song of Songs.* He who has eaten some new fruit, sweet of odor and sweet to the taste, he, perhaps, may imagine—but only up to a sixtieth part of it—the sweetness and pleasure that was mine as I read *The Song of Songs* in my *Siddur!*

After the service, still holding on to my *Siddur,* I watched everybody greeting my father and my father answering their greetings. They ask him for the news of the world, and he answers, sighing.

How happy and proud I was that I had a father with whom everybody was eager to speak! And just as the older people pressed forward to talk to my father, so the younger ones gathered about me and my *Siddur.* I told them it was new and that my father had brought it from the fair. Each took it in his hands, examined it, and kissed it.

I never knew how many good friends I had. There were times when they had annoyed me, and I had been angry with them, but today I saw that what they really felt toward me was love, and that they were my true good friends.

So I stood there among them, like a bridegroom among the guests, and they entertained me with all kinds of stories about prayer books, as, for example, about the prayer book from which the dead pray on the cemeteries when there is an evil edict against the Jews; or about the prayer book that is printed with the soot from the flames which consumed those who perished for the Sanctification of the Name, in which no man, born of woman, may pray, because it is forbidden to derive benefit from the dead—only the Holy One, blessed be He, only He, in the Garden of Eden, toys with it; or, again, about that prayer book in the Great Synagogue in *Buczacz* which, when a wicked man looks into it, a letter flies off and disappears. That *Siddur* has now been hidden away by the officers of the synagogue because they feared—so much has evil increased in our minds—that a single letter wouldn't be left standing in it. Some of my friends felt that it was wrong to hide the *Siddur:* "Let the eyes of the wicked rot!" they said. "They surely have sinned, but why should the *Siddur* suffer?" Others, however, were happy because now they wouldn't have to be put to the test of reading in it.

There was also told the story of the tremendous *Siddur* of Rabbi Meir ben Reb Yitzhak, the Cantor, blessed be the memory of a saint, from the other side of the River Sambation, he who composed the prayer *Akdomas.* It appears the Emperor wanted to garner that *Siddur* into his treasure-house, but couldn't, it was too big. Then there was the *Siddur* of Rabbi Godiel, called the Suckling, because he was as small as an ant, in which are read the litanies: "We have been deemed as sheep for slaughter" and the angel Michael responds: "Repent thine anger, and have mercy on thy chosen ones, thine elect."

God forbid that I should envy or begrudge these famous sacred prayer books, but man is made to hold dear his own, so I returned to my *Siddur,* opened it, and passed it around again among my comrades.

One of them took it in his hand, examined it, and said: Your *Siddur* is nice, all right, but I saw a nicer one that came from Jerusalem. Its boards were made of olive wood, and the Temple was engraved on it, and underneath was written: *Printed here in Jerusalem, the Holy City. May it be rebuilt and established, speedily and in our time, Amen.*

"How do you know," I asked, "that my *Siddur* was not printed in Jerusalem?"

Even as I said it, my heart melted like wax, and my hands grew weak. My friends then took my *Siddur,* opened it, pointed, and read: *Printed here in the sacred community of Pietrkov.*

"I never heard," said one of them, "of a city called Pietrkov."

Said another: "What a funny name!"

Added a third: "It must be a city of the iniquitous realm of the Greeks."

A fourth said: "And I say, that city is called after a *goy.* Pietr, I know, is the name of a *goy.*"

"A fine *Siddur,*" taunted another, "a fine *Siddur* your father brought you!"

Yet another capped it: "A gift to be proud of!"

Thus my friends teased and taunted me. When we parted, they wrinkled their noses, and sneered: "Pietr of Pietrkov!"

Left alone, I looked again into my *Siddur,* and I said: *"Ribono shel Olom,* Master of the World, in your great mercy, rub out from my *Siddur* the word that has brought me so much pain and shame, and inscribe in its stead the word Jerusalem, and I will pray before You every day, even as they do in Jerusalem, Your holy city." Then I looked again into my *Siddur.* Alas, there it still was, *Pietrkov* with every letter big and terrible and frightening like needles in my eyes.

Still, I wasn't downcast. How can one be sorry with such a beautiful prayer book in one's hand? I turned to the other pages—no Pietr, no Pietrkov there, only pure prayers, holy, wonderful, rising from the print.

At random I read: *And bring us back with song to Zion, the city in eternal joy to Jerusalem, the home of thy kingdom.* My heart leaped up, prayer itself leaped, as if unable to remain in its printed place. And not only this prayer, but all prayers for weekdays and Sabbaths, New Moon and holy days, all hopped and leaped and were ready to go. The prayers, too, had a prayer—to go up to *Erez Israel.*

Thus I browsed in my *Siddur,* turned its pages, until at last I came a second time to the Passover *Haggadah.* My friends, my brothers, my beloved holy seed, what shall I tell you that you do not already know? For even as I turned the pages, there they were before me, in very big letters, those wonderful words: NEXT YEAR IN JERUSALEM! My eyes were filled with tears, not tears of shame or pain, but tears of joy. They fell among the letters, until those letters themselves seemed to swim in tears.

What shall I add and what shall I tell and what shall I prolong saying concerning this long Galuth? I kissed my *Siddur,* and I kissed those letters, and I said: "Today, now, both you and I are in Galuth; but next year—Jerusalem!"

This story of Agnon, as adapted and translated by the Canadian Jewish poet Abraham M. Klein, first appeared in English in *The Jewish Spectator* for September 1953. It is reprinted here by kind permission of the editor.

Glossary

Adon Olam Hymn of praise with which the *Siddur* opens.
Alenu Prayer proclaiming God as king.
Amidah The "standing" prayer, the central feature of all Jewish worship.
Amoraim Later talmudic Sages (3rd–6th centuries).
Avodah Service of worship (particularly in temple).
Avodah zarah Idolatry.
Berakhah (pl. berakhot) Blessing, benediction.
Bet Midrash House of Study, also used for prayers.
Binah Lit. "Understanding" – one of the *Sefirot*.
Daven, davening (Yiddish) Pray, praying.
Devekut Lit. "Cleaving" – Devotion.
En Sof (In *Kabbalah*) The ultimate source of divinity, which is beyond human reach.
Gabbai Synagogue warden or treasurer.
Galut The Exile.
Gemara Discussions and debates of the later talmudic Sages (focused on the *Mishnah*).
Geulah Redemption.
Haggadah Story of Exodus as related on Passover eve.
Halakhah Rules and decisions laid down in the Talmud, Codes, etc.

Hallel Psalms of praise said on New Moons and Festivals (Psalm 113–118).
Hasid Lit. "A pious one" – specifically, an adherent of the hasidic movement.
Haskalah Movement of Enlightenment.
Heder School for primary religious education.
Hiddur mizvah The beautifying of the commandments.
Hitkashrut A bond or connection between God and man.
Hitlahavut Enthusiasm, an important ideal of Hasidism.
Hokhmah Lit. "Wisdom" – one of the *Sefirot*.
Iyyun (tefillah) Concentration (on prayer).
Kabbalah The Jewish occult tradition.
Kaddish Aramaic prayer of sanctification sometimes said by mourners.
Kavvanah (pl. kavvanot) Attentiveness (to prayer).
Kedushah Sanctification recited during repetition of the *Amidah* (and on other occasions).
Kiddush The Sanctification for Sabbath and Festivals usually said over a cup of wine.
Kinot Prayers of lament.
Kol Nidre Aramaic declaration annulling vows – made at the beginning of Yom Kippur prayers.
Maariv The evening prayer.
Mahzor Festival prayer book.
Malkhut Lit. "Kingdom" – one of the *Sefirot*.
Malkhuyot Verses of kingship – in the *Musaf* for Rosh Hashanah.
Melamed A teacher (usually in a *heder*).
Mezuzah Sign on doorpost (see Deuteronomy 6:9).
Midrash Rabbinic homily.
Minhag Custom.
Mikveh Ritual bath.
Minhah The afternoon prayer.
Minyan A quorum for worship (consists of ten men).
Mishnah The core document of the Talmud, the first systematization of the Oral Law.
Mishneh Torah The Code of Maimonides (term also used for Deuteronomy).
Mitnagdim (mitnaggedim) Opponents of the hasidic movement.
Mizvah (pl. mizvot) Religious command; also simply "good deed."
Modim "We give thanks" – the penultimate blessing of the *Amidah*.
Musaf The Additional Service for Sabbath, New Moon, and Festivals.
Neilah Lit. "The locking of the gate." Closing prayer for Yom Kippur.
Nosah Rite or style of prayer.
Nosah Ashkenaz The "German" rite, widely accepted in Central, Western, and Eastern Europe.
Nosah Sefarad The "Spanish" rite, largely adopted by the *hasidim* and resembling the modes of prayer of North African and Middle Eastern Jewries.
Payyetan Liturgical poet.

Glossary

Piyyut Liturgical poem.
Posekim Rabbinical decisors.
Raza deshabbat Passage from the *Zohar* recited on Friday evening according to *Nosah Sefarad*.
Rosh Hashanah The New Year.
Sefirah (pl. Sefirot) The ten Divine Emanations according to the *Zohar*.
Selihot Penitential prayers.
Shaharit The morning service.
Shalom-alekhem Lit. "Peace unto you" – opening words of hymn welcoming the angels to the Sabbath table.
Shekhinah The Divine Presence (in many sources represents the female aspect of divinity).
Shema (keriat shema) Declaration of divine unity made morning and evening (Deuteronomy 6:4–9 and other texts).
Shemoneh-esreh The eighteen benedictions of the weekday *amidah*.
Shofarot Verses relating to the blowing of the ram's horn – in the *Musaf* for Rosh Hashanah.
Shul Yiddish for synagogue.
Shulhan Arukh Lit. "A Prepared Table" – Joseph Caro's authoritative code of law (16th century).
Siddur Prayer book.
Tahanun "Supplication" – prayer following the *Amidah*.
Tallit Prayer shawl.
Talmid hakham Student learned in the sacred texts.
Tanakh Bible (acronym for *Torah, Neviim, Ketuvim*).
Tanna (pl. tannaim) Talmud Sages of the earlier, mishnaic period.
Tefillah Prayer.
Tefillin Phylacteries (see Exodus 13:9).
Teshuvah Repentance.
Tiferet Lit. "Glory" – one of the *Sefirot*.
Tikkun Lit. "Repair" – kabbalistic exercise aimed at repairing breaches in the metaphysical order.
Torah Lit. "The Teaching". Specifically, the Pentateuch; by extension, the totality of the Oral and Written Law.
Tosafot Supplementary glosses on the Babylonian Talmud (Rhineland, 12th–14th centuries).
Yehi Razon "May it be thy will." Opening formula for petitionary prayers.
Yekum Purkan Opening words of Aramaic prayer for the community and its leaders. Said on Sabbaths.
Yeshivah (pl. yeshivot) Talmudic academy.
Yom Kippur Day of Atonement.
Zaddik (pl. zaddikim) A righteous man – specifically, spiritual leader of hasidic sect.
Zibbur The community.

Zikhronot Verses on the subject of remembrance—in the *Musaf* for Rosh Hashanah.
Zizit Ritual fringes attached to a four-cornered garment (see Numbers 15: 37–41).
Zohar Central kabbalistic text—in the form of a commentary on the Pentateuch and other portions of Scripture.

Index

Actions, during prayers, 70-71, 230-232
"*Ad Henah*" (story by Agnon), 18-19
Adversity, behavior in, 10-11
Afternoon prayers, 60-61, 222
Agnon, S. Y., 18-22, 25
Albo, Rabbi Joseph, 81, 88-89, 167-168
Alfasi, Isaac, 56
Allegories
   Land of Israel as, 151-152
   in prayers, 194
Amidah, 48
   changes in, 50, 56, 207
   as only prayer, 55, 70
   relevance of, 32-33
Angels, and humans, 218-220
Answers, to prayers, 125, 130-134, 169-170, 172-173
   and human merit, 120, 123
   and necessary belief, 138-139
   risk of receiving, 34, 187

Anticipatory act, prayer as, 165-169
Approaches, to prayer, 71-88
Aramah, Rabbi Yitshak, 83-84
Ascension
   through prayer, 111-112, 115-116, 147-149, 234
   through sacrifices, 154-155
Asher, Rabbeinu, 56-57
Avner, Rabbi, 149
Avot, 62-63, 83
Awe, in worship, 230
Ayin, 153
Azriel, Rabbi, 153

Baal Shem Tov, 79, 233-234, 237
Babylonian Talmud, 50-51
Bahye ibn Pakuda, R., 75
Balance, in prayer, 7
Ben Abuyah, Elisha, 7
Ben Isaac, Rabbi Hayyim (of Volozhin), 80

Ben Rabbi Shimon, Rabbi Meir (of Narbonne), 145
Besht, the, 218, 226, 234, 237
Bialik, Hayim Nahman, 19–21
Bickel, Shlomo, 17, 19
Blessings, 48; *see also Amidah*
 creativity in, 49, 58
Body movements, during prayers, 70–71, 230–232

Cantors, 86, 239
Causation, fixed natural, 131–132
Chaim, Rabbi (of Brest-Litovsk), 75
Charity, and sacrifices, 213
Charms, *mizvot* as, 155–156
Christianity, 46, 171
Cleaving. *See* Clinging
Clinging, to God, 81–82, 146, 158, 232–235
 as stage of ascension, 77–78, 147–150
 in thought, 144–146, 153
Closed canon. *See* Fixed prayer
Cohen, Hermann, 165
Collective prayer. *See* Community prayer
Commandments, 54
 effects of obedience to, 157–158, 220
 fulfillment of, 10, 135–136
Commentary on the Mishnah (Maimonides), 122–124
Community, Jewish
 function of prayer in, 35–36
 importance of, 26–27, 237–239
 lack of faith in, 190–191, 200
Community prayer, 7, 26–27, 37, 85–88, 99, 112
 in experiential services, 201–204
 importance of, 7, 34, 116, 125, 196, 237–239
 vs. personal prayers, 169–172
Conservative groups, 33
Contemplation, of Divine World, 144–146
Continuity, through prayer, 7, 27–28, 35–36, 40

Contradictions, in Maimonides, 119, 136–137
Conversion, and repentance, 16
Corporeality, of God, 127–128
Creativity, in prayers, 36–37, 45–50, 55–60, 114
 personalization, 33–34
Crescas, Rabbi Hasdai, 81
Criticism
 of Jewish prayer, 17, 19–23
 of kabbalism, 145
Cultic act, prayer as, 45–46

Day of Atonement services, 212–213
Dessler, Rabbi Eliyahu, 82
Devekut. See Clinging, to God
Devotion, need for in prayer, 189–190, 192, 206
Dialogue, prayer as, 6, 182–183, 186
Diaspora
 loss of Hebrew during, 50–51
 worship during, 113–114
Didatic prayer, 80–82 Dienemann, Max, 28–29
Divine Presence, prayer as, 157, 223–224, 234–236
Divine Providence, 89, 112, 133–134, 190–191
Divine World, contemplation of, 144–146
Duschinsky, Rabbi J. Z., 59

Education
 during experiential services, 204–205
 failure to teach devotion, 189–190, 192
 religious, 179–188, 192–196
 through prayer, 81, 168
Effects, of prayer, 6–7, 81–82, 99, 153, 172–173, 218–221
 repair, 76–80, 114–115
 theological problems of, 167–169
 unification, 76–80, 148, 152
Effort, prayer not substitute for, 124
Eleh ezkerah, for modern congregations, 212–213

Index

Eliezer, Rabbi, 47–48, 61
Emotions
  and *devekut*, 232–235
  God's, 125–126, 130–132
  in prayers, 53–54, 59, 195, 230
"Enlightened" services, 15
En Sof, 145, 147, 150, 157
Evening prayer, 195, 222
Evil, in world order, 156, 167–168
Existentialist prayer, 83–85, 195
Experiential services, 195, 201–213
Experimental booklets of prayers, 200–213
Ezra, Rabbi, 158–159

Faith
  lack of, 190–191, 200
  as purpose of prayer, 7, 21
  as requirement for prayer, 123–124, 182–188
Fanatics, prayers of, 170–171
Faulty prayers, 34–35
Fixed prayer, 14
  as closed canon, 21–29
  personal contributions in, 207–208
  personal contributions to, 99
  purposes of, 27–28, 86
  vs. spontaneous personal prayers, 45–52
Forsaking, of prayer, 13, 16; *see also* Inhibitions
Frequency, of prayer, 55–57

Gaon, Rabbi Hai, 55–56
Gaon, Rabbi Saadyah, 55
Gaon, Rabbi Sherira, 56
Gaon, Rav Amaram, 50
Gaon of Vilna, 11
Gentiles, need to pray, 7–8
Gerson, Rabbi (of Kitov), 233
Gersonides, 81
Gikatilla, Joseph, 155–157
Glatstein, Jacob, 22

God
  effect of worship on, 157–158, 219–220
  and Holocaust, 9–10
  image of, 92–93, 120, 126–127
  name of, 58, 229
  omnipresence of, 112–113, 221
  and prayer, 54–55, 83–85, 91–92
  prayer as, 223–224
  prayers of, 5
  quarrels with, 28–29
  removal of, 185
God as King theme
  parables about, 210–212, 217–218, 227, 237
  relevance of, 210–212
Godhead, 146–147, 149–150, 157–158
Goethe, Johann Wolfgang von, 171–172
Governance, God's, 131–134
Greenberg, Uri Zvi, 173
Guide of the Perplexed (Maimonides), 119, 126–129
  on petitionary prayer, 122
  on praise, 93
  on religious language, 95

Halakhah, and regulation of prayer, 53–63
Halakhic authorities, 35
  and prayer book changes, 29–30, 51
Halevi, Rabbi Yehudah, 74, 81, 96, 109–117, 155
  on community vs. personal prayer, 86–87, 169–170
Harmony, within Judaism, 16, 18–19
Hasidism, 21, 78, 79, 217–239
Haskalah, 21–22
Hayim, Rabbi (of Volozhin), 157–158
Hazon Ish, 189–190
Hebrew
  loss of, 50–51
  as vernacular, 191–192
Heiler, F., 166–167
Heinemann, Joseph, 69–71
Herberg, Will, 211

Heschel, Abraham Joshua, 83, 88, 99, 206
Hierarchies, 157, 170–171
    prayer and world order, 156
Hirsch, Rabbi Samson Raphael, 83
History, 46, 213
    in experimental prayer books, 203
    of prayers, 5–6, 193, 195
Holdheim, Samuel, 25
Holocaust, the
    effect on prayer, 8–11, 23, 88
    effect on *Siddur,* 28–29
House of Hillel, 61
House of Shammai, 61
Humanism, Jewish, 6
Humans, 6, 171
    limitations of, 145–146
    power of, 218–221
Huna, Rav (the *Tur*), 60–63
Hurvitz, Rabbi Abraham ben Shabtai Sheftel, 86

Ibn Daud, Rabbi Abraham, 97–98
Ibn Gabbai, Rabbi Meir, 155, 157–159
Idolatry, prevention of, 132–133
Inhibitions, to prayer, 57–58, 60, 228
    and changing *Siddur,* 28–30
    irrelevance as, 4, 8–9, 23, 191
    lack of faith as, 39, 184–186, 200
Inquiry, vs. tradition, 20–21
Institutionalized prayer. *See* Community prayer; Fixed prayer
Intellectual activities, 41
    contemplation of Divine World, 144–146
    as prayer, 60, 195–196
    value of, 133–139, 221–223
Intention; *see also* Kavvanah
    God's, 121, 125
Interpretations. *See also* Understanding
    of prayers, 193–195
    of the Torah, 130–133
Isaac, Rabbi (of Acre), 146–151
Isaac the Blind, Rabbi, 144–145

Islam, 46
Israel
    community of, 7, 27, 237–239
    innovations in worship in, 32, 41
    Land of, 151–152
    people of, 111–113
    prayers of, 5–6
    religious education in, 180, 189–192

Judaism, nostalgia for past in, 16–19, 21

Kabbalah, 51, 78
    Spanish, 143–159
    types of prayers in, 73–80
Kadushin, Max, 84–85
Kant, Emmanuel, 91–92
Karo, Rabbi Joseph, 56
Kavvanah, 40, 74–75, 206
    effect on worship, 226–231
    and kabbalism, 144–145
    of prayer, 60–63, 153, 180–181
    prayer without, 228, 231, 233
Kingdom on earth, prayers for, 168–169
Klein, A. M., 212
Kook, Rabbi A. I., 92–93, 95–96, 98–100, 168, 193
Kuzari (Halevi), 110, 113, 117

Land of Israel, as allegory, 151–152
Language, 86
    changes in, 191–192, 210–212
    importance of each word and letter in prayer, 225–226, 228–229
    limitations of human, 92–94, 120–121, 126–127, 129, 139
    limited to Moses', 124–125, 129–130
    of prayers, 50–51, 70–71, 79
    religious, 93–95, 193
    and timeliness of prayers, 165–167, 170–173
Law
    codification of, 122, 124–125
    and piety, 137–138
    secular vs. religious, 61

Laws of Prayer, requirements for, 30, 39–40
Leibovitz, Professor Yeshayahu, 94, 96–97, 100
Levels
  of existence, 110–113, 153
  of prayer, 169–171, 224, 231–232, 234, 236
Literal interpretations, of the Torah, 130–133
Literature, 3, 8
  in prayer books, 202–213
  Siddur as, 192–193
Lowe, Rabbi Judah (of Prague), 76
Luria, Rabbi Isaac (the *Ari*), 22, 80

Magic, 73–77, 155–156
Mahzor; see also Prayer books
  new versions of, 32, 207–211
  supplementary material in, 205–206
Maimonides, 54, 100, 119–140
  on *kavvanah*, 75
  on religious language, 95
  on types of prayers, 56–57, 92–93
Majority/minority, tension between, 14–15
Mana, Rabbi, 61
Martyrology, 212–213
Mavo Lasiddur (Shechter), 195
Meirat Eynayim, 145
Melodies, of *nosahs*, 15–16, 34, 41, 228
  hasidic, 21–22
Middle Ages, halakhic discussion of prayer in, 164
Middot, in revision of *Mahzor*, 208–209
Mikveh, 229
Milhemet Mitzvah (ben Rabbi Shimon), 145
Minimum requirements, for Laws of Prayer, 30, 39–40
Minyan, purpose of, 7, 87
Miracles, 89–90, 183
Mishneh Torah, 124, 126, 138
Mishnah Yoma, 213
Mistakes, in prayers, 34–35

Mizvot, 82
  prayer as, 94, 100
  purpose of, 113, 155–158
Morning prayers, 32, 224
  compared to others, 195, 222
Moses, 139, 150–151
  prayers of, 124–125, 129–130
Motivations, for prayer, 56–57; *see also* Purposes, of prayer
Musar movement, 82
Mysticism
  and mystical prayer, 77–80, 84–85
  and prophecy, 166–167
  in the Spanish *Kabbalah*, 143–159

Nachmanides, 54
Nahman, Rabbi (of Bratzlav), 3, 5, 11
Necessary belief, 138–139
Need, for prayer, 6–8, 96, 100, 139, 168, 235–236
Nefesh Hahayim (ben Isaac), 80
Nonhalakhic prayer, 58–59
Nosahs, 34, 79
  choice of, 15–16, 25–26, 36, 187
  similarities between, 37, 39–40
Nosah Sefarad, 27–28
Nostalgia
  lack of, 37
  vs. needs of new generation, 31–41
  for tradition, 16–19, 21, 25–27
Numerology, 78

Obligatory prayers, 54, 56, 217–218, 222
  emptiness of, 184, 227
  Maimonides on, 122, 124, 129
Olat Reiyah (Kook), 193
Orientation, through prayer, 4–5, 7
Origins, of prayers, 5–6, 36–37, 69–70, 195; *see also* Sources, of prayers
Orthodox Jewry, fixity of prayers of, 48
Otsar Ha-Hayim (Isaac of Acre), 148
Ozick, Cynthia, 210

Parables, 218–219
  about community, 238–239
  about *kavvanah*, 221–222, 227, 228
  about rewards, 236–237
  about selflessness, 80
Paradoxes, of prayer, 88–98
Perfection, and levels of existence, 111–113
Personality, effect of prayer on, 81–82
Personal prayers, 33–34
  and community prayer, 86–87, 169–171
  criticism of, 116, 159
  vs. fixed liturgy, 45–52
  frequency of, 55–57
  value of, 54–55, 207–208
Petitionary prayers, 90–93, 134, 183
  God's response to, 126–127, 130–132, 236–237
  personal requests in, 159, 169–171
  and praise, 173–174
  problems of, 80, 120–123, 167–169
Petuchowski, Jakob, response to, 31, 33, 37
Philosophical prayer, 83–84, 120
Piyyutim, 6, 25
  for modern congregations, 209, 212, 213
  origins of, 49–50
  as tangential, 32–33, 35
Plato, influence of, 111
Poetry, 6
  incorporation of, 21–22, 202–213
Poverty/wealth, 237
Power, of prayer, 5
Praise, 123–125, 218–219
  and image of God, 120, 126–127
  limitations of language for, 129–130
  and petition, 173–174
  before prayer, 92–94
  prayers as, 54, 169
Prayer books, 114; *see also Siddur*
  evolution of, 21–22, 57–58, 207
  experimental, 200–213
  personal relationships with, 241–244
  variations in, 27, 29, 31–41, 48–49

Preparation, for prayer, 61–62, 115, 224, 229
Presence of God, 112–113, 182, 221
Printed texts
  effect on *Siddur*, 27–28
  and fixity of prayers, 48, 50–51, 207
Prophecy, 85, 113
  and prayer, 114, 150–152, 166–167
Prophets, and other humans, 110–111
Protest against heaven, 23
  over Holocaust, 9–11, 28–29
Psalms, 207–208, 233
Purposes, of prayer, 5, 21, 235–236
  obligatory vs. personal, 54, 60, 128
  problems of, 10–11, 165, 167–169
  as repair, 155–158

Raba, 7
Raya Mehemna, 157
Rebellion. *See* Protest against heaven
Rebirth of Israel
  and changes in *Siddur*, 28–29, 32, 40
  effect on prayers, 47, 87
Reform movement, 33, 48, 71
  prayer books of, 25, 203
  synagogues of, 15, 18
Relevance
  of God as King theme, 210–212
  of prayer books, 32–33, 36, 200–213
  of prayers, 32–33, 39, 191
Religiosity, 3–4, 8
Repairs, of Divine needs
  through prayer, 76–80, 155–158
  through sacrifices, 154–155
Repentance
  and conversion, 16
  effects of, 125
Repetition, of prayers, 6, 191
Response to prayers. *See* Answers, to prayers
Responsive readings, 204
Restoration, through prayer, 114–115, 164–165
Revelation, 85, 166

Index

Rewards, 155–157, 236–237
Rosenzweig, Franz, 85, 163–174
Rote prayer; *see also* Fixed prayer; Obligatory prayer
   criticism of, 23–24, 217–218
Rubrics, 62
   for *middot,* 208–209
   for *Mishnah Yoma,* 213
   in revision of *Amidah,* 207

Sacrifices, 56, 154–155, 213
Sadan, Dov, 25–26, 32–33
Sages
   and fixed prayer, 45, 47
   and personal prayers, 48
Samuel, 55–56
Schelling, Friedrich, 166
Scholem, Gershom, 94, 144, 146, 153
Scoffers, prayers of, 171–172
Seder ha-avodah, 212–213
Sefirot, 144, 147–148, 157
Self-abasement, 219
Semantics, of prayer, 71; *see also* Language
Semiotic model, 71
Service, 77, 159
   other methods of, 82, 113–114
   prayer as, 45–47, 98
Services, 41
   Evening, 195, 202
   experimental prayer books in, 202–213
   length of, 27, 29, 31–32
   source of prayers in, 57–58
Shaare Zedek (Gikatilla), 155–156
Shechter, Joseph, 195
Shekhinah. See Divine Presence
"*She-lo Nikashel*" (story by Agnon), 18, 19
Shemoneh Esreh (18 benedictions). *See Amidah*
Shulhan Arukh, 61–62
Siddur, 35, 51, 191; *see also* Prayer books
   changes in, 22, 31–32, 185
   as closed canon, 25–30, 36
   education on, 180–181, 192–196
   personal relationships with, 241–244
   risks of changing, 38, 40
Siddur Tif-ereth David, 27–28
Siegfried Moses Festschrift (Agnon), 25
Simon, Akiva Ernst, 75
Sins, 156, 169–170, 206–207
Soloveitchik, Rabbi Joseph B., 75, 85, 87–88, 98
Souls, 152
   ascension of, 154–155
   immersion in God, 149–150, 153
Sources, of prayers, 37–39, 59, 98–99; *see also* Origins, of prayers
Star of Redemption prayer (Rosenzweig), 163–174
Stein, Leopold, 27–28
Steinsaltz, Rabbi Adin, 109–110
Supplementary material, in prayer books, 202–213
Supplication. *See* Petitionary prayer
Synagogues, 17, 86–87, 200
   destruction of, 28–29
   role of, 26–27, 33, 87–88

Talmud, 54, 58
Teachers/leaders, 150–151
   education for prayer by, 179–188
   education on *Siddur* by, 193–196
   and followers, 14–15, 238–239
Tefillah-bezibbur. See Community prayer
Tenses
   future vs. past, 33, 37
   and language of prayers, 165–167, 170–173
   and vain prayers, 89–90
Tevah, 225
Thanks, 124, 169
Themes; *see also* God as King theme
   in experimental prayer books, 203–213
Theology, 94
   problems of faith in, 182–188
   problems of prayer in, 163–164, 167–169

Theurgic prayer, 96
  and mysticism, 73–77, 79
  and prophecy, 150–152
Tikkune Zohar, 157
Torah
  and prayer, 5–6, 122–123
  theology-less, 94
Tradition
  and changes in *Siddur,* 28–30
  naivete of, 19–21
  vs. needs of new generation, 31–41, 87
  nostalgia for, 25–27
Trust, lack of, 36
Types of prayers, 69–100, 169–171

Understanding; *see also* Interpretation
  as *kavvanah* of prayer, 61–62, 181
  of prayers, 222
  of Scriptures, 122–123
Unification
  of God, 127–128
  with God, 225–226
  through *mizvot,* 158–159
  through prayer, 76, 78–79
Union groups, 33

United States
  changes of prayers in, 27–28, 32, 37
  experimental prayer books in, 201–213

Vain prayers, 89–90, 167
Voluntary prayers; *see also* Personal prayers
  afternoon as, 60–61, 222

Weiss, Rabbi Yitzchok Yaakov, 59
Will, 99–100, 153–154
Women, prayers of, 52, 59
World order. *See* Hierarchies
Worship
  effects of, 219–220
  intellectual activity as, 134–135
  prayer in, 128–129, 165

Yehoshua, Rabbi, 213
Yeshivot, 191
Yesh Nohalin (Hurvitz), 86
Yidn Davenen (Bickel), 17
Yitzhak, Rabbi Levi (of Berditchev), 217–218
Yochanan, Rabbi, 55–56

Zakkai, Rabbi Yochanan ben, 213
Zohar, 76–78, 224

About the Editors

Dr. Gabriel H. Cohn teaches Bible and *Midrash* at Bar-Ilan University in Israel. He was the dean of Gold College for Women, Jerusalem, for more than twenty years and the editor in chief of *Deot,* a religious-academic periodical. Among his publications are *Studies in the Five Megilloth* (Hebrew) and *The Book of Jonah in the Light of Biblical Narrative* (German). Dr. Cohn lives in Jerusalem with his wife, Nechama, and their three children.

Harold Fisch, now professor emeritus in English literature at Bar-Ilan University in Israel, was rector of that university from 1968 to 1971. A graduate of Oxford University, he is well known around the world as a scholar and critic. Among his publications are *A Remembered Future: A Study in Literary Mythology* and *Poetry with a Purpose: Biblical Poetics and Interpretation.* He and his wife, Joyce, are the parents of five children.

GENERAL THEOLOGICAL SEMINARY
NEW YORK